Shakespeare's Poetics

For Marilyn

Shakespeare's Poetics

EKBERT FAAS

The right of the
University of Cambridge
to print and sell
all manner of books
was granted by
Henry VIII in 1534.
The University has printed
and published continuously
since 1584.

CAMBRIDGE UNIVERSITY PRESS

Cambridge

London   New York   New Rochelle

Melbourne   Sydney

Published by the Press Syndicate of the University of Cambridge
The Pitt Building, Trumpington Street, Cambridge CB2 1RP
32 East 57th Street, New York, NY 10022, USA
10 Stamford Road, Oakleigh, Melbourne 3166, Australia

First published 1986

Printed in Great Britain at
the University Press, Cambridge

British Library cataloguing in publication data
Faas, Ekbert
Shakespeare's poetics.
1. Shakespeare, William. Sonnets   2. Shakespeare,
William – Criticism and interpretation
I. Title
821'.3   PR2848

Library of Congress cataloguing in publication data
Faas, Ekbert, 1938–
Shakespeare's poetics.
Bibliography: p.
1. Shakespeare, William, 1564–1616 – Technique.
2. Poetics.   I. Title.
PR2995.F3   1985   822.3'3   85-7903

ISBN 0 521 30825 9

Contents

Introduction

I remember, the Players have often mentioned it as an honour to *Shakespeare,* that in his writing, (whatsoever *he penn'd*) hee never blotted out line. My answer hath beene, Would he had blotted a thousand. Which they thought a malevolent speech . . . Hee was (indeed) honest, and of an open, and free nature: had an excellent *Phantsie;* brave notions, and gentle expressions: wherein hee flow'd with that facility, that sometime it was necessary he should be stop'd. *Sufflaminandus erat;* as *Augustus* said of *Haterius.* His wit was in his owne power; would the rule of it had beene so too.

"[H]ee never blotted out line:" Ben Jonson's complaint is as familiar as his saying that Shakespeare "wanted Arte" and had "small *Latine,* and lesse *Greeke.*" "[T]o powre forth Verses, such as they are, *(ex tempore),*" to Ben Jonson, was typical of poets who, "presuming on their owne *Naturals,*" derided diligence and understanding;[1] and he would not condone such vices even where he was convinced of a poet's greatness, as in Shakespeare's case. On the other hand, his rival showed at least a minimal concern with his art. In his 1623 poem on Shakespeare, Ben Jonson tries to make the most of this effort. In addition to the hundreds of lines he should have blotted, Shakespeare wrote others that were "well torned and true-filed." But in his eulogistic effort, Jonson simply ends up fitting his fellow-playwright into the Prokrustes bed of his own theories:

> Yet must I not giue Nature all: Thy Art,
> My gentle *Shakespeare,* must enioy a part.
> For though the *Poets* matter, Nature be,
> His Art doth giue the fashion. And, that he,
> Who casts to write a liuing line, must sweat,
> (Such as thine are) and strike the second heat
> Vpon the *Muses* anuile.

vii

More than anything else, such reservations confirm Ben Jonson's view of Shakespeare as essentially the poet of nature.

> Nature her selfe was proud of his designes,
> And ioy'd to weare the dressing of his lines![2]

There are few other contemporary comments on Shakespeare's artistry, and none as illuminating as Ben Jonson's. But most of them, whether eulogistic or critical, reflect an obvious consensus. Shakespeare, for better or worse, is the poet, not of art, but of nature. To the admiring Beaumont he sets an example of how far a poet might progress by trusting his natural instinct. Shakespeare's lack of erudite craftsmanship, which Jonson criticizes, becomes a goal for future generations which Beaumont, at least temporarily, embraces as his own. Characteristically, the lines are from his epistle to Ben Jonson:

> . . . heere would I let slippe
> (If I had any in mee) schollershippe,
> And from all Learninge keepe these lines as cleere
> as Shakespeares best are, which our heires shall heare
> Preachers apte to their auditors to showe
> how farr sometimes a mortall man may goe
> by the dimme light of Nature.[3]

By 1647, the notion has already turned into a commonplace. John Denham's prefatory verses to the first Beaumont and Fletcher folio of that year compare Ben Jonson's laborious efforts with "what more easie nature did bestow / On Shakespeares gentler Muse."[4] "Nature was all his Art," comments William Cartwright disapprovingly in the same volume.[5] A little later, in Richard Flecknoe's 1664 *Short Discourse of the English Stage*, the consensus attitude of Shakespeare's contemporaries or immediate followers has become part of an historical assessment crediting Fletcher with wit, Jonson with "Gravity and ponderousness of Style," and Shakespeare with excelling "in a natural Vein." Comparing Shakespeare with Ben Jonson, Flecknoe writes, "you shall see the difference betwixt Nature and Art."[6]

How did Shakespeare respond to being viewed as the poet of nature and what did he have to say about his art himself? To give an answer to this question is far from easy. Unlike Lope de Vega or Sidney, Shakespeare wrote neither a "New Art of Making Comedies" nor a "Defence of Poesie," and the attempt to deduce such a poetics from what his plays and poems seem to imply about it is beset with considerable problems. Most kindred studies chart the outer precincts of this territory, while few venture into the actual center.

Most strikingly, there is no single book to date assessing Shakespeare's sense of his craft and creativity in their multiple aspects. Instead, we have several studies dealing with Shakespeare and music, the fine arts, and other areas marginal to his actual poetics.

> The man that hath no music in himself,
> Nor is not mov'd with concord of sweet sounds,
> Is fit for treasons, stratagems, and spoils.

Words such as these from *The Merchant of Venice* (V, 1) have rightly earned Shakespeare the reputation of a music enthusiast, and much has been written about it.[7] Less enthusiastic, perhaps, but no less well-informed, are the playwright's references to painting and the fine arts. Again, there are several studies on the subject.[8] Scholars have also analyzed Shakespeare's awareness of the *ut pictura poesis* concept, his use of emblems, as well as less obvious connections between, say, Elizabethan painting and "ways of seeing" in his plays.[9] Similar attention has been given to Shakespeare's use of traditional rhetoric,[10] his concepts of language,[11] his imagery,[12] his imagination,[13] the five-act structure of his plays,[14] and his sense of decorum.[15]

By contrast to such book-length studies, analyses of Shakespeare's conception of poetry, such as E. C. Pettet's,[16] and of Shakespeare's poets, like Kenneth Muir's,[17] are usually limited to under two dozen pages. No wonder that their scope is somewhat narrow. E. C. Pettet's essay, however brilliant, is mainly concerned with the concepts of poetic frenzy and "feigning." Kenneth Muir's, though equally insightful, focuses on the various poet-characters in Shakespeare's work, while only commenting on individual concepts of his poetics in passing. Even more selective is Alvin B. Kernan's "Shakespeare's Essays on Dramatic Poesy: The Nature and Function of Theater within the

Sonnets and the Plays," or his more recent *The Playwright as Magician: Shakespeare's Image of the Poet in the English Public Theater*. As these titles suggest, Kernan is concerned with Shakespeare's self-image as poet amidst the conflicting demands of aristocratic patronage and the popular stage, rather than with the playwright's attitude towards the individual aspects of his craft and creativity. The most thorough discussion of Shakespeare's implied poetics to date, then, remains J. W. H. Atkins's, in his history of English literary criticism during the Renaissance.[18]

This is not to ignore the many recent studies in dramatic reflexivity, role-playing, the play-within-the-play, or what is often summarily referred to as metadramatic criticism. What is metatheatre? Since Lionel Abel first used the term on the cover of his *Metatheatre: A New View of Dramatic Form* (1963), similar studies, each with its own terminology, have appeared in great number. Abel himself speaks of plays that are "theatre pieces about life seen as already theatricalized."[19] James L. Calderwood, subsuming Abel's "metatheatre" under his "metadrama," pursues the Shakespearean "metaphor of life-as-drama" towards the playwright's "evolving conceptions of art."[20] More recent studies simply speak of the theatre turning to itself,[21] or define "metadramatic" as "the proposition that plays are in part at least about themselves, some aspect of dramatic or theatrical art, or the responses of spectators."[22]

Useful in the face of such terminological proliferation has been Michael Shapiro's attempt to subsume the whole matter under the related concept of dramatic reflexivity and its various functions. These involve "the audience's degree of involvement in the stage illusion" (an area studied by Doris Fenton, Maynard Mack, Eugene Paul Nassar and others),[23] the "interplay between different planes of illusion"[24] (as discussed in Robert Weimann's monumental *Shakespeare and the Popular Tradition in the Theater*), the "spectators' responses to any given dramatic illusion,"[25] the topos "that life too is a play,"[26] and finally the fact that many plays tend to comment in one way or another upon themselves.[27] Studies of this last type include Anne Righter's pioneering *Shakespeare and the Idea of the Play*, J. L. Calderwood's two books on metadrama, Robert Egan's argument that Shakespeare's "dramas within drama," with their often undeclared audiences, serve as models for the offstage audience, Anthony B. Dawson's *Indirections. Shakespeare and the Art of Illusion,* and Alvin B. Kernan's investigations into Shakespearean self-portrayal as poet in the English public theatre. Another category that might be added to all these concerns the reflexivity derived from an onstage producer–playwright like Iago or Prospero, a field explored in various recent articles.[28]

Yet, as much as the present study is indebted to all these, it by no means fits the same labels. Metadramatic or reflexive criticism deals largely with such themes as the idea of the play, the world as stage, the art of illusion and man as a role-playing animal – all important, but by no means central to our concerns. Of course there is overlap, but it tends to be in areas – such as Shakespeare's understanding of language – which are important, yet not central, to both approaches. While metadramatic criticism emphasizes the interpretation of individual plays in terms of their self-reflexive statements, the present study focuses on the specific concepts of a poetics implied in individual works, as well as in Shakespeare's oeuvre at large.

Such, at least, is its methodological thrust. In practical terms, things turn out to be somewhat different. It would be easy enough, of course, to give lists of the various statements in which Shakespeare, through one of his characters or the speaker-narrator of his poems, comments on such matters as poetic imagination, *furor poeticus,* art and nature, dramatic mimesis, acting, the audience, meter, rhyme, and rhetoric.[29] Most of these comments are contained in a handful of *loci classici* familiar to any reader of Shakespeare (e.g., Theseus' speech on the imagination in *A Midsummer Night's Dream,* V, 1); the rest are easily located with the help of a concordance.

But such mere cataloguing, obviously, would distort rather than reveal what we are after. In Sonnet 105, for instance, we read: " 'Fair, kind, and true' is all my argument." Does such a seemingly straightforward statement tell us anything concrete about the author's idealistic intentions in the Sonnets or perhaps in his work in general? It would be naive to make such a claim. Even if we assume that Will, the speaker of the sequence, stands for William Shakespeare, rather than some persona, there is sufficient reason for distrust or at least caution. Will has already told us that the beauty of his friend's mind, which he proposes to praise, is tainted by "the rank smell of weeds" (69). Rather than celebrate the kind and true, he tends to whitewash his friend's sinfulness –

> Authorizing thy trespass with compare,
> Myself corrupting, salving thy amiss.   (35)

Is such inconsistency meant to dramatize Will's sinful fall from grace into mental and linguistic confusion, as Margreta de Grazia assumes?[30] Or is Shakespeare juxtaposing two contradictory poetics, a serious, orderly, tragic one with another, playful, dissociative, tragicomic, as R. A. Lanham proposes?[31] Whatever the case, we are cautioned against trying to establish Shakespeare's poetics from quoting random lines out of context.

As one might expect, matters in the plays are even more complex. Theseus' speech about lunatic, lover, and poet is spoken in a tone of ironic dismissal of everything poetic, including "antique fables" and "fairy toys:"

> The poet's eye, in a fine frenzy rolling,
> Doth glance from heaven to earth, from earth to heaven;
> And as imagination bodies forth
> The forms of things unknown, the poet's pen
> Turns them to shapes and gives to airy nothing
> A local habitation and a name.[32]

Does Shakespeare identify with Theseus' irony? The consistently negative portrayal of poets in his work might suggest such an attitude. But Theseus' speech, as will be shown in more detail later, is undercut by the context in which it appears. "Poor Theseus," as one critic puts it. "In the play's terms, there are such things as fairies, and, by extension, there is truth in antique fables and fairy toys, in the shaping fantasies of lovers, poets, and madmen. Moreover, to claim to be on the side of reason, as Lysander's case illustrated, is dangerous. Theseus has conveniently forgotten what we remember hearing in the first act: that he, like the lovers, like Bottom, was once a fairy victim too, led 'through the glimmering night' by Titania herself, who has followed his fortunes and come to bless his wedding. "[33] For these and other reasons it seems appropriate to conclude with Kenneth Muir that what "Theseus intends as a gibe against poetry is a precise account of Shakespeare's method in this play."[34]

Of course, not all the evidence to be drawn on for this study is thus refracted by multiple ironies and perspectives. Much, particularly regarding Shakespeare's awareness of specific Renaissance critical concepts, can be gathered from his vocabulary and phrasing. Here the various Shakespeare concordances are of great help. But word-field analyses by and large reveal little regarding the more complex issues. What were Shakespeare's views of the general purposes of drama or of the art of acting? What of theatrical illusion and the role of the audience? What of language in general and poetic language in particular? What was his understanding of the imagination, of creativity, and especially of the creation of supernatural agencies? What, finally, of the relation of art to nature? The answers to most of these questions, which in that order mark our general argument, have to be gathered either by analyzing statements made by individual dramatis personae (e.g., Theseus on the imagination) or by interpreting themes in specific works (e.g., the dismantling of essentialist discourse in *Troilus and Cressida*). The problems and fallacies in either case are the usual ones of interpretation. For even where we analyze no more than a few lines spoken by a specific character we ought to do it, at least ideally, by interpreting the whole play.

Needless to say, no dramatis persona, not even the speaker of the Sonnets, should be identified with Shakespeare. To be precise, the mere possibility of such identification remains forever elusive. For who is thus identified with, say, Theseus or Holofernes? All we are able to reconstruct within the hermeneutic vicious circles is, as W. C. Booth has taught us long ago, the "implied author." Our sense of this complex creature, Booth writes,

includes, in short, the intuitive apprehension of a completed artistic whole; the chief value to which this implied author is committed, regardless of what party his creator belongs to in real life, is that which is expressed by the total form.[35]

A more appropriate title than "Shakespeare's Poetics," then, would have been "The Poetics of the Implied Author in the Works Attributed to Shakespeare." If, here and elsewhere, we nonetheless allow ourselves to speak of "Shakespeare" instead, we really mean this "implied author." In the absence of such documents as diaries and letters, this fictive construct is the closest we shall ever get to the author himself.

In other words, our findings towards Shakespeare's poetics (e.g., his dismantling of essentialist discourse in *Troilus and Cressida* or his inverted Platonism in *Love's Labour's Lost*) largely depend on an interpretative understanding of individual works. Hence, they are open to all the disagreements interpretations are likely to incur. Though to a lesser extent, this is also true of how the implied author stands in relation to the various characters – Berowne, Holofernes, the Will of the Sonnets, Theseus, Hamlet, Cleopatra, the Poet in *Timon*, Prospero, Polixenes – who are made to articulate the more complex concerns of Shakespeare's poetics. Two of these, Will and Theseus, as well as the ironies surrounding them, have already been mentioned. The others, though they will be discussed in more detail later, should at least be introduced at this point.

Berowne and Prospero probably offer the fewest problems. Granted, the plays in which they appear occasionally put us on our guard against them: *Love's Labour's Lost* largely through mocking good humor; *The Tempest* mainly by making us see the protagonist, say, fly into a temper or temporarily lose control of the situation. But such touches serve the purpose of characterization rather than a radical dissociation from the implied author. As protagonists, Prospero and Berowne act, to a considerable extent, as informing intelligences of their plays. Of course, there are limits to this, particularly in the case of Berowne and the penance imposed upon him at the end of *Love's Labour's Lost*; but by and large, their ideas or actions are made to prevail like those of author substitutes built into the plays. There is little reason, then, why we should not take their comments on creativity as essentially "Shakespeare's."

Irony, similar in complexity to that surrounding Theseus' comments on the imagination, refracts the well-known art–

nature dispute between Polixenes and Perdita.[36] All this, of course, has been discussed in various places. Polixenes, while determined to prevent Florizel, his "bud of nobler race," from marrying Perdita, "a bark of baser kind," advocates horticultural grafting as "an art / That nature makes;" Perdita, convinced of being a real shepherdess who is about to marry a prince, seems to oppose the idea. But the debate is a specious one; in fact, there is no genuine dissent. After listening to Polixenes' argument, she simply murmurs assent: "So it is."

The reasons she gives for continuing to dislike the "streak'd gillyvors" merely shift the debate onto different ground. While endorsing Polixenes' advocacy of an art which is itself nature, Perdita now treats these bastard flowers as symbolic of an excessive use of artifice. Her imagery here –

> I'll not put
> The dibble in earth to set one slip of them;
> No more than were I painted I would wish
> This youth should say 'twere well, and only therefore
> Desire to breed by me –

introduces an issue as familiar from Shakespeare's other works as his "art / That nature makes." Invectives against "painted rhetoric" or the "painted flourish" of eulogistic praise are found in *Love's Labour's Lost* (IV, 3; II, 1), while Will, in the Sonnets, inveighs against an unnamed rival poet who is "Stirr'd by a painted beauty to his verse" (21). We shall see from the songs concluding *Love's Labour's Lost* what type of "painting" Shakespeare favors instead. To use an apt phrase from the Sonnets, it is the kind "with Nature's own hand painted" (20), a notion well in tune with Polixenes' basic argument.

A more difficult case is that of the Poet in *Timon* who, like his friend the Painter, turns out to be a flattering opportunist. But we know nothing of that in the opening scene, where he makes his crucial statement about poetry oozing like a gum "From whence 'tis nourish'd." This in itself, of course, would not be sufficient cause for agreeing with E. C. Pettet that the words read "like the self-analysis of a practitioner" like Shakespeare, who "admits the subconscious nature of poetic composition."[37] What may be sufficient, however, is the fact, noted by Kenneth Muir, that there is little reason for doubting the Poet's sincerity at this point.[38] Though to a lesser extent than Prospero or Berowne, the Poet too, at least here at the beginning, is an agent in the play's underlying thematic dynamics. His allegorical poem dedicated to Timon, which shows Fortune in her fickleness towards her favorites, will come true at a later point. It is only towards the end that we are made to lose trust in his role as part of the play's informing intelligence.

The opposite is true of Cleopatra. Given her general readiness for lying and blackmail, we have good reason to distrust her words on most occasions. But by the time she utters her crucial words on the mythopoeic imagination (V, 2), the Queen, now full of longings to join her "husband" Antony in Elysium, has transcended these limitations. In turn, there is something almost superfluous about her prolix comments on her dream of Antony. To a greater or lesser extent, most related statements made by Theseus, Berowne, Polixenes, or the Poet strike us as similarly gratuitous. Were one to omit them, the works in which they occur would hardly suffer as poetic artefacts. We know that Theseus' words on the poet are probably due to marginal addition to an already completed text. At least metaphorically speaking, there is a similarly marginal feel about most comparable statements by Berowne, Polixenes, the Poet, and Cleopatra.

But to return to the various implied-author-persona relationships, there is, in fact, little controversy in the cases discussed so far. Most critics, for good reason, argue that Theseus, Will, Berowne, Prospero, Polixenes, Perdita, the Poet, and Cleopatra, in what they say about poetry and art, stand, in one form or another, for the implied author of the work in question; just as few would disagree that what Holofernes tells us about similar concerns is for the most part to be laughed at like the pedant himself. The only major mouthpiece of Shakespeare's poetics who has caused fundamental disagreement, then, is Hamlet. Readers to whom the Prince's views on drama and acting should be either linked with or dissociated from those of the implied author fall into neatly opposed groups.

For a long time critics simply identified the protagonist with Shakespeare. Roy Battenhouse, in 1970, listed over half a dozen such, and there have been more since.[39] Others, more recently, have put us on our guard against such simplistic equation. As S. L. Bethell wrote in 1944,

Hamlet is praising a type of dramatic composition in favour among the aristocratic dilettanti, but never successful on the popular stage; and it is difficult to believe that Shakespeare would wholeheartedly approve a mode of construction which he must himself have deliberately avoided. Hamlet, on the other hand, the aristocratic amateur, might well have shared Sidney's preference for the neo-classical. This would confirm my conclusion that the passage is meant to be taken as a serious expression of Hamlet's opinion, but not of Shakespeare's.[40]

Other critics, more convincingly, have associated Hamlet's theories with those of Ben Jonson.[41] But we have more than such external evidence for establishing the distance between Shakespeare and his dramatis persona.

As in Theseus' case, Hamlet's words are undercut by the context in which they appear. The Prince advises the players not to overstep "the modesty of nature" (III, 2) in their acting. But how would the player acting Hamlet acquit himself on the many occasions in which the protagonist vows to eat a crocodile, hems and haws, rants and raves, and all in ways repeatedly commented on by other characters? If ever the playwright wrote a part suggesting that its impersonator "tear a passion to tatters" and "split the ears of the groundlings" (III, 2), it was that of Hamlet. The irony speaks for itself.

But all this only begs another question. If Hamlet's theories of drama and acting seem to be like Ben Jonson's rather than the author's, what, then, were Shakespeare's own ideas about such matters? Needless to say, we shall never attain the complete answers we crave. But a lot that might bring us closer to them still lies unexplored in the vast regions of Shakespeare's work as a whole. What, for instance, were the playwright's favored modes of acting? As Daniel Seltzer notes, critics have strong opinions about the original Shakespeare productions as having been either highly "formal" or downright "realistic," even "naturalistic." But few attempts have been made to back up such claims by researching, say the printed and "implicit" stage directions in the texts themselves, or the various, though hardly numerous, comments on acting in commendatory poems, eulogies, and similar contemporary materials. Seltzer's 1971 conclusion, that the body of that evidence has not been collected and published,[42] remains true to date, despite his own efforts in sifting through over two hundred texts, from the earliest interludes to late Jacobean drama. In addition, there are Barbara Mowat's brilliant though controversial analyses on "Stage-Gesture in Shakespeare," as well as sporadic comments on the subject in various places.[43] But matters such as these are easily smothered under the researcher's theorizing and need to be documented in ways which will allow the reader to draw his own conclusions. After Seltzer's and Mowat's pioneering efforts, a volume on this subject remains to be written. Whatever is said about Shakespeare's concepts of acting in the second chapter makes no claim to fill this gap; rather, it needs to be tested by just such future research.

The same applies to much else in this volume. The task I have set myself is a near-impossible one, even in terms of the approach to be adopted in its pursuit. To discuss briefly one further example, the purpose of playing, in Hamlet's view, "is to hold, as 'twere, the mirror up to nature; to show virtue her own feature, scorn her own image, and the very age and body of the time his form and pressure" (III, 2). Interpreting similar statements in the context of the entire play, we have to be on our guard against simply taking the protagonist's words as Shakespeare's.[44] But a look into Elizabethan and Renaissance criticism can show that Hamlet, while not necessarily voicing the implied author's opinion, echoes a commonplace of the period. The Latin "Comoedia est imitatio vitae, speculum consuetudinis, et imago veritatis," which Donatus attributes to Cicero, was widely quoted by writers in England and abroad. Particularly fond of it among Shakespeare's contemporaries was Ben Jonson, who repeatedly used the image of the stage as a mirror of life in his own plays. But what was Shakespeare's own opinion on the matter? After all, the fact that the play undercuts Hamlet's comments on acting does not necessarily mean a similar inversion regarding his views on the purpose of dramatic art in general. In the absence of further evidence for establishing

Shakespeare's attitude to his character from the play itself, we are sent back to the playwright's oeuvre at large.

The area entered at this point, of course, must be explored with great caution. But, depending on the appropriateness of the questions raised in this pursuit, not all will be mere speculation. Does Shakespeare show preference for Hamlet's mirror-play analogy elsewhere? Does he tend to use the terminology of mimetic imitation wherever else he comments on similar matters? If not, what other terms does he prefer? Required at this point, then, are extensive word-field analyses, another area which has begun to attract systematic interest only more recently.[45] What is more, Hamlet, in stating that dramatic art should "show virtue her own feature, scorn her own image, and the very age and body of the time his form and pressure" (III, 2), can be compared with other advocates of didacticism and satire (e.g., Jaques in *As You Like It* and the Poet in *Timon of Athens*) whom Shakespeare presents in more directly ironical fashion.[46]

In sum, the attempt to deduce Shakespeare's poetics from the statements put into the mouths of his characters, follows a three-step approach. Each such statement is to be interpreted (1) within the context of the work in which it occurs, (2) within the context of Shakespeare's oeuvre in general, and (3) against the background of comparable non-Shakespearean writing of the period. Not each interpretation, of course, will proceed precisely according to that sequence. To add to the critical analogues scholars have found for the art–nature debate in *The Winter's Tale* (IV, 4), for instance, would be like carrying owls to Athens. Similar attention has been given to parallel instances in Shakespeare's works in general. But what is the result of all this research? The common assumption is that the Perdita–Polixenes debate simply repeats the current commonplaces of the time. And, prima facie, this is indeed the case. Even if it is assumed that Shakespeare upholds Polixenes' "an art / That nature makes" as his artistic credo, there is enough from other sources which seems to express the same idea. "Nature is more noble than Matter or Forme," we read in Palingenius' highly popular *Zodiake of Life*.[47] Here as elsewhere, then, Shakespeare's "ideas," as one critic puts it, seem to "belong to the common thought of his age."[48]

But is this really true in our case? *The Zodiake of Life*, while pro-
moting the superiority of nature over art, tells us on the very same
page, that nature is "nothing els but the law of God." The reason
for ranking nature above art, in other words, is that "nature" was
equated with the "order of the vniuerse" (J. Huarte),[49] which
itself was commonly thought of in teleological or Christian providential terms. As will be shown in more detail later, this, then,
was the overriding conviction of the age: the laws of art simply
derive from the cosmic laws of nature, the *ministra et factura dei*.
Would Shakespeare differ from that norm? The general answer is
"no"; but simply, I think, because critics take for granted that
Shakespeare's use of "nature" in the Polixenes–Perdita debate
conforms to the teleological understanding of the word prevalent
during the Renaissance. For a fresh look at this matter, we shall
therefore – as step one of our approach – try to establish the
meaning of "nature" from an interpretation of the entire play.
Time, the Chorus, from the opening of Act IV, offers the best
access to such an analysis.

But before dealing with these perhaps most comprehensive
issues of Shakespeare's poetics in the last chapter, this study will
have to come to grips with more mundane matters. Its first part
starts by assessing Shakespeare's awareness of general critical
issues against the background of related Renaissance writing.
Here already, we see the playwright evolve his ideas in partial
opposition to the consensus of his time. While Renaissance critics
drew sharp distinctions between invention and delivery (alias
imagination and composition), Shakespeare emphasizes the
spontaneous simultaneity of both (Chapter i). Similar discrepancies are found by comparing Shakespeare's attitudes towards
acting and drama with their mimetic and satirical counterparts in
Ben Jonson (Chapter ii). But most idiosyncratic regarding the
actual theatre, perhaps, is the playwright's attitude towards his
audience. The apologists of the three unities were divided in their
demands for either coercing spectators into believing that what
they saw was real, or for arguing that they could not but be aware
of the signifier–signified nature of theatrical events at all times.
Shakespeare, by contrast, not only ignored the unities, but also
prompted his spectators to range over a far-reaching spectrum

between the extremes of a nearly alienation-effect-type self-awareness and a complete absorption in the illusion of the spectacle (Chapter III).

It should be obvious even from this first part that "poetics," in the sense in which the word is used here, is by no means limited to concerns of mere craftsmanship. The second part will cast the net even wider. Here we shall explore Shakespeare's sense of language in general (Chapter V) and of poetic language in particular (Chapter VI); his ideas of creativity and the imagination (Chapters VI and VII); his theories regarding mythopoeic dramatizations of the supernatural (Chapter VIII); and, finally, his views on nature, art and artifice (Chapter IX). Except for his mythopoeic creativity, in which he seems to rely on some of the basic beliefs of his age, Shakespeare, as regards most of these issues, strikes a highly original, idiosyncratic, and sometimes surprisingly "modern" note. But for all its dissent from mainstream Renaissance theorizing, his poetics is by no means an isolated phenomenon. Many of its specific aspects, and, more importantly, its basic underlying assumptions, are also found with the two perhaps most eminent philosophers of his age, Montaigne and Bacon. It is only natural, then, that a separate chapter on the ideas which they shared should preface the more philosophically oriented second part of this book (Chapter IV). A few hints and examples as to these affinities between Shakespeare, Montaigne, and Bacon must suffice in this introduction.

Most crucial here, as will be shown in detail later, is their common antiessentialism or radical empiricism. Poetry, as a result, no longer serves the bidding of metaphysics or theology in expressing absolute "truths," as it ought to do according to most Renaissance theorizing. For, at least to Bacon and Montaigne, such metaphysical concepts are to be counted among the self-delusions of the human mind and hence have lost their validity. Bacon classifies them among the idols of the mind. Montaigne, in less systematic fashion, writes: "We say indeed 'power,' 'truth,' 'justice'; they are words that mean something great; but that something we neither see nor conceive at all."[50] Yet, however different in their wording, the two philosophers agree that "the inquisition of man," as Bacon puts it, "is not competent to find out *essential* forms";[51] that "there cannot be first principles for men," in Montaigne's words, "unless the Divinity has revealed them."[52] The last words, perhaps, that Shakespeare wrote for the stage sound a strikingly similar note:

> O you heavenly charmers,
> What things you make of us! For what we lack,
> We laugh; for what we have, are sorry; still
> Are children in some kind. Let us be thankful
> For that which is, and with you leave dispute
> That are above our question. Let's go off,
> And bear us like the time.[53]

More specific evidence of Shakespeare's basic antiessentialism and of how it permeates his poetics is found throughout the canon.

Whereas Neoplatonists, for instance, viewed creativity in terms of an ascent towards ideational absolutes, Shakespeare reverses this trajectory for the sake of a hypersensitivity of sensory perception which

> ... gives to every power a double power
> Above their functions and their offices.[54]

While averse to metaphysical speculation, this radical empiricism of quasi-supernatural intensity is open to the world of myth, or in Shakespeare's words, of "antique fables" and "fairy toys."[55] Linguistically, it avoids the apodictic tone of essentialist discourse in propounding its absolute "truths"; indeed, it rarely loses sight of language's limitations in trying to capture the ever-elusive flux of experience. Its ideal but unrealizable medium would be a language of silence, or the "dumb thoughts, speaking in effect," evoked by Shakespeare's Sonnet 85.

Similarly, Renaissance apologists of the *furor poeticus* went out of their way to emphasize, like Pontus, that such frenzy had nothing to do with either "bodily maladies" or any "folly and corruption of the brain." Instead, it is engendered by a "secret divine power, which illuminates the spirit of reason."[56] Even where they advocated a seemingly infinite freedom of "inexcogitable" invention, theorists from Fracastoro to Puttenham were equally intent on dissociating artists who make use of the imagination in the right way (*euphantasioti*) from those who abuse that power in delirium or ecstasy (*phantastici*).[57] In any case, whatever the poet has poured forth in this so-called divine frenzy, has to be revised and given a proper shape under the auspices of cold reason.[58]

Shakespeare's dissent from such ideas, as manifest in Theseus' lunatic-lover-and-poet speech, for instance, is borne out by Ben Jonson, who criticizes his fellow-playwright for his all too free-flowing fantasy and for his reluctance to revise.[59] Here again, Montaigne would probably have sided with Shakespeare. The essayist's self-declared task was to explore the "chimeras and fantastic monsters"[60] of his mind in defiance of all Renaissance prohibitions. As to Theseus' lunatic poet, who sees "more devils than vast hell can hold,"[61] the imagination to him has, and perhaps should have, semi-psychotic potential, just as the poet's fury is a genuinely pathological impulse.[62] True to his basic assumptions, Montaigne let the contents dictate his style rather than the reverse. Written spontaneously, without much revision, his essays, at least in the author's view, came to look much like the chimeras and monsters of his mind – "grotesque and monstrous bodies, pieced together of divers members."[63]

Behind all this is a radical new understanding of the artistic imagination. Bacon's severance of poetry from philosophy and, concomitantly, of the poet's imagination from the philosopher's speculations – for which again we find parallels in both Shakespeare and Montaigne – is surely not the mere repetition of a Renaissance commonplace as has been claimed.[64] Freed from reason's overrule, the imagination, despite Horace's injunctions to the contrary,[65] now "may at pleasure join that which nature hath severed, and sever that which nature hath joined." For the metaphysical restrictions that Fracastoro, Puttenham and Sidney, for example, imposed upon such phantasmagoric imaginings no longer apply. Poetry has been liberated from such bondage. It "wanders forth, and feigns what it pleases."[66] Such words are innovative in more senses than that of introducing a new concept of poetry that "ceases to be knowledge and becomes fiction and play."[67] Bacon, who also had an unprecedented understanding of myth, not only freed the poetic imagination from its traditional subservience to philosophy, but was prepared to elevate it beyond reason. This happens when the poet, with his "similitudes, types, parables, visions, dreams," assumes his role as a purveyor of supernatural inspiration.[68]

All these more rarefied aspects of a poetics, most of which Shakespeare shared with Bacon and Montaigne, will be explored in the second part of this study. But first some of the more immediate of the poet's concerns as craftsman and playwright must claim our attention.

I · Shakespeare, poet of nature

How did Shakespeare himself, whom others both praised and criticized as the poet of nature, view his craft and creativity? The question, raised in the introduction, is dealt with in numerous places in the canon. From the beginning, Shakespeare's comments on the issue have a complexity usually lacking in similar discussions by his contemporaries:

> Look when a painter would surpass the life
> In limning out a well-proportioned steed,
> His art with nature's workmanship at strife,
> As if the dead the living should exceed;
> So did this horse excel a common one
> In shape, in courage, colour, pace, and bone.

Prima facie, this stanza from *Venus and Adonis* (289–94) echoes the traditional assumption that art transcends nature by its tendency to idealize. But then we realize that the painter's more perfect horse only serves as analogue to a real one which Shakespeare, in the following stanza, describes in the most concrete detail.

Even where Shakespeare echoes the commonplace of art's superiority over nature directly, he undercuts his own statement by drawing attention to a lifeless artificiality to all art. "In scorn of nature, art gave lifeless life," he says of a painting described in *The Rape of Lucrece* (1374). "It tutors nature. Artificial strife/Lives in these touches, livelier than life," comments the Poet while looking at a portrait done by the Painter. Only the imaginative cooperation of the beholder can redeem art, at least temporarily, from its deathlike artifice.

> *Poet:* Admirable. How this grace
> Speaks his own standing! What a mental power
> This eye shoots forth! How big imagination

> Moves in this lip! To th' dumbness of the gesture
> One might interpret.
> *Painter:* It is a pretty mocking of the life.[1]

In other words, art, where it is claimed as surpassing nature, does not even equal it. At best, it may be said to reenact natural creation. This is a stance most clearly articulated in the romances. Marina, in Gower's words, "composes / Nature's own shape of bud, bird, branch, or berry" in her needlework – "That even her art sisters the natural roses."[2] Even in the romances, art is essentially lifeless. In order to be brought alive, it is in need of the spectator's imaginative collaboration. In one sense, the creator of a sculpture showing chaste Dian bathing, as described by Iachimo, may seem to have surpassed nature; but in others he clearly lags behind her:

> Never saw I figures
> So likely to report themselves. The cutter
> Was as another nature, dumb: outwent her,
> Motion and breath left out.[3]

The same is true of Julio Romano, who, "had he himself eternity and could put breath into his work, would beguile nature of her custom, so perfectly he is her ape." Emphasized here is that the artist lacked the essential qualities – eternity and the power to give life – which could make him nature's equal. Art, even from his hands, can be no more than life's deathlike "mockery," a term which Shakespeare, along with similar ones like "counterfeit" and "feigning," seems to prefer to the mimetic terminology of either naturalistic or idealistic imitation. "Prepare / To see the life as lively mock'd as ever / Still sleep mock'd death," announces Paulina before unveiling Julio Romano's sculpture.[4]

Shakespeare's continuing, even increased, insistence on the essential lifelessness of art is, of course, by no means his ultimate word on the matter. It simply underscores the stance of a poet who, aware of the limitations of his art, tries to reenact rather than to outdo nature. What is talked about as Julio Romano's sculpture of the dead Hermione, after all, turns out to be the live Hermione. What Shakespeare, through Polixenes, seems to suggest as his own is "an art / That nature makes," not one that presumes to "tutor" nature.[5] But all this takes us far ahead into issues which, more appropriately and in greater detail, will be discussed in a later chapter.

For the time being, a more simple answer to the question of Shakespeare's possible response to being called the poet of nature will have to suffice. This can be found in the extent or lack of the poet's concern with the technicalities and theories surrounding his craftsmanship. Did Shakespeare display an interest in or at least an awareness of such matters as prosody, imagery, poetic structure, and genre theory? How, in all this, does he compare with his immediate contemporaries? Of what range, specificity, and complexity is his aesthetic vocabulary if held up against the same background? To answer questions such as these will also provide us with an introductory survey of Shakespeare's implied poetics in general.

THE PEDANT'S CREATIVITY

One of his most comprehensive early statements on the poet's craft and creativity is put into the mouth of Holofernes. As such it reflects the presumptions of the pedant, and not, ŏf course, the attitudes of the poet. At the same time, Holofernes' words give us valuable evidence as to Shakespeare's familiarity with current poetic theories of his time:

This is a gift that I have, simple, simple; a foolish extravagant spirit, full of forms, figures, shapes, objects, ideas, apprehensions, motions, revolutions. These are begot in the ventricle of memory, nourish'd in the womb of pia mater, and delivered upon the mellowing of occasion. But the gift is good in those in whom it is acute, and I am thankful for it.[6]

Compared with others of "Nature's gifts," such as the "gift of tongue" and "heavenly gift of prophecy,"[7] Holofernes' gift involves the most complex mental activities. Predictably, the pedant describes this functioning of his talent in the terms of traditional facultative psychology.[8] The entire brain is enclosed by a membrane or *pia mater*, a term Shakespeare elsewhere tends to use as a synonym for intelligence in general.[9] It is divided into several portions or ventricles, each of which houses a specific mental faculty such as commonsense, imagination or memory. There were exceptions like Charron and Huarte who opposed this rigid compartmentalizing of the cerebral faculties. But Shakespeare, here and elsewhere, seems to favor localization. Lady Macbeth speaks of the "receipt of reason" (I, 7). Holofernes mentions the "ventricle of memory," usually thought to be the hindmost portion of the brain. This, to him, is the source of all the "forms, figures, shapes, objects, ideas, apprehensions, motions, revolutions" that go into the making of poetry.

Holofernes' account of the creative process leaves out an important preliminary. For the forms and figures which the poet calls up from his memory when writing were originally formed by different agencies of the brain. In this way, the memory is not the source but simply "the Register and Storehouse of all the Idea's and Images first perceiv'd by the Senses, and then collected and seal'd up by the Imagination."[10] Nor do images and ideas simply flow from the memory. Instead, they have to be activated by other mental agencies before they will be released into the creative process. According to Robert Burton, "Memory lays up all the species which the senses have brought in, and records them as a good register that they may be forthcoming when they are called for by phantasy and reason."[11]

But such omission serves the purpose of characterization. For what spills from Holofernes' brain when composing poetry are the ideas and figures of his reading rather than those of his personal experience. Like Launcelot Gobbo, he has "planted in his memory / An army of good words."[12] Hence his verses seem to draw on a very "alms-basket of words." The poem given as an example of his poetic gift is perhaps the most ludicrous in all of Shakespeare. Holofernes announces it as "an extemporal epitaph on the death of the deer" killed by the Princess. But there is little of the spontaneity that, naively, we might associate with such a title. Of course, we are warned that Holofernes' extemporizing will be harnessed to some alliteration which, in the poet's view, "argues facility."[13] But in fact almost every word in Holofernes' extemporal epitaph is pre-programmed by formal devices. These range from rhymed iambic heptameter to intricate schemes such as proparalepsis or the adding of a syllable to a word:[14]

> The preyful princess pierc'd and prick'd a pretty pleasing pricket.

Some say a sore; but not a sore till now made sore with
   shooting.
The dogs did yell; put el to sore, then sorel jumps from
   thicket –
Or pricket sore, or else sorel; the people fall a-hooting.
If sore be sore, then L to sore makes fifty sores o' sorel.
Of one sore I an hundred make by adding but one more L.[15]

Here, then, we have Holofernes' much-advertised ideas and
figures as "begot in the ventricle of memory, nourish'd in the
womb of pia mater, and delivered upon the mellowing of occasion." To call this "extemporal epitaph" a *reductio ad absurdum* of
Holofernes' poetics is putting it mildly. At the same time, Elizabethan spectators may well have found simply parodistic what a
modern audience finds ludicrous. Those familiar with the critical
writings of the time, in fact, were perhaps reminded of an
exercise which Puttenham proposes in his *Arte of English Poesie*.
This "dittie written extempore" according to specific rules is
much like Holofernes' "extemporal epitaph." Though improvised, it is predetermined by the number of its lines, by its
metrical arrangement, by its rhyme scheme, and by its opening
line. Those who successfully complete the exercise will give proof
of all the qualities which Holofernes values so highly. They will
display the accomplishments of "great arte" – a powerful
memory, the copiousness of their discourse, and, needless to
say, their foolish extravagant spirit:

If ye shall perceiue the maker do keepe the measures and rime as ye haue
appointed him, and besides do make his dittie sensible and ensuant to
the first verse in good reason, then may ye say he is his crafts maister.
For, if he were not of a plentiful discourse, he could not vpon the sudden
shape an entire dittie vpon your imperfect theame or proposition in one
verse. And, if he were not copious in his language, he could not haue
such store of wordes at commaundement as should supply your con-
cords. And, if he were not of a maruelous good memory, he could not
obserue the rime and measures after the distances of your limitation,
keeping with all grauitie and good sense in the whole dittie.[16]

Despite all this, not all of the poetic theorizing Holofernes
stands for is parodied. No doubt, Shakespeare agreed with the
schoolmaster's praise of Ovid, one of the playwright's favourite
poets. Equally to the point is Holofernes' critique of Berowne's

sonnet. While showing mechanical correctness of meter, the poem indeed lacks the true essence of poetry. "Here," the pedant comments, "are only numbers ratified; but, for the elegancy, facility, and golden cadence of poesy, caret. Ovidius Naso was the man. And why, indeed 'Naso' but for smelling out the odoriferous flowers of fancy, the jerks of invention."[17]

THE ARTS OF LANGUAGE

If such critical acumen strikes us as limited, there is little of greater perspicacity expressed by Shakespeare in his poems or put into the mouths of his characters elsewhere. Rosaline, half agreeing with Holofernes, finds that the numbers of Berowne's poem are true, but only for the sake of cracking a joke at his hyperbolic praises of her beauty:

> Nay, I have verses too, I thank Berowne;
> The numbers true, and, were the numb'ring too,
> I were the fairest goddess on the ground.[18]

Somewhat more specific is Rosalind's criticism of Orlando's poem in *As You Like It*:

Celia: Didst thou hear these verses?
Rosalind: O, yes, I heard them all, and more too; for some of them had in them more feet than the verses would bear.
Celia: That's no matter; the feet might bear the verses.
Rosalind: Ay, but the feet were lame, and could not bear themselves without the verse, and therefore stood lamely in the verse.   (III,2)[19]

What are we actually told about the nature of metrical language? That some of Orlando's lines have more feet in them than are required by the measure? That the feet he uses are so lame that they have to find their support in the line? It all says little more than what is implied in single phrases like "the very false gallop of verses"[20] and "the even road of a blank verse."[21]

While others were discussing the nature of metrical speech as opposed to prose, Shakespeare, to all evidence, displayed little interest in such theorizing.[22] To Chapman, for instance, poetry and prose are as far apart as the matters they are intended to communicate:

... Truth, with Poesie grac't, is fairer farre,
More proper, mouing, chaste, and regular,
Then when she runnes away with vntruss't Prose;
Proportion, that doth orderly dispose
Her vertuous treasure, and is Queene of Graces;
In Poesie, decking her with choicest Phrases,
Figures and numbers: when loose Prose puts on
Plaine letter-habits; makes her trot, vpon
Dull earthly businesse.[23]

Nothing comparable is to be found in Shakespeare. Hamlet complains that he is "ill at these numbers" and has "not art to reckon [his] groans" (II, 2). Henry V claims that he has "no strength in measure" (V, 2) and Will that his "gracious numbers are decay'd." Longaville, noting that his "stubborn lines lack power to move," may even tear up his poem on stage, and decide to "write in prose."[24] But none of these comments reveals a deeper understanding of the nature of metrical language.

The playwright also lacked a detailed terminological interest along these lines. The word hexameter, which has been called "an obsession of the Elizabethan mind,"[25] is not even mentioned; nor are such concepts as iambic or trochaic. If other technical terms are used, it is mostly in order to parody the characters who employ them. "Come, more; another stanzo: call you 'em stanzos?" sighs the melancholy Jaques.[26] "Let me hear a staff, a stanze, a verse," exclaims Holofernes; and after Nathaniel has recited Berowne's sonnet, he adds: "You find not the apostrophas, and so miss the accent: let me supervise the canzonet."[27] Quince suggests that the prologue introducing Pyramus shall be written in eight and six. But Bottom would prefer it in eight and eight. When the prologue finally appears, we realize that it is written in neither measure, but in the usual ten and ten.[28]

As with meter, so with rhyme. While the opponents and apologists of the device waged a critical war lasting several decades, Shakespeare at best made fun of specific kinds of rhyming.[29] To Benedick, such categories are the very hallmarks of his poetic impotence; "Marry, I cannot show it in rhyme; I have tried; I can find out no rhyme to 'lady' but 'baby' – an innocent rhyme; for 'scorn,' 'horn' – a hard rhyme; for 'school,' 'fool' – a babbling rhyme; very ominous endings. No, I was not born

under a rhyming planet, nor I cannot woo in festival terms."[30]
"Speak but one rhyme and I am satisfied; / Cry but 'Ay me!'
pronounce but 'love' and 'dove'," mocks Mercutio.[31] When
Rosalind reads some of Orlando's verses, Touchstone comments
that the poet's rhymes follow each other like dairy women
walking in single file. "I'll rhyme you so eight years together,
dinners, and suppers and sleeping hours, excepted. It is the right
butter-women's rank to market."[32] Other, more intriguing, references to the poet's own "barren" or "poor" rhyme, as found in
the Sonnets, apply not so much to specific rhyme schemes as to
the poems in general.[33]

More widespread and serious than Shakespeare's theoretical
concern with prosody, was his interest in poetic diction and
rhetoric. Best-known here, of course, are the poet's protests
against affectation. The garrulous Polonius is reminded to
provide "More matter, with less art."[34] Berowne, while inveighing against "Three-pil'd hyperboles" and "Figures pedantical,"
claims: "Honest plain words best pierce the ear of grief."[35]
Shakespeare himself voices analogous concerns in the Sonnets.
While claiming to speak "In true plain words by [a] true-telling
friend," he accuses his rival poets for using whatever "strained
touches rhetoric can lend" (82) and for

> Making a couplement of proud compare
> With sun and moon, with earth and sea's rich gems,
> With April's first-born flowers, and all things rare
> That heaven's air in this huge rondure hems.   (21)

We all know, of course, that Shakespeare is not above using
such hyperbole and other devices himself. More than that, he
often displays a distinct awareness of such techniques in talking
about comparisons, conceits, devices, epithets, figures, flowers
of fancy, hyperboles, metaphors and similes. Most striking
perhaps is his concern with poetic comparison. To be sure, here
again a lot is sheer good humor or parody. Particularly adept at
comparison are Falstaff and Prince Hal.

Prince: I'll be no longer guilty of this sin; this sanguine coward, this
bed-presser, this horse-back-breaker, this huge hill of flesh –
Falstaff: 'Sblood, you starveling, you eel-skin, you dried neat's-tongue,
you bull's pizzle, you stock-fish – O for breath to utter what is like

thee! – you tailor's yard, you sheath, you bow-case, you vile standing tuck!

The Prince, after this, promises to wait until Falstaff has tired himself "in base comparisons";[36] Falstaff, after a similar exchange, compliments Hal for his "most unsavoury similes" calling him "the most comparative, rascalliest, sweet young prince."[37] Whether things are thus matched "in comparisons with dirt"[38] or praised to the sky, comparison is most frequently used for hyperbole. Romeo, in the Nurse's view, is "past compare" (II, 5). Adonis, to Venus, is "sweet above compare."[39] "I am compar'd to twenty thousand fairs," mocks Rosaline after reading Berowne's verses.[40] Demetrius, after waking in the presence of Helen, exclaims: "To what, my love, shall I compare thine eyne? / Crystal is muddy."[41] We know that one of Shakespeare's most famous sonnets (18) raises a similar question and arrives at an analogous answer. Troilus proposes the ultimate in such comparative hyperbole to the future poets that will remember his story:

> when their rhymes,
> Full of protest, of oath, and big compare,
> Want similes, truth tir'd with iteration –
> As true as steel, as plantage to the moon,
> As sun to day, as turtle to her mate,
> As iron to adamant, as earth to th' centre –
> Yet, after all comparisons of truth,
> As truth's authentic author to be cited,
> 'As true as Troilus' shall crown up the verse
> And sanctify the numbers.   (III, 2)

We learn most about the possibilities which Shakespeare associated with comparison, whenever the figure becomes part of a poetics documented in the very process of poetic creativity. The best-known example occurs in Sonnet 18. Here Shakespeare asks himself if he should compare his friend to a summer's day, and in his answer ends up pointing at the "eternal summer" captured in the *monumentum aere perennius* of the very lines raising that question. Another sonnet shows how comparison, if usurped by the "madness of discourse," which from time to time haunts the poet, can turn into a tool of insidious self-deception:

> No more be griev'd at that which thou hast done:
> Roses have thorns, and silver fountains mud;
> Clouds and eclipses stain both moon and sun,
> And loathsome canker lives in sweetest bud.
> All men make faults, and even I in this,
> Authorizing thy trespass with compare,
> Myself corrupting, salving thy amiss,
> Excusing thy sins more than thy sins are.   (35)

How such "false compare" (130) figures within the sonnet sequence as a whole will be discussed at a later point. There also we shall look at Richard II's prison soliloquy beginning "I have been studying how I may compare / This prison where I live unto the world" (V, 5). In evolving various comparisons, the King, as we shall see, provides us with a running commentary on the way in which a poet, according to Theseus' well-known words, gives "a local habitation and a name"[42] to the ill-defined thoughts of the original creative impulse.

Only second to Shakespeare's concern with poetic comparison is his interest in the conceit. This word, of course, stands for various other concepts such as understanding and imagination as much as for the strictly artistic device. Even as such it applies to the fine arts as much as to poetry. The figures woven into a napkin are called "conceited characters."[43] The painter of the sack of Troy described in *The Rape of Lucrece* is labeled "conceited" for creating a powerful effect of pathetic fallacy whereby the clouds overhanging Ilium seem to kiss the city's turrets (1371). In the same poem, the word "conceit" also serves to describe the technique of creating the effect of optical illusion:

> For much imaginary work was there;
> Conceit deceitful, so compact, so kind,
> That for Achilles' image stood his spear,
> Grip'd in an armed hand; himself, behind
> Was left unseen, save to the eye of mind:
>   A hand, a foot, a face, a leg, a head,
>   Stood for the whole to be imagined.   (1422–8)

Linguistic just as much as artistic conceits are characterized by their *pars pro toto* ingenuity. Sometimes merely enigmatic, they can also be downright deceptive. Basset, in *1 Henry VI*, is said to "set a gloss upon his bold intent" "with forged quaint conceit"

(IV, 1). Other conceits are so ingenious that a "conceit's expositor" like Berowne may be needed to explain them.[44] The ladies' witty repartees in *Love's Labour's Lost*, as described by Boyet, give ample evidence of such wilful obscurity:

> The tongues of mocking wenches are as keen
> As is the razor's edge invisible,
> Cutting a smaller hair than may be seen,
> Above the sense of sense; so sensible
> Seemeth their conference; their conceits have wings,
> Fleeter than arrows, bullets, wind, thought, swifter things.   (V, 2)

Another expert at playing on both words and occasions is Launcelot Gobbo. He simply will not put up with his master's wish of seeing his orders answered and followed in straightforward fashion:

Lorenzo: . . . I pray thee understand a plain man in his plain meaning: go to thy fellows, bid them cover the table, serve in the meat, and we will come in to dinner.
Launcelot: For the table, sir, it shall be serv'd in; for the meat, sir, it shall be cover'd; for your coming in to dinner, sir, why let it be as humours and conceits shall govern.[45]

Grumio, in *The Taming of the Shrew*, on a similar occasion has to serve as his own "conceit's expositor" to his master Petruchio. This little *explication de texte* occurs when Petruchio rejects the tailor's gown for Katherine and asks his servant to "take it up unto [his] master's use:"

Grumio: Villain, not for thy life! Take up my mistress' gown for thy master's use!
Petruchio: Why, sir, what's your conceit in that?
Grumio: O, sir, the conceit is deeper than you think for. Take up my mistress' gown to his master's use! O fie, fie, fie!   (IV, 3)

Shakespeare says less about specifically poetic conceits whereby poets, to quote William Webbe, "drawe mens mindes into admiration of theyr inuentions."[46] But what little he hints at along these lines suggests that ingenuity at the expense of meaningfulness should be kept within limits. His ideal here may well have been what Juliet calls "Conceit, more rich in matter than in words." The heroine here probably uses "conceit" in the sense of understanding rather than of rhetorical device. At the same time, her words contain a clear retort to Romeo's over-elaborate ingenuity of language. In six lines, building up to a single conceit, the protagonist has just invited Juliet to indulge in similar jerks of invention. Juliet's refusal therefore sounds only too convincing at this point.

> *Romeo:* Ah, Juliet, if the measure of thy joy
> Be heap'd like mine, and that thy skill be more
> To blazon it, then sweeten with thy breath
> This neighbour air, and let rich music's tongue
> Unfold the imagin'd happiness that both
> Receive in either by this dear encounter.
> *Juliet:* Conceit, more rich in matter than in words,
> Brags of his substance, not of ornament.
> They are but beggars that can count their worth;
> But my true love is grown to such excess
> I cannot sum up sum of half my wealth.   (II, 6)[47]

Of similar spirit are the lines from a sonnet which, though probably by Richard Barnfield, was published under Shakespeare's name in *The Passionate Pilgrim* of 1599. Here Spenser is said to have such "deep conceit" or understanding that he passed "all conceit" or play of fancy (VIII, 7, 8).

Apart from his obvious fascination with the nature of conceit and comparison, Shakespeare's concern with the nomenclature of related devices rarely seems to rise above a humorous dismissal of the "Sweet smoke of rhetoric."[48] Touchstone's terminological legerdemain is a case in point. His example of a "figure in rhetoric" is "drink, being pour'd out of a cup into a glass, [which] by filling the one doth empty the other."[49] Otherwise, the playwright and his characters have little good to say about rhetoric *per se*. In the Sonnets, the poet opposes the "true plain words by [a] true-telling friend" to the "strained touches rhetoric" can lend to the verse of his rivals (82). There is similar contrast between the "painted rhetoric" of the poetasters in *Love's Labour's Lost* (IV, 3) and "the heart's still rhetoric disclosed" by the King's eyes after he has fallen in love with the Princess (II, 1).

The few times Shakespeare uses the word "metaphor," he makes fun of it.[50] "Syllogism" is mentioned once, again for the sake of a joke: "Clown: . . . virtue that transgresses is but patch'd with sin, and sin that amends is but patch'd with virtue. If that this simple syllogism will serve, so; if it will not, what remedy?"[51] Shakespeare's most conspicuous use of "hyperbole" is found in Berowne's denunciation of "Three-pil'd hyperboles"[52] and in Ulysses' condemnation of Patroclus' fustian imitation of Agamemnon: "and when he speaks, / 'Tis like a chime a-mending; with terms unsquar'd, / Which, from the tongue of roaring Typhon dropp'd, / Would seem hyperboles."[53] Needless to say, Shakespeare frequently uses the words "epithet" and "simile." He specifies similes of comfort and epithets of war, or characterizes the two words by a variety of often interchangeable adjectives such as "sweetly varied," "most singular" and "choice," "swift" and "unsavoury."[54] But, characteristically, he prefers the simple word "phrase" to the more specific terms of rhetoric proper. The epithets characterizing "phrase" in Shake-speare's works are almost as diverse as the "mint of phrases"[55] in Don Armado's brain. There are "phrase[s] of war," phrases of sorrow and soft phrases of peace. There are "soldier-like phrase[s]," "red-lattice phrases," "Taffeta phrases," "grandsire phrase[s]," not to mention the phrases that are termed "good," "poor," "stewed," "ill," and "vile."[56] And, finally, there are the precious phrases "by all the Muses fil'd" to which the poet opposes his "dumb thoughts, speaking in effect."[57]

The absence of related, more technical, terminology from Shakespeare's works is in direct proportion to their ubiquity in Elizabethan critical and non-critical writings. Even such simple terms as "monosyllable," "similitude,"[58] "elocution," and "alle-gory,"[59] which are widely used by other writers, are simply non-existent in Shakespeare's vocabulary. Of course, this does not mean that Shakespeare was unaware or ignorant of such matters. Although the playwright never uses the word "Euphuism," for instance, Falstaff's parody of that style is as well informed as anyone's who ever read Lyly's novel.[60] All one might claim at this point is that Shakespeare's terminological unconcern in some cases stands out all the more when we remember how consistently he returns to a handful of his favorite poetological concepts and interests.

On the other hand, there is no doubt that Shakespeare drew on the rich arsenal of the Renaissance arts of language. Sister Miriam

Joseph purports to identify in his work over two hundred figures of speech and devices of language, each one equipped with its special label ranging from "acyron" to "zeugma:"

The formal training which Shakespeare received, [she argues] contributed not only to the breadth and stature of his thought but also to the richness of the gorgeous panoply with which he invested it. His language, fresh, vibrant, exuberant, and free, makes use of the schemes of words as well as the schemes of construction. He effects sudden and vivid concentration of meaning by a poetically superb and daring use of anthimeria (nouns as verbs), catachresis (verbs and adjectives employed in a transferred sense), hypallage (the transferred epithet), the compound epithet, metaphor, metonymy, syllepsis of the sense, negative and privative terms. He secures swiftness of movement, compactness, and emphasis through anastrophe (inverted word order), parenthesis, zeugma (one verb serving two or more subjects), brachylogia and asyndeton (omission of conjunctions).[61]

The value of such analyses, particularly regarding individual lines and passages, is often considerable. At the same time one wonders how Shakespeare might have felt after reading Sister Miriam Joseph's learned study. Perhaps he would have reacted like Montaigne in the essay "Of the Vanity of Words:"

When you hear people talk about metonymy, metaphor, allegory, and other such names in grammar, doesn't it seem that they mean some rare and exotic form of language? They are terms that apply to the babble of your chambermaid.[62]

POETIC STRUCTURE AND GENRE

The discrepancies between Shakespeare's poetological interests and those of his peers is probably greatest where issues of poetic structure and genre are concerned. Matters such as these, of course, did not elicit the highest critical acumen of the Elizabethans.[63] Nevertheless, there was enough that could have, but did not, arouse the interests of a poet as alive to related issues as Shakespeare. Critics and writers other than the playwright discussed such matters as the structure of dramatic plot, the difference between tragedy and comedy, or the nature of tragicomedy and romance.

Before Richard Flecknoe, in his *Short Discourse of the English Stage*, said that spectators of a play "shu'd be led in a Maze, but not a Mist,"[64] playwrights had been commenting on similar concerns for several decades. To describe the nature of a dramatic plot as a maze, in fact, had long been a commonplace. Fletcher, in the Prologue to *The Woman's Prize*, warns his spectators not to expect "the mazes of a subtle plot."[65] Cartwright praises Ben Jonson for not making a "strange perplexed *maze*" pass for a dramatic plot.[66] Other writers took a more liberal attitude towards the issue. A certain Jay, commenting on Massinger's *A New Way to Pay Old Debts*, praises the "craftie *Mazes* of [its] cunning plot."[67] D'Amville, in Tourneur's *The Atheist's Tragedy*, describes a plot in which every circumstance of "persons, dispositions, matter, time / or place" was made part of a complicated murder story, and "yet nothing from / The induction to th' accomplishment seem'd forc'd, / Or done o' purpose, but by accident" (II, 4).[68] Lyly, in the Epilogue of *Sapho and Phao*, congratulates himself for having led his spectators successfully through "a Labyrinth of conceites" towards a conclusion which ties in with "where [he] first beganne."[69] Romelio, in Webster's *The Devil's Law Case*, expresses the hope that "the last act be the best i' th' play" (II, 3).[70] Ben Jonson, with characteristic thoroughness, has certain characters in *The Magnetic Lady* (I, 7, Chorus) discuss the nature of the dramatic plot in terms of protasis, epitasis and catastrophe, and in his *Discoveries* describes the ideal plot as one which "being compos'd of many parts . . . beginnes to be one, as those parts grow, or are wrought together."[71]

While they could be extended, these examples are sufficient to highlight the scarcity of similar comments in Shakespeare. The playwright once refers to his *mediis in rebus* technique, twice has characters point out the fact that at the end of the play Jack will either have or not have Jill,[72] and in *As You Like It* has Hymen, in true comedy fashion, bring about the "conclusion" by joining eight men and women in wedlock. Otherwise, he sometimes makes an epilogue announce the end of the play, but without commenting on the conclusion as such. Clifford's "La fin couronne les oeuvres"[73] and Hector's

The end crowns all;
And that old common arbitrator, Time,
Will one day end it[74]

refer to the character's understanding of his particular situation
rather than to the end of the play. The same is true of Edmund's
"Pat! He comes like the catastrophe of the old comedy" when he
sees Edgar run into the trap he has laid for him.[75] The use of
"catastrophe" and "conclusion" regarding the story of King
Cophetua and the beggar maid in Armado's letter to Jaquenetta
serves to parody the writer, not to make a significant statement
about the terms.[76] Or there is Desdemona's comment on the
"most lame and impotent conclusion" of one of Iago's "old fond
paradoxes."[77]

More significant are two comments on the conclusions of
musical compositions. One suggests how "music at the close, /
As the last taste of sweets, is sweetest last,"[78] the other how a
musical piece may end with all its components "Congreeing in a
full and natural close."[79] As far as dramatic "plots" are concerned, Shakespeare never once seems to use the word in that
specific sense.[80] Parolles' "Who cannot be crush'd with a plot?",
for instance, refers to part of what we have seen in *All's Well
That Ends Well* (IV, 3), but only obliquely to the play's plot
structure.

Hardly more insightful, though far more extensive, are Shakespeare's comments on the use of prologues, epilogues, and
choruses – another widely debated set of issues in Renaissance
poetics. Needless to say, the playwright displays no consistent
theoretical attitude towards such matters. Much of the satire in
the performance of "Pyramus and Thisbe" focuses on the Athenian workmen's "vilely penn'd" prologues,[81] explaining what is
all too obvious. But Shakespeare, as we know, uses prologues in
several of his own plays, and on occasion, justifies such practice
to the audience. In *Troilus and Cressida*, a prologue is introduced
to help the "fair beholders" leap "o'er the vaunt and firstlings" of
the war left unpresented in the play. In *Henry V*, it tries to enlist
the spectators' imaginative collaboration and to help them
bridge some of the gaps which the author had to leave in his
play:

For 'tis your thoughts that now must deck our kings,
Carry them here and there, jumping o'er times,
Turning th' accomplishment of many years
Into an hour-glass; for the which supply,
Admit me Chorus to this history;
Who, prologue-like, your humble patience pray
Gently to hear, kindly to judge, our play.

Shakespeare's justification of his Chorus here contrasts with the ironical use of the word in the exchange between Ophelia and Hamlet while the two watch "The Mouse-trap":

Ophelia: You are as good as a chorus, my lord.
Hamlet: I could interpret between you and your love, if I could see the puppets dallying. (III,2)

Pragmatically ambivalent in a similar way is Shakespeare's attitude towards epilogues which he makes fun of on the one hand, and uses on the other. In at least one instance, he does both. In *As You Like It*, the Epilogue, in the person of Rosalind, appears on stage only to tell the audience that "a good play needs no epilogue." But even that attitude is quickly exchanged for another.

Rosalind: ... If it be true that good wine needs no bush, 'tis true that a good play needs no epilogue. Yet to good wine they do use good bushes; and good plays prove the better by the help of good epilogues. What a case am I in then, that am neither a good epilogue, nor cannot insinuate with you in the behalf of a good play!

Shakespeare displays an equal lack of theoretical interest in questions of genre. The person who raises the matter in most explicit terms is scatterbrained Polonius. To him the players, come to act at the court of Denmark, are the best "in the world, either for tragedy, comedy, history, pastoral, pastoral–comical, historical–pastoral, tragical–historical, tragical–comical–historical–pastoral."[82] The terminological confusion so typical of Shakespeare's time is satirized, but no attempt is made to correct it. The attitude, of course, is by no means uniquely Shakespearean: "Wee present neither Comedie, nor Tragedie, nor storie, nor anie thing," announces the Prologue to Lyly's *Endimion*.[83] Similar indifference is shown by Dekker, who seems unable to decide whether the play he is talking about be "Pastoral

or Comedy, Moral or Tragedie."[84] Some of Shakespeare's contemporaries would obviously have shared the playwright's
mocking attitude towards the genre-conscious garrulity of a
Polonius or towards the terminological legerdemain of the Athenian workmen who indiscriminately call their "Pyramus and
Thisbe" a play, an interlude, a "most Lamentable Comedy," a
"tedious brief scene" and "very tragical mirth."[85] "Is't comedy,
tragedy, pastoral, moral, nocturnal, or history?" asks one of
Marston's characters. The answer is "Faith, perfectly neither; but
even What You Will."[86] Needless to say, the last words spell out
the play's title, which may have been inspired by Shakespeare's
preference for similar ones such as *As You Like It* and *Twelfth
Night: Or, What You Will.*

As J. W. H. Atkins points out, there is a minor exception to
Shakespeare's manifest indifference to terminological issues of
genre: "towards one type of play – the pastoral – he betrays a
critical attitude which is of some significance. In *As You Like It*, for
instance, the artificiality of pastoralism is derided by Touchstone's solemn fooling; Jaques scoffs at the idea of Arcadia as 'a
free republic'; and by means of both satire and parody the ethical
motive of pastoralism is held up to ridicule. In *The Winter's Tale*,
however, a more sympathetic attitude is adopted." Otherwise, so
Atkins concludes, Shakespeare makes no definite pronouncements with regard to his views on the different "kinds."[87]

But more can be said about the issue if we look at some of the
negative evidence. Shakespeare's terminological range concerning genre, especially when compared with that of his contemporaries, is conspicuously limited. In addition to the terms
already quoted, it includes ballad, canzonet, carol, dirge, ditty,
elegy, fable, hymn, masque, ode, pageant, psalm, roundel,
satire, and song.[88] But other terms, such as bucolic, dramatic,
eclogue, epic, epithalamium, lyric, panegyric, parody, romance,
and tragicomedy, which were well familiar to the Elizabethans,[89]
are absent from Shakespeare's vocabulary. What is more, even
the playwright's use of terms as crucial to his art as comedy,
tragedy, and history, let alone any sense of what distinguishes
these various genres, never rises above the commonplace.

Not all theorists, for instance, confined themselves to the

notion that "Poets *Tragicall*," to quote Puttenham, "set forth the dolefull falles of infortunate & afflicted Princes."[90] Thomas Lodge had read in Donatus that both tragedy and comedy "wer inuented by lerned fathers of the old time to no other purpose but to yeelde prayse vnto God for a happy haruest or plentiful yeere."[91] Puttenham himself speculated that tragedy, via the cothurn, was somehow connected with certain sacrifices surrounding the god Pan.[92] By contrast, Shakespeare only hints at the notion of tragedy as a fall of princes,[93] and commonly uses the term in the even more simplistic sense of calamity, murder, and butchery. Typical here are associations such as "bitter, black, and tragical," "tragic melancholy night," and "act of tragic violence."[94] At that, "tragedy," except where the word occurs in the titles of actual plays or in descriptions of plays-within-the-play,[95] usually has a metaphorical rather than directly dramaturgical sense. Even rare expressions such as "tragic scene" and "tragic volume"[96] usually refer not to literary matters, but to the death of phoenix and turtle or to a messenger's ill-boding brow. In turn, "Black stage for tragedies"[97] serves as a poetic description of the night rather than of theatrical matters. Equally unrevealing in this way is the mention of the "English tragedians," whose talents, in Buckingham's description, are reminiscent of corny dilettantes rather than professional actors:

> Tut, I can counterfeit the deep tragedian;
> Speak and look back, and pry on every side,
> Tremble and start at wagging of a straw,
> Intending deep suspicion.[98]

A counterpart to this "deep tragedian" is the spectator "turn[ing] white and swoon[ing] at tragic shows" in the possibly apocryphal *A Lover's Complaint* (308). But neither this nor an intriguing question raised by Marcus at the sight of his mutilated niece Lavinia –

> O, why should nature build so foul a den
> Unless the gods delight in tragedies? – [99]

are enough to give us positive clues as to Shakespeare's deeper understanding of the genre in which he most excelled.

Even less discriminating is Shakespeare's use of the words

"comedy" and "comic." While his contemporaries evolved theories of laughter (e.g., "Laughter proceeds / From absurd actions that are harmless"), attempted to work out what distinguishes comedy from tragedy, or tried to define the nature of tragicomedy,[100] Shakespeare seemed content with the obvious. That Jack and Jill should have each other at the end of a comedy; that a comedy contains more pleasing stuff than a "Christmas gambold or a tumbling-trick"; that it can frame the spectator's "mind to mirth and merriment"[101] – such and similar comments voiced by some of the characters suggest the extent of the playwright's enquiries along similar lines. Some light on comic acting is shed by the mention of the comedian who "can say little more than [he has] studied."[102] Similarly, there is Cleopatra's complaint about the "quick comedians" who stage things "Extemporally" (V, 2), or Hamlet's warning that the "clowns speak no more than is set down for them" (III, 2). But in sum Shakespeare displays as little theoretical concern with the comic and comedy as with the tragic and tragedy. As far as tragicomedy and romance are concerned, he does not even mention the terms.

MAJOR FORM AND INVENTION

What, finally, can we say about Shakespeare's sense of the overall design of a play or poem in general? To Renaissance aestheticians, such major form was defined by the poet's invention.[103] In George Gascoigne's view, "The first and most necessarie poynt that euer I founde meete to be considered in making of a delectable poeme is this, to grounde it upon some fine inuention."[104] Except in terminological differences, critics had little disagreement regarding the matter. What to Gascoigne is the invention or device is the "*Idea* or fore-conceite of the work" to Sidney,[105] and the "Fable and Fiction" to Ben Jonson.[106] But whatever they call it, all three consider major form to be the most important part of the poem as well as of the creative process. "[F]or any vnderstanding knoweth the skil of the Artificer standeth in that *Idea* or fore-conceite of the work, and not in the work it selfe," writes Sidney.[107] "[H]ee is call'd a *Poet*," argues Ben Jonson, "not hee which writeth in measure only; but that fayneth and formeth a fable, and writes things like the Truth. For, the Fable and Fiction is (as it were) the forme and Soule of any Poeticall worke, or *Poeme*."[108]

Shakespeare uses some of the same vocabulary, while varying it with other terms. "And for thy fiction," Timon tells the Poet, "Why, thy verse swells with stuff so fine and smooth / That thou art even natural in thine art" (V, 1). Of course, "fiction" here, quite apart from Timon's duplicity in using the word, has a vaguer meaning than in Ben Jonson. More direct are Puck's description of *A Midsummer Night's Dream*'s "weak and idle theme" (V, 1), Ophelia's and Claudius' references to the "argument" of "The Mouse-trap," and Prince Hal's use of the same word when Falstaff proposes that they should "have a play extempore:" "Content – and the argument shall be thy running away."[109] Elsewhere "argument" is used almost synonymously for "invention," which Shakespeare, like his contemporaries, employs most frequently in this context. " 'Fair, kind, and true' is all my argument," protests the sonneteer, " 'Fair, kind and true' varying to other words; / And in this change is my invention spent" (105). *Venus and Adonis*, as Shakespeare states in the Dedication, was "the first heire" of his "invention." When Lucrece tries to write her husband a letter after being raped, her inventions are so many that they smother her ability to express herself.

> Conceit and grief an eager combat fight;
> What wit sets down is blotted straight with will;
> This is too curious-good, this blunt and ill:
>> Much like a press of people at a door,
>> Throng her inventions, which shall go before.
>
> (1298–1302)

Claudio, who believes he has caused the death of his beloved Hero by suspecting her innocence, is asked if he "Can labour aught in sad invention" and "Hang her an epitaph upon her tomb." The melancholy Jaques has composed a poem to a tune "in despite of [his] invention." Ganymede, alias Rosalind, is angry at the "Ethiope words," "cruel style," and "giant-rude invention" of a letter sent her by Phebe. Sir Toby advises Sir Andrew to be "eloquent and full of invention" in his challenge to

Cesario, alias Viola. Characteristically, Iago's invention, when
asked to praise Desdemona with his paradoxes, "comes from
[his] pate as birdlime does from frieze – it plucks out brains and
all."[110]

But most revealing here are the Sonnets, where "invention,"
upon its first occurrence, appears together with its twin-concept
"argument:"

> How can my Muse want subject to invent,
> While thou dost breathe, that pour'st into my verse
> Thine own sweet argument . . .
> For who's so dumb that cannot write to thee,
> When thou thy self dost give invention light?   (38)

Just as the poet's invention or argument is directly prompted by
experience (the love for his friend), so his words are a direct
expression of his emotions:

> Why write I still all one, ever the same,
> And keep invention in a noted weed,
> That every word doth almost tell my name,
> Showing their birth, and where they did proceed?
> O, know, sweet love, I always write of you,
> And you and love are still my argument.   (76)

In other words, experience gives the poet's pen both its "skill and
argument" (100). The remaining sonnets in which "argument"
and "invention" appear side by side (79, 103, 105), are variations
on the same theme. The poet pretends that his friend's "lovely
argument / Deserves the travail of a worthier pen"; but in fact he
is saying that his rival's supposedly superior invention will, like
his own, be nothing more than what is prompted by reality or the
friend who provides it (79). The poet's "bare" argument and
"blunt invention" can never equal, let alone "mend," the
"subject" (103). In all this, the playwright, though sharing certain
tendencies with a Sidney, Puttenham, or Ben Jonson, reveals a
distinctly Shakespearean bias.

All four writers seem to agree in crediting "invention" with
some of the powers we now tend to associate with the Romantic
imagination.[111] If Ben Jonson speaks of the "state of poesie" as
"Blessed, aeternall, and most true deuine," it is mainly because of
"her peculiar foode, / Sacred inuention."[112] In Puttenham's view,

the poet, if equipped with "an excellent sharpe and quick inuention, holpen by a cleare and bright phantasie and imagination," becomes the equal of God, "who without any trauell to his diuine imagination made all the world of nought."[113] The equation, first evolved, under Ficino's influence, by Florentine Neoplatonist Cristoforo Landino, was a familiar one to Renaissance poets and critics like Tasso and Scaliger.[114] Like the divine Creator, so Puttenham puts it,

> Even so the very Poet makes and contriues out of his owne braine both the verse and matter of his poeme . . . even as nature her selfe working by her owne peculiar vertue and proper instinct and not by example or meditation or exercise as all other artificers do, [he] is then most admired when he is most naturall and least artificiall.[115]

Although Sidney avoids the equation of the poet with God, he credits poetic invention with much the same special powers. "Onely the Poet," he writes,

> lifted vp with the vigor of his owne inuention, dooth growe in effect another nature, in making things either better then Nature bringeth forth, or, quite a newe, formes such as neuer were in Nature, as the *Heroes, Demigods, Cyclops, Chimeras, Furies,* and such like: so as hee goeth hand in hand with Nature, not inclosed within the narrow warrant of her guifts, but freely ranging onely within the Zodiack of his owne wit.[116]

Shakespeare, at least, in the opening Chorus of *Henry V,* speaks of the poetic invention in the same demiurgical terms, praying

> . . . for a Muse of fire, that would ascend
> The brightest heaven of invention.

But elsewhere the playwright reveals a more original attitude concerning the issue. However Romantic they sound, critics like Ben Jonson, Puttenham, and Sidney limit the poet's semi-divine powers to the act of poetic invention, as distinct from the actual writing process. Ben Jonson may grant that the poet, unlike other artists, raises himself "as by a divine Instinct" and "utters somewhat above a mortall mouth";[117] but he has mere contempt for those who confuse such poetic frenzies with the process of composition.[118] Puttenham, in a similar way, distinguishes demiurgical invention from three other stages of the creative process. These are deliberate and rational where invention can be spontaneous and imaginative. All four are spoken of in terms of the several roles which the poet should play, not simultaneously, but one after the other. Spontaneous invention, in other words, is succeeded by the laborious process of highly conscious crafts-manship – "as first to deuise his plat or subject, then to fashion his poeme, thirdly to vse his metricall proportions, and last of all to vtter with pleasure and delight, which restes in his maner of language and stile as hath bene said, whereof the many moodes and straunge phrases are called figures."[119] Composition, then, is not to be identified with the "invention" preceding it. Most categorical in this respect is Sidney, who distinguishes between the "*Idea* or fore-conceite of the work" and the "deliuering forth" of this invention. "Which deliuering forth," he stresses, ". . . is not wholie imaginatiue, as we are wont to say by them that build Castles in the ayre."[120]

Altogether, Renaissance aestheticians had few things to say about the writing process. Particularly, they had little sense of a simultaneity of imagination and delivery so familiar to post-Romantic critical theory. The few critics who did have any such sense rarely went beyond listing a mechanical sequence of activities. Fracastoro, said to be one of the most "Romantic" of Renaissance critics,[121] is representative of the rest, although he inverts the usual sequence of events. The poet, like the orator, begins by exercising his conscious craft, which finally transports him into the state of divine frenzy:

First he began to modulate sounds, to select the musical, and reject the unmusical, or slur them as much as possible, to delight especially in metaphors, to give attention to sonority and smoothness, and in short to all the other beauties of language. Then he proposed to consider feet and meters, to make verses and to see what was appropriate for each idea. For subject matter he desired to select as far as possible only the beautiful and admirable excellent and to ascribe to it only beautiful and admirable qualities. If these were lacking he proposed to form them through metaphor, to search for digressions, and comparisons, to omit none of the other devices which make for the excellence of speech, arrangement, transitions, figures, and other ornaments . . . As soon as he had joined all the beauties of language and subject and had spoken them, he felt a certain wonderful and almost divine harmony steal into him, to which no other was equal. And then he observed that he was, as it were, carried out of himself. He could not contain himself, but raved like those who take part in the mysteries of Bacchus and Cybele when the pipes are blown and the drums re-echo.[122]

Like any poet, Shakespeare must, at least occasionally, have shared his contemporaries' sense of distinction between the work of art and what it deals with – between the many details, digressions, formal elements, etc., and the major theme, invention, argument, or fiction these serve to express. The Prologue to *Romeo and Juliet*, for instance, tells us that the play is about a "pair of star-cross'd lovers . . . / Whose misadventur'd piteous overthrows / Doth with their death bury their parents' strife." And it is true that the tragedy bears out this proposition with almost theorematic consistency. But *Romeo and Juliet* is, in this, by no means typical of Shakespearean drama,[123] quite apart from the fact that the question as to whether Shakespeare wrote the play with a preconceived idea remains open. The tragic theme of human sacrifice leading to progress might well have emerged in the process of writing and the Prologue have been composed after the tragedy had been completed.

That at least is the bias – so contrary to Renaissance criticisms in general – suggested by Shakespeare's more directly theoretical statements on the matter. We have already seen how the Sonnets stress a simultaneity, even oneness, of poetic invention and composition. A related notion, that of an inventionless or unpremeditated creativity, recalls Ben Jonson's critique of Shakespeare's fantasy as flowing with too much facilty.[124] It is voiced by one of Shakespeare's characters. Winchester suspects Gloucester to have come with "deep premeditated lines" and "written pamphlets studiously devised," and challenges him to speak spontaneously and from the heart instead:

> Do it without invention, suddenly;
> As I with sudden and extemporal speech.[125]

The only time that a poet, in Shakespeare's oeuvre, describes his creativity in some detail, the statement sounds all too similar:

> Our poesy is as a gum, which oozes
> From whence 'tis nourish'd. The fire i' th' flint
> Shows not till it be struck: our gentle flame

Provokes itself, and like the current flies
Each bound it chafes.[126]

"Invention," let alone the separation between "fore-conceite" and delivery, is not even mentioned. To speak in Holofernes' terms, there is no distinction between "the jerks of invention" and the "odoriferous flowers" plus "golden cadence of poesy" with which the poet is supposed to invest his original argument.[127] Compared with the pedant's description of the creative process, or similar ones found in various Renaissance poetics, the Poet's words do not mention a single one of the terms we would expect in such a context.

Where we would usually hear of "imaginatiue groundplot[s] of a profitable inuention,"[128] we are told of gum oozing from a tree. Where we expect to be informed of how the poet applies his knowledge of prosody and poetic rhetoric, we are given another metaphor – a flame provoking itself – hinting at the same kind of almost involuntary self-generation. Where we are prepared for the customary lesson as to how to apply conscious craft to the effusions of invention, this poet is said to flee from, as much as to work within, the boundaries of a formal restraint. There is no word of any of the figures, metrical proportions, devices, conceits, and other ornaments that are the stock in trade in comparable Renaissance descriptions of the creative process. We might find ideas similar to the poet's elsewhere; but both the language and general drift of his statement are highly original. As E. C. Pettet put it so well over thirty years ago, "it reads like the self-analysis of a practitioner ... Shakespeare admits the subconscious nature of poetic composition; but in the place of divine *inflatus* he advances a theory of spontaneous generation and internal stimulus."[129]

This theory is not so much stated as exemplified by imagery, syntax, and prosody. Instead of a discursive sequence imposed from without, there is an internal undercurrent of associations, with words, images, and ideas prompting further words, images, and ideas. The deepest notion, probably, is that of flux. It is there in the gum that flows from the tree which nourishes it; then it temporarily disappears in the image of the flame that provokes itself; but it reemerges in the current that flies each bound it chafes. The syntax, as it constantly overwhelms the iambic pentameter line, suggests a similar flow. Sentences usually end in midline, one sentence generating the next without conjunctions or rational links of any kind. All this is further enhanced by the repeated midline pause. There is variation in the sound pattern, appropriately found in the one sentence – "[t]he fire i' th' flint / Shows not till it be struck," – which modifies the overall statement. But as well as the shrill tones heard here, there is a bass tone of dark vowel sounds running right through the poet's words. In sum, these seem to embody, not to explain, their theoretical message. Creativity, rather than being sequential, with invention preceding delivery, is a self-generative process of psychophysiological spontaneity, imagination, and composition occurring in near-simultaneous unison. If Shakespeare ever intended to reply to Ben Jonson's charge that "hee flow'd with that facility, that sometime it was necessary he should be stop'd," he could have found no better words than those of the Poet in *Timon of Athens*.

II · Acting and Drama

HAMLET'S ADVICE to the players, as various critics point out, reflects an essentially neoclassical viewpoint particularly reminiscent of Ben Jonson.[1] The Prince is clearly aware of following a time-honored tradition in stating his most central concept. The purpose of playing, "both at the first and now," he argues,

> was and is to hold, as 'twere, the mirror up to nature; to show virtue her own feature, scorn her own image, and the very age and body of the time his form and pressure. (III, 2)

Speaking in more historical terms, he also calls the players "the abstract and brief chronicles of the time." In the protagonist's view, one had better have "a bad epitaph after death than their ill report" while alive (II, 2).

Though ultimately stemming from Plato and Aristotle, Hamlet's theory of drama as mimesis derives from a phrase Donatus attributes to Cicero: "Cicero ait Comoedia est imitatio vitae, speculum consuetudinis, et imago veritatis."[2] The statement is one of the most popular commonplaces of the Renaissance. It is quoted by Minturno and Jaques Grévin as well as paraphrased by Cervantes. In England, it is found in Lodge's *Defence of Poetry*, Heywood's *Apology for Actors*, and other texts. Sidney's definition of comedy as "an imitation of the common errors of life" seems to draw on it. Spenser, lamenting the decline of classical comedy – "By which man's life in his likest image / Was limnèd forth" – may refer to it. If Shakespeare ignored all these, there was also Ben Jonson's *Every Man Out of His Humour*, a play performed in 1599 at the Globe, not long before the writing of *Hamlet*. Cordatus, friend of the author and a man of "discreet, and vnderstanding iudgement," evidently proposes the Latin phrase as Jonson's own understanding of comedy. "Quid sit

28

Comoedia?" he asks, and lacking a better answer, proposes Cicero's alleged "Imitatio vitae, speculum consuetudinis, et imago veritatis" as the most appropriate one (III, 6).[3]

HAMLET AND BEN JONSON

Like Hamlet, Ben Jonson uses the word "mirror" as his most central concept of dramatic art and never tires of repeating it. The opening of *Every Man Out of His Humour* invokes "a mirrour / As large as is the stage, whereon we act." Probee, in *The Magnetic Lady* (II, 7, Chorus), defines comedy as a "Glasse of custome . . . so held up to me, by the Poet, as I can therein view the daily examples of mens lives, and images of Truth." Ben Jonson himself, in a preface to *Love's Triumph through Callipolis*, declared categorically that all representations, "especially those of this nature in court, publique Spectacles, eyther haue bene, or ought to be the mirrors of mans life."[4] Here, as in surveying other of Jonson's ideas about drama, it must not be forgotten, of course, that whatever Jonson the classicist might theorize, his practice, to quote Renu Juneja, "was rooted in the techniques and traditions of Elizabethan drama."[5]

The natural correlative of Hamlet's mimetic sense of drama in general is his preference for the well-structured or "excellent play, well digested in the scenes, set down with as much modesty as cunning" (II, 2). Polonius earlier draws a distinction between the "scene individable" conceived according to the "law of writ" and the dramatic "poem unlimited" of imaginative "liberty" (II, 2). Of course, we do not know what exactly Shakespeare associated with these terms. But there is little doubt as to which of the two kinds of drama is advocated by Hamlet. His own model play, of which we hear a long sample, emerges as a neoclassical drama *par excellence*.

The speech itself, as S. L. Bethell shows, has all the salient hallmarks of Senecan rhetoric which Polonius associates with the "scene individable" and the "law of writ:" there is "rant, Latinity, the stock emotive word; classical reference; extended conceit; the classical simile."[6] No doubt the play itself was well digested in the scenes and acts. In Hamlet's description it avoided bawdry –

"there were no sallets in the lines to make the matter savoury" (II, 2). Certainly, it allowed little room for humor, especially of the kind aroused by the clown who, leaving the script, would crack an improvised joke in order to get a cheap laugh from the groundlings while "in the mean time some necessary question of the play" went unheeded. It was a play defined by the rhetoric of its script, a play without the usual "inexplicable dumb shows and noise" for the groundlings (III, 2). Instead, it addressed itself to an elite of the judicious, perhaps like the small circle of scholars and aristocrats assembled around the Countess of Pembroke and her brother, Sir Philip Sidney – it "pleas'd not the million; 'twas caviary to the general" (II, 2).

Of the major Elizabethan playwrights, only Ben Jonson survived the neglect of future generations with such ideas. In *Every Man Out of His Humour* (II, 3), for instance, some of the characters discuss when and why a scene is too long or how the author might "haue altered the shape of his argument, and explicated 'hem better in single *Scenes*." Ben Jonson involves himself in extensive considerations of concepts like protasis, epitasis and catastasis. He also has little patience for the kind of "jig" or "tale of bawdry" which Hamlet contemptuously alleges to be Polonius' favorites (II, 2). At least in theory, the laughter aroused, say, by "a rude Clowne drest in a Ladies habit, and using her actions" should be considered "a fault in Comedie." Ben Jonson claimed to "dislike, and scorne such representations," concurring with the ancient philosophers that laughter is "unfitting in a wise man."[7] Fed by a Pauline distrust of the *concupiscentia oculorum*, such puritanism, averse to anything spectacular,[8] can vent itself in a paroxysm of indignation when confronted with the lurid occasion of some spectators watching a jig and bawdry combined:

> Look, look, how all their eyes
> Dance i' their heads (obserue) scatter'd with lust!
> At sight o' their braue *Idoll*! how they are tickle'd,
> With a light ayre! the bawdy *Saraband*![9]

Needless to say, Ben Jonson also shares Hamlet's contempt for the unskillful groundlings who "are capable of nothing but inexplicable dumb-shows and noise." The Prince's "barren specta-

tors" (III, 2) are Ben Jonson's "*Faeces*, or grounds of your people,"
"the rude barbarous crue, a people that haue no braines," and
"onely come for sight." The playwright's own kind of drama
addresses itself to those whom he prefers to call "auditors" rather
than "spectators." Its priority is a manifest words above action.
The Prologue to *The Staple of News* stresses the author's clear
preference for delivery over stage action

> For your owne sakes, not his, he bad me say,
> Would you were come to heare, not see a Play.
> Though we his *Actors* must provide for those,
> Who are our guests, here, in the way of showes,
> The maker hath not so; he'ld have you wise,
> Much rather by your eares, then by your eyes.[10]

Jonsonian drama, then, is addressed to the "learned ears" of
those whom Hamlet calls the "judicious" (III, 2): "To Schollers,
that can iudge, and faire report / The sense they heare, aboue the
vulgar sort / Of Nut-crackers, that onely come for sight." A
remark in Ben Jonson's *Poetaster* seems to parallel Hamlet's
concern with "judicious" auditors, who overweigh "a whole
theatre of others" (III, 2). The Author about to attempt tragedy
after comedy has proven "so ominous" to him, is more than ever
committed to his elitist audience:

> Where, if I proue the pleasure but of one,
> So he iudicious be; He shall b' alone
> A Theatre vnto me.[11]

It is quite likely that some of their more sophisticated spectators
noticed the parallel between Shakespeare's and Ben Jonson's
words.[12]

Quite generally speaking, the relationship between stage
action and delivery was a crucial issue to Elizabethan playwrights. One character in Tomkis's *Lingua* (IV, 2) complains that
his speech has no action in it – "for . . . the hand (you knowe) is
harbinger to the tongue, and prouides the words a lodging in the
eares of the Auditors." By contrast, Communis Sensus, in the
same play, emphasizes delivery over action and ridicules the old
kind of pantomimic action advocated by Phantastes.[13] Dekker's
Sir Quintilian in *Satiromastix* (V, 1) draws the same distinction,

wondering if a fellow-actor has failed his role – "Disranckt the lynes? disarm'd the action?"[14] The dichotomy between "action and deliuerie"[15] was a familiar one, and obviously known to Shakespeare: "How can I grace my talk, / Wanting a hand to give it that accord?" exclaims Titus Andronicus (V, 2).

The distinction between action and delivery is also central to Hamlet's art of acting. A player, in his view, affects both "eyes" and "ears" of his audience (II, 2). Yet like a good neoclassicist, the Prince stresses words over spectacle. The players should neither saw the air too much with their hands nor split the ears of the groundlings with their bellowing. Hamlet concedes that they ought not to be too tame either. Their action should be suited to the delivery, and the delivery suited to the action, but only by strictly observing the limits imposed by "the modesty of nature." Proper delivery – "trippingly on the tongue" – is recommended as the very means of staying within these boundaries:

Speak the speech, I pray you, as I pronounc'd it to you, trippingly on the tongue; but if you mouth it, as many of our players do, I had as lief the town-crier spoke my lines. Nor do not saw the air too much with your hand, thus, but use all gently; for in the very torrent, tempest, and, as I may say, whirlwind of your passion, you must acquire and beget a temperance that may give it smoothness. O, it offends me to the soul to hear a robustious periwig-pated fellow tear a passion to tatters, to very rags, to split the ears of the groundlings, who, for the most part, are capable of nothing but inexplicable dumb shows and noise. I would have such a fellow whipp'd for o'erdoing Termagant; it out-herods Herod. Pray you, avoid it . . . Be not too tame neither, but let your own discretion be your tutor. Suit the action to the word, the word to the action; with this special observance, that you o'erstep not the modesty of nature; for anything so o'erdone is from the purpose of playing.   (III, 2)

Hamlet has already demonstrated how to achieve such tempered smoothness by reciting some lines "with good accent and good discretion" (II, 2).

Like Hamlet, Ben Jonson predictably opposes any "*scenicall* strutting, and furious vociferation." Instead, he recommends an acting style more in tune with his aim of sporting with human follies, not with crimes. Essential to it is an external mimicking of idiosyncratic character traits, an interest shared by Hamlet, with his fondness for certain stock characters such as the sighing lover and the humorous man (II, 2). In *Every Man in His Humour*

(III, 5), Ben Jonson seems to give us an example of such acting techniques. We are told of someone who, in imitating certain military men, proceeds by "obseruing euery tricke of their action, as varying the accent, swearing with an *emphasis*, indeed all, with so speciall, and exquisite a grace, that (hadst thou seene him) thou would'st haue sworne, he might haue beene Serieant-*Maior*, if not Lieutenant-*Coronell* to the regiment."[16] Such skill would also find the approval of Hamlet. Characteristically, the Prince remembers some actors who, by their strutting and bellowing, "imitated humanity so abominably" that the characters they tried to represent were hardly recognizable as human beings (III, 2).

Speaking of the ultimate goal of such acting, both Hamlet and Ben Jonson subscribe to a clearly didactic understanding of drama. Characteristically, Cicero's alleged "Imitatio vitae, speculum consuetudinis, imago veritatis," so central to either's theorizing, is given a markedly didactic twist by both. Ben Jonson's Cordatus, after quoting the Latin phrase, claims that this purpose of drama ought to be "accommodated to the correction of manners." Elsewhere, the playwright adds similar afterthoughts about anatomizing the time's deformity to the profit of the auditors, wherever he uses the metaphor of the mirror. While subscribing to Horace's *prodesse et delectare*, Ben Jonson clearly stresses the profit rather than the delight of his audience.[17] In turn, Hamlet insists that the theatre, in holding the mirror up to nature, "show virtue her own feature, scorn her own image, and the very age and body of the time his form and pressure" (III, 2). Like Jonson, he is interested in the profit rather than the delight of his audience.

DRAMATIC MIMESIS AND THE AUDIENCE

Hamlet's admirers may have reason to wonder why Shakespeare should have made their hero the mouthpiece of a theory of drama so obviously out of tune with his actual practice. To try to resolve this problem would mean resketching a somewhat unflattering portrait of this "spoilt favourite among Shakespearean characters" (S. L. Bethell)[18] which I attempted elsewhere.[19] All I shall try to establish here is to what degree Hamlet's poetics of drama differs from or agrees with similar statements in other of Shakespeare's works. Of course, there is a third possibility. A major principle enunciated by Hamlet might find no, or next to no, analogues elsewhere in the canon. Yet even such negative evidence can be of interest. The very fact of Shakespeare's deliberate or unconscious reticence concerning a given notion might hint at the playwright's attitude towards it.

Hamlet's mimetic concept of drama as a mirror held up to nature with actors "imitating" humanity is a case in point. Shakespeare commonly uses the word "mirror" and its synonym "glass" in the sense of model. Henry V, for instance, is "the mirror of all Christian kings" (II, Prologue). Hamlet himself is reputed to have been "the glass of fashion" by Ophelia (III, 1). Or Cressida may find less of Troilus "in the glass of Pandar's praise" (I, 2) than in the actual person of her lover. But, except in Hamlet's phrase, the word "mirror" or "glass" meaning mimesis, a metaphor so very popular with Ben Jonson, is absent from Shakespeare's works.

It is almost the same with "imitate" and "imitation," words well-known in their mimetic sense at least since Roger Ascham's *The Scholemaster* (1570). "The whole doctrine of Comedies and Tragedies," we read there, "is a perfite *imitation*, or faire liuelie painted picture of the life of euerie degree of man."[20] "Poesie," Sidney wrote several years later, "is an arte of imitation, for so *Aristotle* termeth it in his word *Mimesis*, that is to say, a representing, counter-fetting, or figuring foorth."[21] But Shakespeare never once used the word "mimesis," only rarely spoke of mimetic "imitation," and showed little interest in or awareness of the Aristotelian doctrine where he employs synonyms like "to present" or "to counterfeit." Apart from Hamlet's "they imitated humanity so abominably" (III, 2), the same terminology is only once employed in an unmistakable sense of dramatic mimesis. Patroclus' vaudeville impersonations of his superiors are called "imitation" by the impersonator. Characteristically, Ulysses has a distinctly low opinion of such mimetic efforts:

> And with ridiculous and awkward action –
> Which, slanderer, he imitation calls –
> He pageants us. Sometime, great Agamemnon,

Thy topless deputation he puts on;
And like a strutting player whose conceit
Lies in his hamstring, and doth think it rich
To hear the wooden dialogue and sound
'Twixt his stretch'd footing and the scaffoldage –
Such to-be-pitied and o'er-wrested seeming
He acts thy greatness in.[22]

Holofernes' "Imitari is nothing"[23] probably refers to the slavish imitation of other literary texts. In another instance, the connotation of mimesis in the use of "imitate" is more oblique. "Describe Adonis, and the counterfeit / Is poorly imitated after you," protests the sonneteer (53). Shakespeare, in talking of such matters, obviously preferred terms such as "to present," "to counterfeit," or "to mock." But even here he shows little concern for the concepts so central to Hamlet's advice to the players. For instance, there is Warwick's

Why stand we like soft-hearted women here,
Wailing our losses, whiles the foe doth rage,
And look upon, as if the tragedy
Were play'd in jest by counterfeiting actors?[24]

As in this case, "to counterfeit," when applied to some form of artistic or histrionic imitation, usually retains a strong connotation of fakery. The same is true of "to mock," as in Leontes' "we are mock'd with art"[25] when looking at Hermione's statue; or of "to present," when Cleopatra voices her misgivings about the "quick comedians:"

Extemporally [they] will stage us, and present
Our Alexandrian revels; Antony
Shall be brought drunken forth, and I shall see
Some squeaking Cleopatra boy my greatness
I' th' posture of a whore.   (V, 2)

Otherwise, "to present" is mainly used in connection with the pathetic mimetic efforts we witness in the Pageant of the Nine Worthies and in the tragedy of Pyramus and Thisbe, where the word is employed some dozen odd times.

We are equally disappointed in looking for further discussion, outside *Hamlet*, of the "scene individable" conceived according to "the law of writ" and of the "excellent play, well digested in the scenes, set down with as much modesty as cunning" (II, 2).[26] Berowne in *Love's Labour's Lost* may remark that the wooing will not end "like an old play" with Jack getting his Jill (V, 2), a notion echoed by Puck in *A Midsummer Night's Dream* (III, 2). Or he may comment that "a twelvemonth an' a day" is "too long for a play" (V, 2).[27] In turn, various choruses may describe the duration of a play in performance as "the two hours' traffic of our stage,"[28] warn the audience that the playwright has turned "th' accomplishment of many years / Into an hourglass," and digested "Th' abuse of distance" by roaming freely from country to country.[29] Or they might draw attention to the fact that the action, following the Horatian *mediis in rebus*, will begin "in the middle, starting thence away / To what may be digested in a play."[30] But, unlike Hamlet's pronouncements of the "excellent play, well digested in the scenes" (II, 2), such statements are humorously descriptive or apologetic rather than normative and programmatic. Instead of calling his scenes well-digested, Shakespeare, when talking to us more directly, has a tendency to speak of his "swelling," "fast-growing," or "swift" scene, which "flies / In motion of no less celerity / Than that of thought."[31] "Scene," in these cases, of course, tends to designate the play as a whole as much as its individual units.

Shakespeare also shows few signs of sharing Hamlet's or Jonson's contemptuous attitude towards the "barren spectators" and their favorite type of popular drama. Sly, with his preference for a "Christmas gambold or a tumbling-trick," may nod while watching a "comonty" like *The Taming of the Shrew* (Induction, 2); the aristocratic spectators of "Pyramus and Thisbe" and the Pageant of the Nine Worthies might be exposed to our ridicule in trying to ridicule the lowly actors. But such irony and humor lack the acerbity of Hamlet's contempt for the unskillful groundlings or Ben Jonson's for "the sordid multitude" as well as the "neater sort of our *Gallants*."[32] In general, Shakespeare's attitude towards his audience seems to be one of conciliatory though ironical self-ingratiation throughout.[33]

This is all the more surprising since Shakespeare, as actor and playwright, frequently voices his disgust with himself and the "harlotry players," "quick comedians," and "counterfeiting actors" that formed his daily company:[34]

> Alas, 'tis true I have gone here and there
> And made myself a motley to the view,
> Gor'd mine own thoughts, sold cheap what is most dear,
> Made old offences of affections new.[35]

Such lines about himself, or those about the "strutting player, whose conceit / Lies in his hamstring,"[36] seem to suggest that Shakespeare, at some point in his career, went through a temporary "disillusionment with the stage"[37] which was finally overcome in the romances. But, unlike Ben Jonson and Hamlet, he never vented such feelings on the audience.

To his "gentles," "fair beholders," and "Gentle spectators" Shakespeare is simply the "humble" and "bending author" with his "rough and all-unable pen."[38] The anonymous author of the Reader's address to the 1609 quarto of *Troilus and Cressida* may speak of the "dull and heavy-witted wordlings as were never capable of the wit of a comedy"; or praise the play under hand because it has been neither "clapper-clawd with the palmes of the vulger" nor "sullied, with the smoaky breath of the multitude."[39] Similarly, Fletcher, collaborating with Shakespeare on *Henry VIII*, distinguishes between those who come to "sleep an act or two" and others who only attend the theatre so as to "hear the city / Abus'd extremely, and to cry 'That's witty!'" (Epilogue). Shakespeare himself had a strikingly different attitude. Except for Hamlet's harangues against the "barren spectators" (III, 2), there is little evidence that he ever addressed his audience, including the unskillful groundlings, in any but the most respectful and deferential terms. In various prologues and epilogues he calls them gentlemen and gentlewomen, apologizes for his "weak and idle theme," for disgracing the battle of Agincourt by representing it with "four or five most vile and ragged foils, / Right ill-dispos'd in brawl ridiculous," or simply for a recent "displeasing play," for which he promises a better one.[40]

A possible exception is *Troilus and Cressida*. With uncommon indifference, the Prologue bids the audience to either "Like or find fault" just as their "pleasures are," and Pandarus, in his final "Hypocrite spectateur, – mon semblable, – mon frère!" address to the audience, calls those who care to identify with him "Good traders in the flesh" and promises to bequeath them his venereal diseases. But *Troilus and Cressida* is Shakespeare's most bitter play, while Pandarus speaks *in propria persona* rather than for the author. Where the playwright addresses his gentles more directly there is nothing but fearing displeasure, asking for patience or pardon, promising amends, striving to please, and begging for applause.

Nor do we find the invectives frequent in Ben Jonson and others against the improvising clown catering to the "gallery-Commoner"[41] who, so Henry Medwall had complained long ago, "lokis and gapys / Only for suche tryfles and japys."[42] Hamlet's words to similar effect again are the curious exception. Would a playwright as intent on entertaining his audience as Shakespeare object to the laughter raised by some improvised joke of a Feste or Falstaff? Falstaff's tendencies to extemporize, as built into the text,[43] suggest the very opposite. After all, even Ben Jonson, though in principle convinced that laughter is "unfitting in a wise man," was not averse to stuffing out the scenes of *A Tale of a Tub* with "*acts of* Clownes *and* Constables" (Prologue).[44]

Quite consistently, Shakespeare, by contrast to Hamlet and Ben Jonson, stresses action over delivery and appeals to his spectators' eyes rather than their ears. Characteristically his gentles and fair beholders are not once in direct address named "auditors" – Ben Jonson's favorite term – or even "audience." Where the Chorus in *Henry V* pleads with us to "eke out [the] performance with [our] mind[s]" (III, Prologue), his appeals to "behold" and to "see" are far more numerous than those directed to our hearing. At the same time he draws attention to simple noises like the neighing of horses or the "shrill whistle which doth order give / To sounds confus'd" (III, Prologue) rather than to the smooth delivery of his characters. His general aim, then, like Gower's in *Pericles*, seems to be "To glad your ear and please your eyes" (I, 1).

Where Ben Jonson tries to isolate his auditors' ears as much as possible from their eyes, Shakespeare's aim, to all evidence, is the very opposite: "Your ears unto your eyes I'll reconcile." Action is allowed to take over wherever the word has played out its role:

"[W]hat need speak I," asks Gower before letting a dumb show demonstrate what remains unsaid. In turn, no effort is spared to explain otherwise inexplicable dumb shows to the groundlings: "What's dumb in show I'll plain with speech."[45] So there is little to suggest that Shakespeare shared Hamlet's and Ben Jonson's puritanical distrust of anything spectacular in general and of the bawdy and obscene in particular. A poet who made his characters joke about erections and impotence or who wrote the following lines in a sonnet, would hardly squirm at the odd "tale of bawdry" or "sallet" in the lines of a play:

> My soul doth tell my body that he may
> Triumph in love; flesh stays no farther reason,
> But, rising at thy name, doth point out thee
> As his triumphant prize. Proud of this pride,
> He is contented thy poor drudge to be,
> To stand in thy affairs, fall by thy side. (151)

Even the more puritanically minded critic would find it hard to deny that Shakespeare displayed a certain zest for such matters. Roy Battenhouse, surely no free-thinker in such matters, suggests that the playwright may even have meant to satirize his hero along these lines.[46] Hamlet's puritanical indignation at salacious sallets, jigs, and tales of bawdry is contradicted by his own use of bawdy innuendo, in, say, taunting Ophelia or calling himself, not inappropriately, a "jig-maker" in the same scene (III, 2).

THE ART OF ACTING

But what, if not Hamlet's, was Shakespeare's view of the art of acting? Here again, the playwright's sporadic suggestions seem to be all but in opposition to the protagonist's. Nor did Shakespeare share Ben Jonson's aversion to anything smacking of "*scenicall* strutting, and furious vociferation."[47] His players, if we can trust these descriptions, had little in common with the Roman actors of old, believed to be full of "formal constancy."[48] The very scripts of Shakespeare's plays told them to behave in a rather more histrionic fashion. As in Norfolk's description of Cardinal Wolsey, their "strange postures" and ways of delivery were usually meant to signal the character's state of mind:[49]

>   My lord, we have
> Stood here observing him. Some strange commotion
> Is in his brain: he bites his lip and starts,
> Stops on a sudden, looks upon the ground,
> Then lays his finger on his temple; straight
> Springs out into fast gait; then stops again,
> Strikes his breast hard; and anon he casts
> His eye against the moon. In most strange postures
> We have seen him set himself.[50]

There was hardly a part of the body that was not involved in these "strange postures." There was biting of lips and thumbs, knitting of brows, scratching of heads, sucking of teeth, changing color, and shedding of tears (sometimes with a little help from an onion or a cup of sack), quite apart from the usual sighing, musing, and staring.[51] Actors would roll their eyes, cross their arms, make an angry wafture with their hand, beat at their heart in grief, stamp the ground with their foot, spurn at straws, paddle a lady with the palm of the hand, and practice less direct forms of non-verbal communication like making mouths, coyly declining the head into the bosom, or just winking and nodding.[52] Techniques of emotion-charged verbal delivery included speaking "in starts distractedly," making "periods in the midst of sentences," letting the tongue stumble in articulating words, and even "murder[ing]" the breath "in middle of a word."[53]

Shakespeare's endorsement of such techniques is probably clearest in *Hamlet*, whose protagonist is made to behave in precisely the histrionic manner condemned in his advice to the players. The Prince would like to hear dramatic speeches pronounced "trippingly on the tongue" (III, 2). But even before he utters such neoclassical principles, we have heard him rant, rave, and bellow ("I should 'a fatted all the region kites / With this slave's offal: bloody, bawdy villain!"), make periods in the middle of his sentences, and speak in "Hum[s]" and starts distractedly, as in "Fie upon't, foh! About, my brains" (II, 2). Later, in alleged competition with Laertes, he vows to "drink up eisel," "eat a crocodile," weep, fight, fast, and tear himself all in one. "Nay, an thou'lt mouth, / I'll rant as well as thou," he assures his opponent (V, 1), obviously oblivious of his previous prohibitions to the players to neither "mouth" their words nor "tear a passion to tatters" (III, 2). Dover Wilson has noted seven seizures of "ungovernable agitation" in Hamlet's behavior,[54] something also remarked by the characters in the play. Horatio comments on his "wild and whirling words" after the Prince has first seen his father's ghost (I, 5). Ophelia, after the nunnery scene, finds his reason "Like sweet bells jangled, out of time and harsh" (III, 1). Gertrude wonders why his tongue, "In noise so rude," "roars so loud and thunders in the index" (III, 4).

Similarly, Hamlet's stage action serves to parody his neoclassical censures of anything in the players' histrionics that might overstep "the modesty of nature" (III, 2). How other than in the strangest postures would the actor playing the Prince acquit himself of his task where Gertrude describes her son as talking to something invisible to her?

> Alas, how is't with you,
> That you do bend your eye on vacancy,
> And with th' incorporal air do hold discourse?
> Forth at your eyes your spirits wildly peep;
> And, as the sleeping soldiers in th' alarm,
> Your bedded hairs like life in excrements
> Start up and stand an end.   (III, 4)

In fact, it is Hamlet's reported demeanor at this point that gives reason to assume that some of Shakespeare's obviously more extreme accounts of the actor's histrionics – like Suffolk's self-taught art of invoking curses – may not be all that exaggerated after all: "My tongue should stumble in mine earnest words, / Mine eyes should sparkle like the beaten flint, / Mine hair be fix'd an end, as one distract."[55]

Long before Hamlet castigates such excesses, we learn that his penchant towards self-dramatization probably exceeds that of any major Shakespearean character, including Petruchio. Ophelia gives a striking description of her one-time lover after he assumes his "antic disposition" (I, 5): Hamlet appeared to her with his doublet unbraced, bare-headed, his muddied stockings ungartered and hanging down over his ankles, with a look so piteous that his impressionable victim is reminded of a ghost freed from hell to speak of infernal horrors. The rest of this speechless pantomime, complete with shaking of arms, heaving up and down of head, profound sighing as well as less cliché-ridden gestures, is too well known to need quoting (II, 1).

But Shakespeare makes Hamlet contradict his advice to the players in even more direct ways. Before the Prince advises the players not "to split the ears of the groundlings" (III, 2), he seems to approve of and, in fact, to covet such histrionic talents himself. Hamlet has just heard a player recite his favorite speech about Priam's slaughter and Hecuba's grief, and in a mixture of self-disgust and amazement, admires the very acting which, when in a more conscious mood, he will later condemn:

> O, what a rogue and peasant slave am I!
> Is it not monstrous that this player here,
> But in a fiction, in a dream of passion,
> Could force his soul so to his own conceit
> That from her working all his visage wann'd;
> Tears in his eyes, distraction in's aspect,
> A broken voice, and his whole function suiting
> With forms to his conceit? And all for nothing!
> For Hecuba!
> What's Hecuba to him or he to Hecuba,
> That he should weep for her? What would he do,
> Had he the motive and the cue for passion
> That I have? He would drown the stage with tears,
> And cleave the general ear with horrid speech.   (II, 2)

Hamlet's words at this point recall similar accounts of acting given by other characters. Julia, in *The Two Gentlemen of Verona*, when once acting Ariadne grieving over Theseus' perjury and flight, shed genuine tears and hence made her audience weep too (IV, 4). Other feats, said to be the "deep tragedian['s]," are mentioned by the future King Richard III, where he wonders if Buckingham can "quake and change [his] colour, / Murder [his] breath in the middle of a word, / And then begin again, and stop again, / As if [he were] distraught and mad with terror" (III, 5). The deep tragedian, so these and Hamlet's words seem to suggest, can shed real tears, change color, and give himself the appearance of real distraction. For once, Shakespeare seems to use his protagonist for making more direct statements about the art of tragic acting. In other words, there is reason to assume that the player's loss of self "in a fiction, [and] a dream of passion," which amazes the Prince, may well have been what the play-wright strove for in his own histrionic efforts.

THE PURPOSES OF DRAMA

What, finally, was Shakespeare's attitude towards the notion that a play should profit the audience? Again it is easy to show that the playwright by and large had little sympathy for either Hamlet's or Ben Jonson's didactic and satirical impulse. It is true that the Chorus in *Henry V* sounds somewhat chauvinistic in his praises of "warlike Harry" (I, 1); and that Gower's moral summing-up of *Pericles* gives a clearly didactic retrospect on what we have seen. But these rare examples of propagandist and didactic commentary hardly apply to Shakespeare's drama-tic art in general. Statements of such manifesto-like nature in other of his prologues, choruses, and epilogues strike instead a consistently undidactic note. Here the playwright, again and again, insists on one half of the Horatian formula of profit and delight,[56] but consistently omits the other. "But that's all one, our play is done, / And we'll strive to please you every day," we are told at the end of *Twelfth Night*. *All's Well That Ends Well* predictably concludes on a similar note:

> The King's a beggar, now the play is done.
> All is well ended if this suit be won,
> That you express content; which we will pay
> With strife to please you, day exceeding day.

Eager for some play "To ease the anguish of a torturing hour," Theseus rejects a satire – " 'The thrice three Muses mourning for the death / Of Learning, late deceas'd in beggary' " – but finds pleasure in the " 'tedious brief scene of young Pyramus / And his love Thisbe.' " "This palpable-gross play," he concludes after the performance, "hath well beguil'd / The heavy gait of night."[57] Instead of quoting further examples, it may suffice to say that Shakespeare not once links this notion of pleasure with that of profit in talking about his dramatic art. And even where he connects the two terms in different context, he gives the Horatian formula a characteristic twist. There is no profit without pleasure. Such at least is Tranio's advice to his master

Lucentio in planning on a "course of learning and ingenious studies:"

> Music and poesy use to quicken you;
> The mathematics and the metaphysics,
> Fall to them as you find your stomach serves you.
> No profit grows where is no pleasure ta'en. [58]

Sometimes the pleasure-oriented function of drama – "To glad your ear and please your eyes" [59] – is expanded to include certain psycho-therapeutic effects. The story we are about to witness in *Pericles* is said to have had a regenerating effect on earlier readers: "And lords and ladies in their lives / Have read it for restoratives," announces Gower (I, 1). More tongue in cheek are the words of the messenger who tells Sly that a comedy might help cure him of his alleged lunacy. The tinker, after all, is perfectly sane, and the acting of *The Taming of the Shrew* is part of a frame-up to make him believe in his alleged former madness and new identity as a lord. Nonetheless, the messenger's words are basically in tune with the notion of drama as a "restorative" and with Tranio's sense that music and poetry will "quicken" those who enjoy them:

> Your honour's players, hearing your amendment,
> Are come to play a pleasant comedy;
> For so your doctors hold it very meet,
> Seeing too much sadness hath congeal'd your blood,
> And melancholy is the nurse of frenzy.
> Therefore they thought it good you hear a play
> And frame your mind to mirth and merriment,
> Which bars a thousand harms and lengthens life.
>
> (Induction, 2)

Even Claudius, after all, has hopes that the players might alleviate Hamlet's madness and asks Rosencrantz and Guildenstern to make the protagonist focus his mind on the delights of the forthcoming performance (III, 1).

To give pleasure and perhaps regenerate the human mind would be primarily the effect of comedy and romance. What, then, is the function of tragedy? One of the rare Elizabethan allusions to the catharsis concept is found in *Galateo of Manners and Behaviours* (1576), translated from Casa's Italian by R. Peterson. The translator points out that tragedies cause people to shed

tears and hence cure them "of their infirmity." But he only says so
by way of making fun of the idea. The same results, he adds, can
be achieved by simpler means such as a smoky dwelling or strong
mustard. Otherwise, the Aristotelian concept is practically
ignored by English writers before Milton, and Shakespeare is no
exception.[60] Yet even if the playwright knew of it, as he may have
from, say, an Italian source like L. Giacomini's *Sopra la purgazione
della tragedia*, the notion was unlikely to appeal to him. Catharsis,
to Giacomini as to most other critics, was understood to be, in
B. Weinberg's phrase, "a pedagogical device or an instrument to
moral improvement."[61] Just as comedy, "by means of laughter
and jokes, calls men to an honest private life," argues L. O.
Giraldi, so tragedy, purging men's minds through terror and
pity, induces them "to abstain from acting wickedly."[62]

Apparently more to Shakespeare's liking, though not part
of his actual poetics of drama, was the notion of the play as the
thing to catch the conscience of the King. It is hard to imagine that
Shakespeare in writing, say, *Macbeth* hoped that the play might
elicit a fit of guilt-ridden anguish or even confession from some
murderous male or female hidden in the audience. But such
stories evidently were around, and he was not averse to using
them, at least once, for their dramatic effect in *Hamlet*. The
protagonist himself claims to have heard

> That guilty creatures, sitting at a play,
> Have by the very cunning of the scene
> Been struck so to the soul that presently
> They have proclaim'd their malefactions.   (II,2)

Shakespeare, here, may be recalling an older play, the anonymous *A Warning for Faire Women*, which had been acted by
Shakespeare's company and was printed in 1599. Predictably,
the person in this drama who is brought to confession by the
cunning of the scene is some Lady Macbeth from Norfolk who
inadvertently watched a tragedy played by some travelling
players. The character who tells her story goes out of his way to
stress what caused her to reveal her crime:

> The passion written by a feeling pen,
> And acted by a good Tragedian –

> She was so mooved with the sight thereof,
> And openly confess[ed] her husband's murder.[63]

Similar stories of the suggestive power of drama to catch the guilty conscience of some spectator are told in Thomas Heywood's *Apology for Actors* and other texts.

All this, of course, is still no answer as to what Shakespeare may have seen as the purpose of tragedy. Even a playwright who did believe that his play might catch the conscience of some guilty individual, could hardly be said to give his dramatic art a clear function. For what in this case would be the effect of his tragedies on the innocent? Such thoughts must have concerned Shakespeare in writing the speech in which he makes Hamlet express what may well be the playwright's own ideas about acting. Here, the Prince, as we recall, covets the very power to "cleave the general ear with horrid speech" (II, 2) that he later disapproves of in telling the players not "to split the ears of the groundlings" (III, 2). At the same time, Hamlet's emotional turmoil at this point serves to exemplify whatever impact such acting can have on an audience. Without a specifically didactic design, it confounds the ignorant, while it amazes the visual and aural faculties of those who know. If it affects man's moral nature, it does so for guilty and innocent alike and without any immediately recognizable pedagogical purpose. A good tragic actor would drown the stage with tears

> And cleave the general ear with horrid speech;
> Make mad the guilty, and appal the free,
> Confound the ignorant, and amaze indeed
> The very faculties of eyes and ears.   (II, 2)

The main function of tragedy, then, is to overwhelm with amazement. It is to confound the "ignorant" with the same techniques as will dislodge the wise from their all too habitual views of life. We have at least one contemporary witness who, like the audiences he refers to, was thrall to such amazement, while being bored by Ben Jonson's erudite insistence. Leonard Digges, who must have known Shakespeare through his stepfather Thomas Russell, is referring to a performance of *Julius Caesar*:

> ... oh how the Audience,
> Were ravish'd, with what wonder they went thence,
> When some new day they would not brooke a line,
> Of tedious (though well-laboured) *Catilines*;
> *Sejanus* too was irkesome, they priz'de more
> Honest *Iago*, or the jealous Moore.[64]

In sum, Shakespeare's dramatic art, so the playwright seems to suggest, was to please and amaze rather than to moralize and to teach. Equally unsympathetic to Shakespeare was the consistent design of the dramatic satirist. Such an attitude is implied in *As You Like It*. Jaques, who has a natural tendency to draw moral lessons from things, displays a conspicuously Jonsonian bias for wishing to "Cleanse the foul body of th' infected world" by speaking his mind. But Duke Senior reveals what is hidden behind such puritanical zeal:

> Most mischievous foul sin, in chiding sin;
> For thou thyself hast been a libertine,
> As sensual as the brutish sting itself;
> And all th' embossed sores and headed evils
> That thou with license of free foot hast caught
> Wouldst thou disgorge into the general world.   (II, 7)

More elaborate, though somewhat obscured by textual problems, is the similar unmasking of the satirist in *Timon of Athens*. It is all the more effective for coming somewhat as a surprise. Like no other work by Shakespeare, the play opens with the words of a Poet who will present the protagonist with one of his works. What's more, this poem, of which the author gives an account to a Painter, prophetically foreshadows what is about to happen in the play. It is an allegorical work about Timon's protectress Lady Fortune, "feign'd" to be enthroned on "a high and pleasant hill," but fickle in her favors:

> When Fortune in her shift and change of mood
> Spurns down her late beloved, all his dependants,
> Which labour'd after him to the mountain's top
> Even on their knees and hands, let him slip down,
> Not one accompanying his declining foot.   (I, 1)

At the same time, the Poet discusses various principles of the kind of allegorically didactic poetry he professes. Mumbling what seem to be some recently created lines, he argues that the glory of verse in praise of the good is stained by poems which for recompense eulogize the vile. He also seems to take issue with satire, suggesting as his own ideal a poetry which, though following a clear didactic and allegorical design, avoids the excesses of both panegyrical and satirical verse. "[N]o levell'd malice," he protests,

> Infects one comma in the course I hold,
> But flies an eagle flight, bold and forth on,
> Leaving no tract behind.   (I, 1)

As Kenneth Muir points out, there is little reason for questioning the Poet's sincerity at this point.[65] Did Shakespeare, then, intend to give this unfinished play a kind of allegorically didactic framework? Despite the Painter's somewhat dismissive remarks concerning the Poet's efforts, all seems to point in this direction.

> 'Tis common:
> A thousand moral paintings I can show
> That shall demonstrate these quick blows of Fortune's
> More pregnantly than words. Yet you do well
> To show Lord Timon that mean eyes have seen
> The foot above the head.   (I, 1)

Even when Apemantus calls the Poet a liar for "feigning" Timon "a worthy fellow," we tend to side with the Poet rather than the fool.

Apemantus: . . . How now, poet!
Poet: How now, philosopher!
Apemantus: Thou liest.
Poet: Art not one?
Apemantus: Yes.
Poet: Then I lie not.
Apemantus: Art not a poet?
Poet: Yes.
Apemantus: Then thou liest. Look in thy last work, where thou hast
feign'd him a worthy fellow.
Poet: That's not feign'd – he is so.   (I, 1)

Timon, at this point, no doubt *is* a worthy fellow, though a gullible one. What is more, the defense of the poet against the charge of lying was an approved argument in Renaissance poetics.[66] It was known both to the Elizabethan apologists of poetry and to Shakespeare himself. As Touchstone puts it, "the

truest poetry is the most feigning."[67] Why then should the Poet in
Timon of Athens feel a liar for feigning Timon to be a worthy man
who will be abandoned by both Fortune and friends? This, after
all, is what we are about to witness in the play.

But the exemplum-like plot of Timon's downfall both fulfills
and disrupts this didactic framework. The Poet was right in
predicting that the protagonist, once cast down by Fortune,
would be abandoned by all his friends. But little in the play, let
alone in the tradition of such inspired prophecies, makes us
expect that the prophet will simply become another example of
his predictions. As long as things went smoothly, he may well
have thought himself to be exempt from such fallibility. But, to all
evidence, he finally acts no differently from all others he spoke of
in his poem. Like them, who "labour'd after" Timon "to the
mountain's top / Even on their knees and hands," he lets his
former benefactor "slip down," not even "accompanying his
declining foot" (I, 1). Now that Timon is rumored to have
recovered his riches, he and the Painter are back, pretending to
be unaware of Timon's newfound gold – "'tis not amiss we
tender our loves to him in this suppos'd distress of his; it will
show honestly in us" (V, 1). Needless to say, the two artists have
had little time to work on new presents for their old benefactor.
So for the time being they agree to feed him with promises
instead: "To promise is most courtly and fashionable; performance is a kind of will or testament which argues a great sickness in
his judgment that makes it." But the Poet already has an idea: he
will write a satire for Timon:

I am thinking what I shall say I have provided for him. It must be a
personating of himself; a satire against the softness of prosperity, with a
discovery of the infinite flatteries that follow youth and opulency.
(V, 1)

In sum, *Timon of Athens*, in anticlimactically disrupting its
exemplum-like framework, presents us with Shakespeare's final
portrait of the didactic poet. When the protagonist, who has been
spying on the two, comments on the Poet's plans in an aside, the
playwright reiterates an insight already voiced in an earlier play.
Essentially Timon's words repeat Duke Senior's character analysis of Jaques. The fierceness with which satirists castigate the sins

of others is often in over-compensation or, if you like, reaction formation regarding their own sins.

> *Timon* [aside]: Must thou needs stand for a villain in thine own work?
> Wilt thou whip thine own faults in other men?   (V, 1)

What is more, Timon articulates one of Shakespeare's most cherished ideas – the essential barrenness of poetic discourse – where he responds directly to the Poet's extempore realization of his satiric plans:

> *Poet*: Sir,
>   Having often of your open bounty tasted,
>   Hearing you were retir'd, your friends fall'n off,
>   Whose thankless natures – O abhorred spirits! –
>   Not all the whips of heaven are large enough –
>   What! to you,
>   Whose star-like nobleness gave life and influence
>   To their whole being! I am rapt, and cannot cover
>   The monstrous bulk of this ingratitude
>   With any size of words.
> *Timon*: Let it go naked: men may see't the better.   (V, 1)

This is moments before Poet and Painter, slapstick-comedy style, are beaten off the stage by Timon. Of course, none of all this is to say that Shakespeare is thus forswearing satire altogether. On the contrary: the Poet, Jaques, Hamlet – all bear witness to the playwright's superb satirical talents, even though the aim may be satire itself. The Poet wants to write "a satire against the softness of prosperity, with a discovery of the infinite flatteries that follow youth and opulency" (V, 1). Jaques wants to "Cleanse the foul body of th' infected world" by speaking his mind.[68] "Let the galled jade wince, our withers are unwrung," protests Hamlet before the performance of "The Mouse-trap." Hamlet, like his two brethren in spirit, protests his innocence, while lashing out against others – "we that have free souls, it touches us not" (III, 2). But, as in the case of Jaques and the Poet, we know better. There is something rotten not only in the state of Denmark, but also perhaps in Hamlet's soul.

What is more, there is abundance of satire in works such as *Love's Labour's Lost*. But it is one thing to be satiric and/or didactic by main design, like Ben Jonson, and another occasionally to display such tendencies, like Shakespeare. Except in *Troilus and Cressida*, perhaps, the playwright never once seems to have worked from an ultimately pedagogical impulse, and even that play bespeaks deep disillusionment rather than the reformatory zeal of the truly satirical poet. To let "the galled jade wince," even merely to "show virtue her own feature, scorn her own image," might have been Hamlet's main goal in directing "a cry of players" (III, 2). But it was hardly Shakespeare's.

III · Shakespeare and his audience

To SAY that Shakespeare defied the unities of action, time and place is merely to state the obvious.[1] It is also well known that he repeatedly implied or defended his attitude towards them. While both *The Tempest* and *The Comedy of Errors*, for instance, observe the unity of time, other of his plays, like *Pericles* and *The Winter's Tale*, jump over gaps of up to sixteen years. Hiding behind his Chorus, the playwright, in both these dramas, tries to elicit the audience's consent for his unorthodox method.[2] Shakespeare, in various places, also discusses how he collapses far-distant sites in one and the same play, moves freely between them, and condenses vast geographical spaces into the small imaginary space of the stage:

> Can this cockpit hold
> The vasty fields of France? Or may we cram
> Within this wooden O the very casques
> That did affright the air at Agincourt?

The answer is no, unless the spectator is prepared to eke out with his thoughts what the playwright can merely suggest. This, then, is what the Chorus in *Henry V* enjoins upon his audience while he wafts them back and forth across the English Channel and "digest[s] / Th' abuse of distance:" "Then brook abridgment; and your eyes advance, / After your thoughts, straight back again to France."[3] Similar comments on how the playwright, with the help of the spectator's imagination, allows himself to journey "From bourn to bourn, region to region," are put into the mouths of Gower in *Pericles* (IV, 4) and of Time, the Chorus, in *The Winter's Tale* (IV, 1).

Most prominent, and ranging from *The Comedy of Errors* to *The Tempest*, are Shakespeare's direct and indirect hints as to how he handles time. On one level, of course, there are the characters informing us of the time of day and the time elapsed within the action of the play. On the other, there are authorial comments relating this imaginary time to the actual time spent by the spectator in the theatre. For the most part such comments relate to wide discrepancies between real and imaginary time. Thus Berowne protests that "a twelvemonth an' a day" is "too long for a play."[4] But usually Shakespeare seems to be arguing for the opposite point of view, "jumping o'er times" and appealing to the spectator's imagination to help him turn "th' accomplishment of many years / Into an hour-glass." Appropriately, the longest plea of this kind to "brook abridgement" and to "admit th' excuse / Of time" is uttered by Time himself.[5]

His speech introducing Act IV of *The Winter's Tale* has been called "Shakespeare's most extensive direct comment on the doctrine of the unity of time."[6] The playwright had good reason for introducing this device. The sixteen years elapsed since the end of Act III are even longer than the fourteen-year gap in *Pericles*. It is the boldest leap of its kind found in any play in the canon. To put it in perspective, one only has to remember that many critics like Robortello would not even allow for Aristotle's "single revolution of the sun," trying to restrict the duration of a play to the daylight time of twelve hours.[7] Understandably, Time, under these circumstances, does not even plead with the spectators to eke out with their imagination what the author has to omit from the play. He instead advises them to imagine that they slept through the interval:

> Impute it not a crime
> To me or my swift passage, that I slide
> O'er sixteen years . . .
> . . .   Your patience this allowing,
> I turn my glass, and give my scene such growing
> As you had slept between.

Also characteristically Shakespearean is the technique, reminiscent of non-perspectival Elizabethan painting,[8] of presenting scenic slices of time, not in temporal sequence, but in lateral simultaneity. Again and again, writes Renu Juneja, the playwright "juxtaposes spatially organized back-to-back scenes so that his audience moves not consequentially but pictorially from

Brutus and Portia to Caesar and Calpurnia, from an unrepentant
Claudius at prayer to a conscience-stricken Gertrude bending
under Hamlet's indictment."[9] Turning directly to his spectators,
Shakespeare points out an example of such scenic simultaneity in
his Prologue to Act IV of *Henry V*. The armies of the French and
English, each of them described in a lengthy passage, are brought
together in the expectation-ridden intensity of a morning before
battle, when time seems to stand still:

> From camp to camp, through the foul womb of night,
> The hum of either army stilly sounds,
> That the fix'd sentinels almost receive
> The secret whispers of each other's watch.
> Fire answers fire, and through their paly flames
> Each battle sees the other's umber'd face;
> Steed threatens steed, in high and boastful neighs
> Piercing the night's dull ear; and from the tents
> The armourers accomplishing the knights,
> With busy hammers closing rivets up,
> Give dreadful note of preparation.
> The country cocks do crow, the clocks do toll,
> And the third hour of drowsy morning name.

Spellbound by the atmosphere rather than eager for sequential
action, we are allowed to listen to what the soldiers on both sides
– "the confident and over-lusty French" and the "poor condemned English" – have to tell each other at this crucial moment.

THE PRESENTATIONAL THEATRE

But some of this is well known, and most of it has been dealt with
in various places. Usually ignored, however, is the extent to
which Shakespeare's continued concern with the unities goes
beyond the traditional discussions of such issues. Exploring this
angle will also give us the answers to several crucial questions.
How did the playwright see the nature of dramatic fictionality?
Were stage events to him mere signs pointing to something else,
or did they have their own reality however illusionist? What in all
this was the role of the spectator?

   None of these deeper issues is raised by, say, Sidney, the first
systematically to expound the unities in England. Here is how

Sidney criticized *Gorboduc* for being "faulty both in place and time, the two necessary companions of all corporall actions:"

For where the stage should alwaies represent but one place, and the vttermost time presupposed in it should be, both by *Aristotles* precept and common reason, but one day, there is both many dayes, and many places, inartificially imagined. But if it be so in *Gorboduck*, how much more in al the rest? where you shal haue *Asia* of the one side, and *Affrick* of the other, and so many other vnder-kingdoms, that the Player, when he commeth in, must euer begin with telling where he is, or els the tale will not be conceiued. Now ye shal haue three Ladies walke to gather flowers, and then we must beleeue the stage to be a Garden. By and by, we heare newes of shipwracke in the same place, and then wee are to blame if we accept it not for a Rock. Vpon the backe of that, comes out a hidious Monster, with fire and smoke, and then the miserable beholders are bounde to take it for a Caue. While in the meantime two Armies flye in, represented with foure swords and bucklers, and then what harde heart will not receiue it for a pitched fielde? Now, of time they are much more liberall, for ordinary it is that two young Princes fall in loue. After many trauerces, she is got with childe, deliuered of a faire boy; he is lost, groweth a man, falls in loue, and is ready to get another child; and all this in two hours space: which how absurd it is in sence euen sence may imagine, and Arte hath taught, and all auncient examples iustified, and, at this day, the ordinary Players in Italie wil not erre in.[10]

Before criticizing the critic is it worth recalling, of course, that the "grosse absurdities"[11] Sidney quotes as his examples may well have been just that – "grosse absurdities" with nothing in them to elicit a willing suspension of disbelief. Around 1583, when *An Apologie for Poetrie* was written, Shakespeare still lived in Stratford, and none of the major Elizabethan plays by Lyly, Kyd, Marlowe, or Greene had yet been performed. It is easy for us to see the limitations of Sidney's stance through their works. But too much of what Sidney witnessed probably had a near children's-play-like improbability, and to a scholar familiar with continental criticism the unities must have suggested themselves as the appropriate cure for such infantilism.

This also, however, may account for the fact that Sidney, in his demand for the three unities, did not confront the deeper issues involved. Why should a drama differ, say, from an epic in not covering several places and periods? Just because one is read while the other is presented on stage? Sidney, indeed, draws a distinction between "reporting" and "representing." He also lists various devices like the *nuntius* or beginning *mediis in rebus* for coping with such problems in drama. But all this only begs a further question which remains unanswered: are we really meant to accept what is presented to us on stage as "reality"? If not, then why should drama not avail itself of the usual methods of leaping through space and time, while leaving the gaps untold, and of *pars pro toto* symbolism, suggesting, say, the battle of Agincourt, with "four or five most vile and ragged foils."[12] We know that such synecdochical substitution is an essential part of all art and communication. Should drama, just because it uses real human bodies on stage, try to exempt itself from this general principle? Or is it just a matter of proportion, so that a drama performed in, say, two hours should cover less time than an epic, whose perusal might take several days? In *An Apologie for Poetrie* none of these questions is raised, let alone answered.

In Sidney's view, to break the unities of action, time and place simply results in "grosse absurdities." A play that covers "both many dayes, and many places" is "inartificially imagined," probably meaning that an artful imagination would have availed itself of *mediis in rebus* and *nuntius* devices instead. The playwright's attempts to suggest, say, a garden, a shipwreck, a rock, a monster, a cave, or a battlefield as actually located on stage (as in some Shakespeare plays) are all dismissed by mere irony: "we must beleeue the stage to be a Garden;" "wee are to blame if we accept it not for a Rock;" "the miserable beholders are bounde to take it for a Caue"; "what harde heart will not receiue it for a pitched fielde?" Plays spanning two generations or more in the course of two-odd hours are not even worth considering. "[H]ow absurd it is in sence," writes Sidney, "euen sence may imagine, and Arte hath taught, and all auncient examples iustified."[13]

There are few Renaissance critics whose discussion and justification of the unities reach deeper than Sidney's. One of them is Castelvetro, who was also the first to demand explicitly a unity of place in addition to those of time and action. A caustic rationalist with a tendency to rough and ready categorizations, he decided that poetry, and particularly drama, "was invented for the pleasure of the ignorant multitude and of the common people, and not for the pleasure of the educated." But Castelvetro's ignorant crowds have little in common with Shakespeare's unskillful groundlings. Not only do they lack an understanding for the subtle reasons of both philosopher and poet "in establishing the rules of the arts"; they are also extremely deficient in imagination. All they are able to believe in is their senses. "Nor is it possible to make them believe that several days and nights have passed when they know through their senses that only a few hours have passed, since no deception can take place in them which the senses recognize as such."[14] Here perhaps we have the direct source for Sidney's indignant "how absurd it is in sence, euen sence may imagine." But the difference is that Castelvetro tries to explain where his follower is content to dismiss the matter with a rhetorical flourish.

Whatever else might be said about him, Castelvetro had the courage of his convictions. An audience is basically ignorant and unimaginative; it should be coerced into believing that what it sees on stage is the truth. Only what is absolutely like reality will fulfill this requirement. The result is that plays are judged in terms not of artistic but of natural verisimilitude. Criticizing Terence, for instance, he finds it improbable that Pamphilus in the *Andria* should walk home from the forum in complete silence and suddenly begin shouting as he approaches his house. A line like "Ex ara hinc sume verbenas" is unacceptable because altars covered with sacred boughs are not a common sight in the public streets.[15] The true test of drama, then, is its historical or factual verisimilitude. In other words (Castelvetro's own) "we cannot imagine a king who did not exist, nor attribute any action to him."[16] No doubt the question as to how many children Lady Macbeth had would have been crucial to this critic.

Nor was Castelvetro by any means the only one to pursue this line of argument. Commenting on Aristotle's distinction between poet and historian, Robortello, in his 1548 commentary on the *Poetics*, clearly inverts the Greek philosopher's dichotomy. The true poet does not present the "kind of thing that might happen, i.e., what is possible as being probable or necessary,"[17] but what has happened in actual fact. This is particularly true of tragedy with its function of arousing pity and fear:

For men by their very nature are prone to pleasant things but averse to unpleasant ones; they cannot, therefore, easily be impelled to sorrow. It is thus necessary for them first to know that the thing actually happened in such and such a way. Thus if a tragic plot contained an action which did not really take place and was not true, but was represented by the poet himself in accordance with verisimilitude, it would perhaps move the souls of the auditors, but certainly less. For, if verisimilar things give us pleasure, all the pleasure derives from the fact that we know these things to be present in the truth; and, in general, to the extent that the verisimilar partakes of truth it has the power to move and to persuade.[18]

Of course there were variations: for instance, as to what was believed to be actual fact – the facts considered objectively, let us say, or what, in Maggi's words, is "received in the opinion of the crowd."[19] But most critics concurred with Vettori that the poetic art, and drama in particular, "is in subjection to the beliefs of the listeners, and . . . attempts to insinuate itself, with every means possible, into their minds."[20] At the same time it was assumed that the spectator's imagination could play no part in this process. The only role it was allowed was submission to the simulation of authentic fact. To Beni, writing in 1600, this means that the playwright must even dispense with verse. In comedy and tragedy, he wrote, "we imitate human actions properly with prose, less properly – nay, even absurdly – when bound by the limits of verse. Therefore prose is to be practiced, verse rejected, . . . since poetry is an imitation of human actions either as they actually were done or as they should have been done, neither of which can be achieved in comedy and tragedy through an imitation bound down by verse."[21]

For good reason, the examples discussed here tend to represent the doctrine in some of its bizarre extravagance. But that drama, by its close-to-fact verisimilitude, should cater to a basically unimaginative audience, was one of the central assumptions of late Renaissance criticism. Sidney was not the only one to echo it in England. Before him, George Whetstone had inveighed against the popular playwright who, "most vaine, indiscreete, and out of order," roams through the entire world in three hours.[22] After Sidney, it was chiefly Ben Jonson who continued the same line of argument. Of course, Jonson's attitude towards the unities was, to say the least, an ambivalent one. Cordatus, his spokesman in *Every Man Out of His Humour*, for instance, rejects the need for having the argument of a comedy "fall within compasse of a dayes businesse." The playwright himself declares in *Discoveries* that a tragedy or comedy must not exceed "the compasse of one Day." Then again we find him admitting to the readers of *Sejanus* that this tragedy was "no true *Poëme*; in the strict Lawes of *Time*." Yet he reaffirms the principle in *Volpone*, which, as the Prologue tells us, observes the "lawes of time, place, persons."[23] Except for his tendency to turn whatever he did into a hard and fast theory, Jonson's practice, to all evidence, was not too different from Shakespeare's. The same with the unity of place. While allowing himself to roam around England within a single play, he made fun of plays which take you across the sea.

But such inconsistencies do little to abate his critical fury when inveighing against others, and particularly against fellow-playwright William Shakespeare. Some of the following lines from the 1616 Prologue to *Every Man in His Humour*[24] cast an ironical glance at *Henry V* as well as at Shakespeare's earlier dramatizations of the Wars of the Roses. Ben Jonson is listing some of "the ill customes of the age" such as

> To make a child, now swadled, to proceede
> Man, and then shoote vp, in one beard, and weede,
> Past threescore yeeres; or, with three rustie swords,
> And help of some few foot-and-halfe-foote words,
> Fight ouer *Yorke*, and *Lancasters* long iarres:
> And in the tyring-house bring wounds, to scarres.
> He rather prayes, you will be pleas'd to see
> One such, to day, as other playes should be.
> Where neither *Chorus* wafts you ore the seas;
> Nor creaking throne comes downe, the boyes to please.

Ben Jonson is equally inconsistent in trying to explain the deeper rationale for either retaining or rejecting the unities. For instance, he largely shares Castelvetro's attitude towards the ignorant multitude of theatregoers; but, unlike the Italian, he feels that this is a reason for relaxing rather than enforcing the rules. "[If] it be obiected, that what I publish is no true *Poëme*; in the strict Lawes of *Time*," he writes of *Sejanus*, "I confesse it . . . Nor is it needful, or almost possible, in these our Times, and to such Auditors, as commonly Things are presented, to obserue the ould state, and splendour of *Drammatick Poëmes*, with preseruation of any popular delight" ("To the Readers"). On the other hand, he seems to follow Castelvetro's basic argument that the playwright has to cater to a basically unimaginative audience. To cross the sea in the middle of a play, for instance, would, as Cordatus explains in *Every Man Out of His Humour*, "out-run the apprehension of [the] auditorie". Even here, however, Ben Jonson remains inconsistent. In the same play, Cordatus adopts the Shakespearean trick of asking the spectator to eke out with his thoughts what remains unpresented on the stage: "let your imagination be swifter then a paire of oares: and by this, suppose PVNTARVOLO, BRISKE, FVNGOSO, and the dogge arriu'd at the court gate, and going vp to the great chamber" (IV, 8).[25] Even this most neoclassical of major English playwrights was never ready for long to subject successful practice to abstract theory.

THE REPRESENTATIONAL THEATRE

But deviations from the practice and theory of the three unities were not an exclusively English achievement. In Spain, Lope de Vega, in his *Arte Nuevo de Hacer Comedias* (1609), while blaming his more "vulgar" techniques on the need to satisfy popular audiences, ignores the unity of place and makes fun of the unity of time.[26] Spanish theoreticians of drama often show much the same attitude or expand Aristotle's unity of action to what Pinciano calls "la acción doblada."[27] Similar tendencies are found in Italy.

Even where critics did not attack the unities as such, they questioned the alleged rationale behind them. Five years after Castelvetro's *Poetica d'Aristotele vulgarizzata et sposta*, Alessandro Piccolomini published his *Annotationi ... nel libro della Poetica d'Aristotile*, second of the great commentaries in the vernacular. Much in the book is entirely traditional. Like Castelvetro, Piccolomini insists that the action of the tragedy must be confined to one day. Like his predecessor, he concludes that poetry, and particularly drama, is designed to please the multitude, and that the extent of such pleasure in tragedy depends upon the play's verisimilitude. For this reason, characters "known with clear and definite certainty" ("persone, per chiara, & per risoluta certezza note") are preferable to those who have to be "entirely invented" ("totalmente finte").[28]

But there is at least one important difference. Piccolomini's audience, unlike Castelvetro's, has intelligence. It is always aware of the difference between fact and fiction and could never be coaxed into believing that what it sees on the stage "is the truth." Hence there is no need for the playwright to strive for perfect natural verisimilitude. Artistic verisimilitude in most cases is sufficient. In Piccolomini's view,

the spectators of tragedies and comedies have an awareness and knowledge of the fact that the things that are done and said on the stage do not happen there and then as true things and without any feigning ("senza fintione alcuna") . . . Therefore, we must not imagine that the cause that might diminish the pleasure of the spectators would be the happening, on the stage, of something that would make them realize that it was not really taking place there, but only as a fiction; but the cause would rather be the lack of resemblance which is required of imitation.

It has to be taken for granted that the actors walking on stage cover less ground than the men and women they represent as walking around the real world; or that asides are supposed to be heard by the audience but not by the other characters on the stage. Such breaches of natural verisimilitude

do not offend the spectators at all . . . [because] just as imitation is not truth itself, but is lacking in some part of truth (for if it were not so lacking it would not be an imitation, but the real thing), so also it is necessary that in imitating, certain things should be done which do not accord completely with the truth of the things imitated . . . The spectators . . . grant and concede ["donano, & concedono"] to the imitators everything far from the truth that the art of imitation necessarily brings and requires.

Here, then, we already find some of Shakespeare's tendency to ask the audience to "grant" and "concede" to the playwright what, though far from the real truth, may be required by the dramatic presentation. Piccolomini's audience, not unlike Shakespeare's, is glad to "pardon" and "excuse" what other theoreticians would term an "error":

if at times the poet should be . . . by the course of the plot and by some legitimate consideration . . . unable to escape such violation in order to achieve something which might be more important, he will deserve pardon and excuse and it will not be counted against him as an error ["meriterà egli perdono, & scusa & non gli sarà attribuito per errore"].[29]

It was only a step from this to a totally artistic and, in a way, symbolist understanding of drama. This was taken in the *Discorsi poetici nella Accademia fiorentina in difesa d'Aristotile* which Francesco Buonamici delivered around 1597. The person, he felt, Aristotle needed defending against was his renowned predecessor Castelvetro. Buonamici draws heavily on Plato's idealism to help him along in this task. Far from catering to an ignorant multitude, the poet is concerned with higher truths. In feigning, say, an individual, "he considers in him the idea, which is universal, so that he does not describe exactly what he is and what he did, but he raises the actions and the character to the highest level of which human nature is capable." In turn, an audience finds little difficulty in appreciating that the particular stage event always points to some "idea abstracted from matter." The spectators' alleged ignorance, in fact, is Castelvetro's own inability to differentiate between fiction and fact:

By not distinguishing them, Castelvetro generates confusion, and he also confuses the nature of the thing represented with the nature of the thing representing ... And he gives little credit to the intelligence of the auditor of the representation, if the latter cannot discern the time of the representation from that represented.[30]

Piccolomini had ventured to "suppose" that the spectators of a tragedy or comedy have an awareness of the fact that the things done and said on stage do not happen there.[31] But to Buonamici there was no doubt at all as to such an awareness. Spectators, not just occasionally, but at all times, were conscious of the distinction between the "signs" of a dramatic action and the actual "things signified." Watching a spectacle, in fact, amounts to a non-stop feat of mental acrobatics, a jumping from one to the other. No matter how hard the playwright might try to suggest to the spectator the illusion of real life, "the work of verisimilitude in the spectator can never cause him – unless he be an imbecile – to mistake the thing representing for the thing represented" ("la cosa rappresentante per la rappresentata"). In turn, there is nothing wrong with representing, say, the sun, a light source so many times the size of the earth, by a little light streaming in from a window; or the troops and courtiers of a king with a mere handful of actors. In neither case would the audience have great trouble interpreting the "sign" ("il segno") in terms of that "of which it is a sign" ("di cui é segno").[32]

Nonetheless, there are distinct and rather narrow limits to such synecdochical substitution.[33] The spectators would always be aware, for instance, that the time of the presentation only points to the time of what is presented. But, as devout Platonists such as they ought to be, their minds (or imaginations) have a yearning for the unified and one rather than for the dispersed and multiple. However, no plot, yoking widely disparate time blocks by violence together, could ever fulfill that demand. Hence Buonamici, though for different reasons from Castelvetro's, sounds remarkably like his predecessor in discussing the unity of time. "It is true," he writes, "that the more the time of representation conformed to the time of the action represented, the easier it would be to imagine it. And, therefore, for the ease of imagination of the spectators ['per la facilità dell' imaginazione delli spettatori'], who must be present at the whole plot, it is not a great paralogism to understand the action of a day as set forth in a few hours, whereas if it were perchance an action of a long time, the imagination would with difficulty be induced to imagine it."[34]

In the final analysis, Buonamici, like other of his neoclassical confrères, shows little trust in the spectators' imagination. Nothing less than a breach of the traditional unity of time is, in his view, beyond its scope. In fact, Buonamici's audience is, in one sense, even less imaginative than Castelvetro's. Here, at least, were spectators who, however ignorant, could be made to identify with what they saw. By contrast, Buonamici's auditors, though willing to suspend their disbelief about, say, a dress made of damask representing the purple and pearls of a kingly robe, would never once lose themselves in the spectacle. Instead of eking out what was left unsaid and unpresented with their imagination, they would simply draw neat, and preferably Platonic, equations between signifier and signified with their reason.

THE THEATRE OF MULTIPLE RESPONSE

But what, if anything, has all this to do with Shakespeare? Needless to say, it would be foolhardy to identify the playwright with either Castelvetro's or Buonamici's attitude. For one thing, Shakespeare defies the unity of time defended by both critics. But he also seems to have little sympathy for either Castelvetro's coercive illusionism or Buonamici's rigid signifier–signified symbolism. Fabian's "If this were play'd upon a stage now, I could condemn it as an improbable fiction," when watching Malvolio's antics in *Twelfth Night* (III, 4), is only the best-known example of how Shakespeare, again and again, reminds his audience that what they are watching is a play and not reality. Deliberate disruptions of illusionism, of course, were an intrinsic part of Elizabethan drama and, as Anne Righter informs us, by no means an invention of Shakespeare. What his plays were to rely on here was first worked out in most of its details in Kyd's *The Spanish Tragedy*. Kyd rarely allows us to forget that we are watching a play, despite the excitement and melodrama he creates: "Through the actor-spectator Don Andrea, through certain deliberate uses of the world as a stage image in the form both of simple statement and of plays within the play, the relation of illusion to reality, actors to audience, is constantly being examined and redefined."[35]

But what does this mean? Should we fight shy of being drawn into the illusionist realm of the dramatic fiction at all times? Must we interpret what we hear and see on stage as mere signs pointing to the higher meanings which these stand for? Shakespeare's way of addressing his audience in *Henry V* and elsewhere suggests the opposite:

> Play with your fancies; and in them behold
> Upon the hempen tackle ship-boys climbing;
> Hear the shrill whistle which doth order give
> To sounds confus'd; behold the threaden sails,
> Borne with th' invisible and creeping wind,
> Draw the huge bottoms through the furrowed sea,
> Breasting the lofty surge. O, do but think
> You stand upon the rivage and behold
> A city on th' inconstant billows dancing;
> For so appears this fleet majestical,

> Holding due course to Harfleur. Follow, follow!
> Grapple your minds to sternage of this navy,
> . . .
> Work, work your thoughts, and therein see a siege;
> Behold the ordnance on their carriages. (III, Prologue)

Work your thoughts, behold, listen, and follow, follow! We are drawn into a fictional realm whose sights and sounds absorb our attention by their very particularity. Nothing here, at least immediately, points to abstractions beyond the profusion of details which an almost hypnotic suggestiveness imprints on our imagination.

Moreover, there is evidence that plays, and particularly Shakespeare's, managed to entrance spectators to the point where they completely lost themselves in the spectacle: "Frozen with griefe we could not stir away / Untill the Epilogue told us 'twas a Play," reports one witness.[36] Exaggerated as such accounts may be, they tell us something about the potential of the plays, the intentions of the authors, and the mental attitude of the theatregoers. The ideal playwright, according to Dekker's portrait in the Prologue to *If This Be Not a Good Play*, "Commands the *Hearers*, sometimes drawing out *Teares*, / Then smiles, and fills them both with *Hopes* and *Feares*."[37] According to Nashe, Shakespeare fully commanded such powers even in his early history plays. At least ten thousand spectators, he reports, at several times cried to see Talbot fight and die in the first part of *Henry VI*.[38] "[O]h how the Audience, / Were ravish'd" in watching *Julius Caesar*, exclaims Leonard Digges.[39]

What we find, then, is a paradox. While consistently disrupting the illusion of the stage action, Shakespeare, with equal deliberateness, tried, at least temporarily, to make the spectators lose themselves in the spectacle.[40] The satirical comments implied in two of his plays-within-the-play, the Pageant of the Nine Worthies in *Love's Labour's Lost* and "Pyramus and Thisbe" in *A Midsummer Night's Dream*, further underline this attitude.[41] As they suggest, a strict adherence to either illusionism à la Castelvetro or signifier–signified symbolism à la Buonamici is, in Shakespeare's view, open to equal ridicule. An audience is never quite stupid enough to be coerced into believing that what is fiction is fact. Nor is it so self-conscious at all times as not to allow itself to get lost in the spectacle.

Shakespeare's first attack here seems to be leveled at the kind of position held by Buonamici. Costard, Armado, Nathaniel, and Holofernes make no bones about the fact that they "present" whatever roles they have decided to play. Before it all starts, Costard, in fact, announces that "every one pursents three" such parts (V, 2). Costard, Nathaniel, and Holofernes all begin by identifying whom they impersonate (e.g., "I Pompey am"), while Holofernes introduces the Boy who represents Hercules: "Great Hercules is presented by this imp / ... / Ergo I come with this apology." When things go wrong with Nathaniel–Alexander, Costard assumes the additional role of a stage critic, commenting that Nathaniel was "a little o'erparted." But the spectators are not amused. Where the actors, à la Buonamici, keep on reminding them what they stand for, they pretend to want to see more illusionism à la Castelvetro. When Costard announces that he is Pompey, Berowne accuses him of lying. When Armado appears as Hector, nobody is content with the semblance:

Boyet: But is this Hector?
Dumain: I think Hector was not so clean-timber'd.
Longaville: His leg is too big for Hector's.
Dumain: More calf, certain.
Boyet: No; he is best indued in the small.
Berowne: This cannot be Hector.

Poor Armado is given no chance at all to go "forward with [his] device." Where the actors try to present their pageant in strict adherence to a signifier–signified concept of drama, their spectators only take delight in watching the collapse of such pedantic efforts. Our own attitude is little different. Although we feel pity for the lowly actors, even perhaps indignation at the cruelty of the spectators, we cannot help but laugh to see the players confounded by their insistent endeavors to explain what they represent. Their performance, as the Princess observes, indeed

> Dies in the zeal of that which it presents.
> Their form confounded makes most form in mirth.   (V, 2)

By contrast to Costard and his confrères in *Love's Labour's Lost*, Bottom and the Athenian workmen in *A Midsummer Night's Dream* start planning rehearsal for their "Pyramus and Thisbe" from the precisely opposite premise. Bottom, in particular, is all out to ravish the audience with his various skills. Playing the lover, he protests, "will ask some tears in the true performing of it. If I do it, let the audience look to their eyes; I will move storms; I will condole in some measure" (I, 2). But when he offers to play the lion in similar vein Quince objects that roaring, if it be done too much to the life, might frighten the ladies and get the actors hanged. Their future spectators, then, at least in the estimation of the players, are of the kind envisaged by Castelvetro. They are thought to be capable of complete and consistent identification with the illusion created by the stage action. Accordingly, the actors try to cater to them with the utmost verisimilitude. Pyramus and Thisbe meet in moonlight, and moonlight should be there actually shining through an open window:

Snout: Doth the moon shine that night we play our play?
Bottom: A calendar, a calendar! Look in the almanack; find out moonshine, find out moonshine.
Quince: Yes, it doth shine that night.
Bottom: Why, then may you leave a casement of the great chamber window, where we play, open; and the moon may shine in at the casement. (III, 1)[42]

But fears of how such acting might affect the ladies make them change their tactics during rehearsal. Even Bottom, perhaps mindful of Quince's warning, exchanges a Castelvetro-type approach for one reminiscent of Buonamici's. With the help of various devices, almost everyone and everything in the performance will be explained in terms of the signifier–signified duality. A prologue will announce that Pyramus does not kill himself *de facto* and, for even "better assurance," that Pyramus is not Pyramus, but Bottom the weaver. When Snout suggests a similar prologue for the lion, Bottom proposes a visual trick instead. Half the face of the person acting the beast must be seen peeping through the hide and tell the ladies not to be afraid, saying the lion is not a lion but "a man as other men are" (III, 1).

In all this, Shakespeare makes the actors use, or misuse, the kind of terminology central to Buonamici's understanding of drama. One person, equipped with a bush of thorns and a lantern, so Quince proposes, will explain that "he comes to disfigure or to present the person of Moonshine." Another, with some plaster, loam or rough-cast about him, so Bottom suggests, will "signify" wall. The actual performance only takes this self-parody to its *ne plus ultra*. In one sense, Quince and his troupe sound like followers of Buonamici trying to teach Castelvetro's ignorant multitude how to distinguish between fiction and fact, signifier and signified. Both Quince and Snout invoke the real "truth" behind the various devices of the spectacle. The Prologue announces that "This man, with lime and rough-cast, doth present / Wall." When Wall speaks *in propria persona*, he repeats this explanation with multiple variations:

> . . . I, one Snout by name, present a wall;
> . . .
> This loam, this rough-cast, and this stone, doth show
> That I am that same wall; the truth is so;
> And this the cranny is, right and sinister,
> Through which the fearful lovers are to whisper.

Again and again, the spectators are told that this or that "presents" or "is" this or that other which it stands for. Snout even refers to the "part" he has discharged as Wall – "And, being done, thus Wall away doth go." But, unlike Castelvetro's ignorant theatregoers, Shakespeare's intelligentsia aristocrats, just like their counterparts in *Love's Labour's Lost*, are hardly in need of a lesson in Buonamici's semiotics of drama. If anything, they know too much of it already, and merely add sarcasm to self-parody. A sophisticated cynicism like theirs will neither be caught in primitive illusionism nor tolerate the consistent pedantry of the opposite.

But Shakespeare adds a final note when he makes Theseus defend the actors' efforts with a phrase which appropriately counts among the poet's most famous: "The best in this kind are but shadows; and the worst are no worse, if imagination amend them" (V, 1). The words also stand out in other ways. For one, they seem to be out of character when we consider Theseus' speech, earlier in the same scene, mocking lunatic, lover, and poet, "of imagination all compact." They are also somewhat out of line with Theseus' consistent mockery during the performance. There is reason to claim, then, that Shakespeare is using the Duke to make a major statement about his art.

Be that as it may, the success of a play, in Shakespeare's mind, no doubt depended on the imaginative participation of the audience. Only given this collaboration could the playwright steer clear of both Castelvetro's consistent illusionism and Buonamici's anti-illusionist symbolism. For if the spectators are prepared to "piece out" the script's and spectacle's "imperfections with [their] thoughts," there is no need for either. The same "imaginary forces" which transmute four or five "vile and ragged foils" into the battle of Agincourt will transcend the duality implicit in this very act of imaginative projection.[43]

Buonamici's audience never does more than transliterate a sign (either heard or seen on the stage) into that of which it is a sign. Even minimal demands of imaginative expansion that would upset this nearly one-to-one equation (by, say, breaking the unity of time) must be avoided so as not to disturb "the ease of the imagination of the spectators" ("la facilità dell' imaginazione delli spettatori").[44] The audience, then, is credited with the analytical power to distinguish the signifier witnessed on stage from the signified it stands for in reality. But it is not, or to no major extent, believed to have the power imaginatively to expand the signifier into something it barely hints at.

By contrast, Shakespeare credits his audience with both. Spectators who are told to see a thousand men where there is only one, or a battle where there are "four or five most vile and ragged foils, / Right ill-dispos'd in brawl ridiculous,"[45] would, needless to say, have a clear awareness of the signifier–signified duality involved in any dramatic spectacle. But at the same time this awareness, as in the examples given from *Henry V*, is rarely one of mere duality. Where the spectacle shows us one man, the spectator is to imagine a thousand. Where four or five actors cross an equal number of ragged foils, we are supposed to see a battle. From what is said and done by the actors playing the King, Nym, Bardolph, Pistol, a Boy,

Gower, and Fluellen, we are to imagine the siege of Harfleur complete with town wall, breach, mines, countermines, trumpet sounds, and parley.

In each case the spectator's imagination is called upon to expand a visual image on the stage into an imaginary one often a thousand times its size and complexity, or to create a perhaps equally amplified image in the mind from what is a passing word of one of the actors. Such imaginative projection and amplification invariably aim at the concrete and particular, rather than at the abstract and idealized as in Buonamici. The spectator is asked not only to witness, listen and behold, but virtually and physically to mingle with the action.[46] At least temporarily, his place will not be in the audience, but in the imaginary realm evoked by the play. In his mind, he will see himself, say, stand on a beach and watch a whole fleet of warships dance on the billows.

Needless to say, such imaginative projection tends to transcend the conscious signifier–signified transference that is its starting-point; or it will sometimes lose itself completely in its largely self-created world. All this may never last for long, and Shakespeare himself, as we have seen, felt a need, again and again, to jolt his audience out of it. So Henry V reminds us, right there before the battle, that what is about to happen will be a story told by future generations, just as it is in the play at hand (IV, 3). But, at the same time, Shakespeare spares no effort to send the spectator's imagination on a trajectory far beyond all analytical awareness, at least of any fact–fiction duality. It would take a volume by itself to document this fact in the plays. In this context, it is enough to recall how Shakespeare, speaking through the choruses in *Henry V*, repeatedly tries to lure us into this state of mind.

THE SPECTATOR'S CREATIVE PARTICIPATION

Apart from being so obviously Shakespearean in kind, this chameleon-like attitude towards the audience also seems to be Shakespeare's in origin. There is little resembling it in the Renaissance criticism surveyed by Spingarn, Weinberg, and others. J. W. H. Atkins, author of *English Literary Criticism: The Renascence*, with its extensive chapter on dramatic criticism from both treatises and plays, mentions the "happy collaboration between artist and hearer (or reader)" demanded by Shakespeare.[47] But Atkins obviously lacks precedents for the same principle in England. English plays using similar audience address all seem to be later than *Henry V* and probably prompted by Shakespeare's play.[48] The idea, and perhaps the practise, was quickly picked up by Drayton, Beaumont, Fletcher, Dekker, and others, and became widely popular. Sometimes, as in the Prologue to *The Merry Devill of Edmonton*, the Shakespearean influence seems to be unmistakable:

> Imagine now that whilst he is retirde
> From Cambridge backe vnto his natiue home,
> Suppose the silent, sable-visagde night
> Casts her blacke curtaine ouer all the world.[49]

Similarly, Dekker, in the Prologue to *Old Fortunatus*, parallels Shakespeare's apologies for cramming the "vasty fields of France" into "this cockpit" or "wooden O."[50]

> And for this smal Circumference must stand,
> For the imagind Sur-face of much land,
> Of many kingdomes, and since many a mile,
> Should here be measurd out: our muse intreats,
> Your thoughts to helpe poore Art.[51]

Analogous excuses for "this narrow Stage" and "what we cannot / With fit conveniency of time, allow'd / For such Presentments, cloath in vocal sounds" are made by the Chorus in Fletcher's *The Prophetess* (IV, 1).[52]

Did Shakespeare, then, evolve these ideas all on his own? J. W. H. Atkins, though unable to show precedents in Renaissance English literary criticism, tries to answer this question by referring to the "Literary Criticism in Antiquity" which he deals with in a comprehensive survey having that title. In asserting the need for "a happy collaboration between artist and hearer (or reader)," he writes, Shakespeare "brought to light again the profound doctrine enunciated by Theophrastus and other writers of classical antiquity."[53] Theophrastus is reported to have said that not all possible points of an oration "should be punctiliously and tediously elaborated." Instead, something should be left to the comprehension and inference of the hearer. For when he perceives what you have left unsaid he becomes not only your hearer but "a very friendly witness," since he was given a chance to show his intelligence.[54] Plutarch, one of the playwright's favorite authors, extends this Theophrastian principle in a more Shakespearean direction. But this point may need some further elaboration.

According to Aristotelian critics, whether à la Castelvetro or à la Buonamici, the playwright has, and is supposed to have, a distinct design on his spectators. He should try either to coerce them into accepting fiction as fact or to make clear to them that what they witness on stage points to a separate, preferably Platonic, level of truth. Both attitudes, as we have seen, are satirized by Shakespeare, who in his own dramatic art seems to be bent on freeing the spectators from this unilaterally manipulative approach. To take one example: the Chorus in *Henry V* simply asks the spectators to let the full spectacle reify itself in their imagination. Of course, there is what the author's script causes to happen on the stage; but more important is what will take place by virtue of the spectator's imaginative effort as well as of his volition. The Chorus in *Henry V* is quite explicit concerning the distinction. The spectators are not only asked to evoke what had to be left unpresented "In the quick forge and working-house of thought"; they are also requested to let these things happen by their imaginative permission

> Now we bear the King
> Toward Calais. Grant him there. There seen,
> Heave him away upon your winged thoughts
> Athwart the sea . . .
> . . . So let him land,
> And solemnly see him set on to London.   (V, Prologue)

Taking Theophrastus as his starting-point, Plutarch allows the reader or listener a similar role with regard to the writer or speaker. "For just as in ball-play the one catching must move in accordance with the thrower, so in all discourse (or reading) there must be a harmonious interchange . . . between speaker (or writer) and listener (or reader)." For, to Plutarch, the human mind is not a vessel to be filled with ready-made knowledge; it is a pile that needs kindling so that it will flare up in pursuit of original thought and truth.[55]

But there is little to show that Shakespeare actually borrowed from these statements in Plutarch's treatise *On Listening*. Instead, he may have evolved his attitude towards the audience from a related concept in the fine arts. In any case, Shakespeare's earliest extensive discussion of imaginative spectator participation occurs in the description of a tapestry or painting in *The Rape of Lucrece*. The young playwright was obviously fascinated by a technique whereby the artist merely suggests what the spectator has to fill in with his imagination. The mind's eye will see an entire figure where the painting only shows part of it.

> For much imaginary work was there;
> Conceit deceitful, so compact, so kind,
> That for Achilles' image stood his spear,
> Grip'd in an armed hand; himself, behind
> Was left unseen, save to the eye of mind:
>   A hand, a foot, a face, a leg, a head,
>   Stood for the whole to be imagined. (1422–8)

Shakespeare, here, was perhaps influenced by Philostratus' description of a painting of the siege of Thebes.[56] He may also have drawn upon Pliny's claim that the painter Parrhasios perfected the arts of painting by not only rendering what they could see but also giving "assurance of the parts behind, thus clearly suggesting even what (the painting) conceals."[57] But none of these precedents speaks of the phenomenon with Shakespeare's terminological precision and sublety. Philostratus, though he mentions figures presented by, say, a mere bust or head, is really concerned with perspectival effect rather than spectator participation. Pliny, though he speaks of how the painter suggests what he conceals, discusses neither the principle of synecdochic substitution – "A hand, a foot, a face, a leg, a head, / Stand for the whole to be imagined" – nor the role of the spectator who imagines in the mind's eye what is missing from the painting. Shakespeare's words, even if they were prompted by Philostratus and/or Pliny, reveal a concern which clearly transcends these possible sources in intensity. This is reinforced by the way in which the poet uses Lucrece as an extreme example of such spectator participation. Herself a victim of rape and violence, she feelingly "weeps Troy's painted woes" (1492) while looking at the painting, and loses herself in her empathetic fantasies to the point where she claws with her nails at the painted figure of the traitor Sinon (1562–3).[58]

The same concern with the evocative powers of painting resurfaced in *The Taming of the Shrew*. Characteristically, the play shows how a person, if surrounded by various theatrical devices, can be made to lose his personal identity. One of these devices, used to lure tinker Sly into assuming his new personality as a lord, takes the form of a description of several pictures. Here again we find the notion that paintings, if the spectator uses his imagination, can suggest things that are not *de facto* depicted:

> *Second Servant*: Dost thou love pictures? We will fetch thee
>   straight
> Adonis painted by a running brook,
> And Cytherea all in sedges hid,
> Which seem to move and wanton with her breath
> Even as the waving sedges play wi' the' wind
> *Lord*: We'll show thee Io as she was a maid
> And how she was beguiled and surpris'd,
> As lively painted as the deed was done.
> *Third Servant*: Or Daphne roaming through a thorny wood,
> Scratching her legs, that one shall swear she bleeds;
> And at that sight shall sad Apollo weep,
> So workmanly the blood and tears are drawn.   (Induction, 2)

It is perhaps no mere accident that a playwright should derive his sense of audience participation from the analogous attitude of someone looking at a painting. Shakespeare, as we saw in the previous chapter, tried to address the eyes as much as the ears of his spectators – and not by mere on-stage spectacle alone. His very language has the same double impact. For good reason, it was one of Goethe's greatest pleasures in life to listen, with his eyes closed, to someone reciting his great predecessor's plays. Shakespeare's language, in other words, has a profoundly sensory, and particularly visual, appeal – but only to those who, whether readers or spectators, have the imagination to visualize in full what a poet can never do more than suggest in part.

This brings us to the end of the first section of this study. Most remarkable in this part, dealing with Shakespeare's immediate theoretical concerns as playwright and poet, is how the author, in uniquely idiosyncratic fashion, disregards, transmutes, and fuses related traditions current during the Renaissance. Both critically and admiringly, contemporaries and next-generation critics called Shakespeare the "poet of nature," a phrase which, however hackneyed, still characterizes this part of his poetics most aptly. Thus Shakespeare can be blithely oblivious of some of the hotly debated issues of Renaissance criticism such as mimesis, genre theory, the difference between prose and poetry, allegory, the nature of prosody, and the uses of rhyme. If he deals with any of these at all, it is usually in a humorous spirit of ironic dismissal.

This, however, is by no means proof either that the playwright was unaware of the Renaissance debates he chose to ignore or that he disregarded such matters altogether. While he never used the word Euphuism, for instance, his ironic skit on this literary fashion shows an acute awareness of its stylistic devices.[59] In turn, Shakespeare could be extremely explicit regarding issues that mattered to him. Such, for instance, were the uses of comparison and poetic conceit or the relationship between invention and delivery. Equally vital to him, as one might expect, were theories of acting, of drama and, above all perhaps, of the audience in relation to the spectacle.

Thus he would even take issue with other poets' theories. This happens in *Hamlet*, whose protagonist is made to articulate drama and acting theories reminiscent of Ben Jonson. Here, as where Shakespeare quarrels with the self-consciously flamboyant rhetoric of the rival poets in the Sonnets (to be studied in Chapter VI), he never attacks his opponents in directly identifiable, let alone name-calling, fashion. The same is true of his response to some of the theories advocated by Renaissance theorists of literature. Scaliger, Castelvetro, Piccolomini, Buonamici, even Puttenham or Sidney – none of them is mentioned, and it remains doubtful precisely how much of their and similar writings Shakespeare knew. But, quite apart from possible influence, Shakespeare's own attitudes with regard to, say, the unities stand out clearly enough against this general background to allow us to draw parallels and contrasts between individual theorists' ideas and his.

Of course, contrasts here tend to outweigh parallels; or, to be more precise, Shakespeare, even where he is found to echo, for instance, Castelvetro's theatrical naturalism, rarely commits himself to an established theoretical attitude. Renaissance theoreticians largely entrenched themselves in rigid either/or polarities. By contrast, Shakespeare, more often than not, reveals an eclectic versatility in subscribing to whatever ideas best serve his immediate demands. In this way, he can poke fun at presentational as well as representational theories of theatrical illusionism in the same play, while, for his own purposes, using both. Depending on the specific theatrical situation, the audience is called upon either to lose itself in or to detach itself from the spectacle. Especially, it must not be rigidly committed to an inflexible mental framework. On the contrary, its most important task is to collaborate imaginatively with an author who, protean and quicksilvery, might lure the spectators into visualizing a whole battle from a few rusty foils, shouts, and alarums one moment, only to shock them out of such illusionism the next.

So far, then, Shakespeare's poetics is characterized by its dissent from, rather than its allegiance to, mainstream Renaissance critical theory. To adduce quickly one further instance, various theorists drew a clear distinction between what Sidney calls the "idea or fore-conceite of the work" on the one hand and the "deliuering forth" of this invention on the other.[60] To Shakespeare, this deliberate succession is fused in a near simultaneity of imagining and writing, or, as Renaissance critics preferred to say, of invention and delivery. A man like Ben Jonson might complain that Shakespeare's fantasy flowed with so much facility "that sometime it was necessary he should be stop'd";[61] but the playwright himself seems to have felt few such compunctions. Some of his comments on the act of creation sound as if Shakespeare tried to dispense with the traditional terminology altogether. "Invention," though it was widely used where we now say "imagination," still retained too much of its intrinsic meaning of looking up commonplaces for the sake of illustrating some abstract idea. Shakespeare's ideal, then, seems almost to be that of one of his characters who advises another to

> Do it without invention, suddenly;
> As I with sudden and extemporal speech.[62]

Shakespeare's comments on the imagination itself, as we shall see, point in the same direction.

But does all this mean that Shakespeare as poet–theoretician was some *Originalgenie* more or less isolated from or ahead of his time? It is true that, wherever he seems to reveal his deepest convictions about his art and creativity, there is little real agreement with the more tradition-bound theorizing of Renaissance criticism; but significant analogues to Shakespeare's poetics, and to its underlying philosophical assumptions, exist elsewhere. What is more, they are found precisely where one might expect them, in the writings of perhaps the two most innovative philosophers of the age. One of them, Michel de Montaigne, was known to Shakespeare in Florio's 1603 translation of the *Essaies*. Whether or not the playwright knew the other, his own countryman Francis Bacon, remains a matter of speculation.[63] But again we are not concerned with possible influence but with the possible affinities of general outlook and poetics between the poet who ranks as the world's greatest and the two philosophers who hold similar eminence within the limits of their epoch.

IV · Shakespeare, Montaigne, and Bacon

T O START with a concrete example of such possible affinities, Montaigne, like Shakespeare, sees little difference
between the poet's invention or "fore-conceite" and the actual
process of writing.[1] Both are part and parcel of the same imaginative impulse. If anything, playwright and philosopher reversed
the emphases of a Sidney, Puttenham, or Ben Jonson, who
distinguished a possibly irrational invention from a strictly
rationalist craftsmanship of delivery. Most revealing here is
Theseus' well-known speech on the imagination,[2] to be discussed in Chapter VII. Once the prelinguistic imagination of the
Duke's poet has bodied forth the "forms of things unknown," the
writing follows almost automatically. In Montaigne's similar
view, words will follow only too readily after imagination has
done its work. To pretend otherwise is mere fakery:

I hear some making excuses for not being able to express themselves,
and pretending to have their head full of many fine things, but to be
unable to express them for lack of elegance. That is all bluff . . . For my
part I hold . . . that whoever has a vivid and clear idea in his mind will
express it, if necessary in Bergamask dialect, or, if he is dumb, by signs:

Master the shift by signs, and words will freely follow.
HORACE

As another said just as poetically in his prose: *When things have taken
possession of the mind, words come thick and fast* [Seneca] And another: *The
things themselves carry the words along* [Cicero].[3]

It all sounds strikingly like what this "unpremeditated and
accidental philosopher" had to say about his own writing. How,
as in writing letters, he was "prone to begin without a plan," the
first remark bringing on the second; how he would let his
subject-matter "make its own divisions without imposing a
rhetorical or logical order upon it; or how the result would be a

"record of various and changeable occurrences, and of irresolute and, when it so befalls, contradictory ideas." Montaigne, of course, was no poet himself and freely admitted to his lack of talent along these lines. But at the same time he saw affinities between his prose style and that "good, supreme, divine poetry [which] is above the rules and reason." "I love the poetic gait," he confessed, "by leaps and gambols. It is an art, as Plato says, light, flighty, demonic."[4]

To be sure, Montaigne's comments on poetry and art, like Bacon's, are both erratic and limited in scope.[5] But they have behind them the weight of a radical new view of life, which also will be found to be Shakespeare's. For lack of a better word, we shall call it their basic antiessentialism. Nearly all aspects of Shakespeare's poetics dealt with in the second part of this study, are prompted or at least permeated by it. As one might expect, they tend to be of a more philosophical, or rather psychophysiological, nature than the predominantly rhetorical, literary, and theatrical concerns studied in the first part. This accounts for a typically Shakespearean paradox. What in Renaissance critical terms might be considered marginal is central to Shakespeare's poetics, as it is to Montaigne's and Bacon's.

To generalize very broadly, all three of them broke with the traditional sense of art as a handmaiden of metaphysics and theology. Freed from this subservience, be it Aristotelian, Neoplatonic or Christian, art becomes an autonomous medium. Rather than depict what ought to be, it reenacts what is. To quote *The Winter's Tale*, an "art / That nature makes" (IV, 4) replaces an art subordinate to speculative reason. The language of poetry, rather than claiming to provide us with access to essentialist absolutes, is content with trying to capture the minute particulars of what is. Form no longer determines content, but content entails its appropriate form. The psychology of spontaneous creation becomes more important than the rationale of rhetorically calculated craftsmanship. The ultimate source of poetry is not reason controlling the imagination, but imagination holding its often dizzying sway over reason. Where it had to illustrate metaphysical or theological convictions, the imagination is allowed to function according to its psychological dynamics.

Hence it opens itself to the realms of hallucination, dream, and myth.

Montaigne's access to these and other convictions seems to have been through introspection. One of his earliest essays, "Of Idleness," describes how he first embarked on his extended self-exploratory odyssey. His original intention, at age thirty-eight, was to withdraw from court and public employment to the life of a private scholar. But several years of such leisure engendered the opposite of the quietude he had hoped for. The human mind, unless kept busy with activities which control it, he found, throws itself "in disorder hither and yon in the vague field of imagination:"

like a runaway horse, it gives itself a hundred times more trouble than it took for others, and gives birth to ... many chimeras and fantastic monsters.

One way of controlling such monstrosities would have been to escape into some form of occupational therapy. Another, recommended by Renaissance psychologists and art theoreticians alike, was to subject the imagination to the control of reason. But Montaigne found a third way which totally contravenes these traditionally approved methods of repression. He decided to make recording the phantasmagoric vagaries of his mind the very means of controlling them. In order "to contemplate their ineptitude and strangeness," he began "to put them in writing, hoping in time to make [his] mind ashamed of itself."[6]

MONTAIGNE AND THE IMAGINATION

For all that, Montaigne fully shared the common Renaissance distrust of the imagination.[7] In fact, there are few other writers of the time who explored the psychosomatic and mind-deranging powers of man's fantasy in greater detail. Being "one of those who are very much influenced by the imagination," he was virtually obsessed with autosuggestive impotence and other symptoms induced by desire and fear. But to try to control such powers through reason, he found, only increased their destructiveness. Instead, one had to treat one's imagination as gently as possible

and relieve it of all trouble and conflict: "We must help it and
flatter it, and fool it if we can." But more therapeutic than all else
to Montaigne was the absolutely authentic and painstakingly
detailed recording of his most bizarre imaginings. No matter if his
essays, in describing the various "chimeras and fantastic monsters" of his mind, turned into just as many "grotesques and
monstrous bodies, pieced together of diverse members, without
definite shape, having no order, sequence, or proportion other
than accidental"![8] What if Horace had opposed the kind of poetry
resembling a "sick man's dream" in which the author's "idle
fancies" assume "a shape that it is impossible to make head or tail
of what he is driving at"? His essays, so Montaigne points out to
the reader, are just like the example of such monstrousness given
by the Latin poet: "Desinat in piscem mulier formosa superne."[9]

So Montaigne persisted in graphing "the course of [his]
mutations," however contradictory and embarrassing they were
to him. Not unlike Ben Jonson's Shakespeare, who never blotted
out line, he did not even allow himself to revise except for minor
corrections. For he wished "to represent the course of [his]
humours," and wanted people "to see each part of [their] birth."
As a result he realized that "himself" at the moment of writing
and "himself" a while ago were "indeed two"; another, that in
graphing this day-to-day, even minute-to-minute, stream of
consciousness, contradictions were inevitable. But not only that.
In a sense, such contradictions were in total accord with the truth.
For Montaigne did not portray "being" but "passing:"

> Not the passing from one age to another, or, as the people say, from
> seven years to seven years, but from day to day, from minute to minute.
> My history needs to be adapted to the moment. I may presently change,
> not only by chance, but also by intention. This is a record of various and
> changeable occurrences, and of irresolute and, when it so befalls,
> contradictory ideas: whether I am different myself, or whether I take
> hold of my subjects in different circumstances and aspects. So, all in all, I
> may indeed contradict myself now and then; but truth, as Demades said,
> I do not contradict.[10]

What is more, unearthing his multiple selves, contradictory
responses, and fantastic chimeras had some clearly beneficent
effects. Any fancy, however frivolous and extravagant could, he
found, be made to benefit the human mind. To let his thoughts

run on, to speak indiscriminately of everything that came to his
mind, to sit constantly brooding over his thoughts, to listen
permanently to his reveries, to spend a lifetime with himself as
the only subject of his thoughts, not only to analyze, but to
"taste" and to "roll about in" himself – most earlier philosophers
would have condemned such activities as dangerous, even
immoral. But Montaigne learnt how to turn morbid introspection
into a pursuit of sanity. As he had anticipated, recording his
fantasies taught him to keep them from losing their way "and
roving with the wind." He even trained himself to dream with
"some order and purpose," found himself dreaming that he was
dreaming, and ended up turning nightmare into burlesque. "I
seldom dream," he confessed towards the end of his life, "and
then it is about fantastic things and chimeras usually produced by
amusing thoughts, more ridiculous than sad."[11]
Introspection, far from enclosing him in his ego, gave him
self-detachment. In learning to regard himself as some object –
"as I do a neighbor or a tree" – potential narcissism was turned
into empathy. Unlike most people, Montaigne felt few incli-
nations to judge others by himself. This was partly because he
had come to see his own self as a conglomerate of multiple
personae and circumstances. Sometimes his empathy was so
strong that people and things left their mark on him: "Anyone I
regard with attention easily imprints on me something of
himself. What I consider, I usurp: a foolish countenance, an
unpleasant grimace, a ridiculous way of speaking."[12] In sum,
Montaigne seems to have had some of the "negative capability"
Keats observed in Shakespeare.[13] The more people differed from
him in temperament and habits, the more he would empathize
with them: "I do not fail, just because I am not continent, to
acknowledge sincerely the continence of the Feuillants and the
Capuchins, and to admire the manner of their life. I can very well
insinuate myself by imagination into their place."[14]

MONTAIGNE'S POETICS

Montaigne, in other words, countered the traditional fear of what
Puttenham calls the "*Chimeres* & monsters in mans imagi-

nations"[15] by a deliberate exploration of such psychological irregularities. Equally original is how the essayist reinterprets the traditional *furor poeticus*. What Renaissance critics viewed as a hyperintellectual ascent towards ideational abstractions becomes a more strictly irrational, or potentially psychotic, impulse to Montaigne. Poets, he writes,

are often rapt in wonder at their own works and no longer recognize the track over which they ran so fine a race. That is what is called poetic frenzy and madness.[16]

Here as elsewhere, Montaigne emphasizes a totally unpremeditated spontaneity instead of insisting on the poet's frenzy-driven ascent towards the absolute. The idea of an intellectual pursuit that tries to leave behind the body was both antipathetic and absurd to the philosopher. In a sense the frenzied poet may transcend his ego, but he can hardly abandon his body. However inspired, man "must order the soul not to draw aside and entertain itself apart, not to scorn and abandon the body (nor can it do so except by some counterfeit monkey trick), but to rally to the body, embrace it, cherish it, assist it, control it." Montaigne's ideal poet is not a Platonist in pursuit of Being, but an empiricist involved with Passing. He "pours out in a frenzy whatever comes into his mouth, like the spout of a fountain, without ruminating and weighing it; and from him escape things of different colors and contradictory substance in an intermittent flow."[17]

At the same time, *furor poeticus* is not a poet's privilege. The best ancient prose, like his own, Montaigne felt, "shines throughout with the vigor and boldness of poetry and gives the effect of its frenzy." The anti-Platonic bias of such statements, though they frequently invoke Plato's testimony, is self-evident. Other Renaissance critics insisted on dissociating the Platonic *divinus furor* from common *insania*. Montaigne, by contrast, saw his imagination's "chimeras and monsters" as a part of both his subject-matter and his style with its "grotesque and monstrous" arabesques:

My style and my mind alike go roaming. A man must be a little mad if he does not want to be even more stupid ... I want the mattter to make its own divisions. It does well where it changes, where it concludes, where it begins, where it resumes, without my interlacing it with words, with links and seams introduced for the benefit of weak and heedless ears.[18]

Characteristically, this psychologically redefined *furor poeticus* is, in Montaigne's view, most operative in the playwright. For the dramatic poet has to draw on self-exploration for his emphatic understanding of others. Far from driving him away from his body towards the absolute, it stirs him "to anger, sorrow, and hatred" in trying to body forth the emotions of his dramatis personae. There is self-transcendence, but only to the extent to which the poet, via an in-depth understanding of himself, makes his own the emotions and personalities of others. The same applies to the audience, which, through its imaginative participation, comes to share this basically irrational experience. Dramatic and other poetry, that is to say "the good, supreme, divine poetry ... above rules and reason," "does not persuade our judgement, it ravishes and overwhelms it:"

The frenzy that goads the man who can penetrate it also strikes a third person on hearing him discuss and recite it . . . And it is seen more clearly in the theater that the sacred inspiration of the muses, after first stirring the poet to anger, sorrow, and hatred and transporting him out of himself wherever they will, then through the poet strikes the actor, and through the actor consecutively a whole crowd.[19]

In sum, Montaigne, while sharing the Renaissance distrust of the imagination, confronts fantasy's "chimeras and monsters" with almost obsessive determination. Introspection, in this pursuit, treats the various manifestations of the "self" like those of an "other." Equally radical is the essayist's reinterpretation of the time-honored *furor poeticus* as a truly psychological frenzy, rather than as a hyperintellectual ascent towards the absolute. For what, in Montaigne's view, could the frenzied philosopher–poet possibly ascend to? One of the essayist's main convictions is that all metaphysical speculation about essences and first principles is mere self-delusion. Reason, "that semblance of intellect that each man fabricates in himself," can afford us no such insights. Hence "there cannot be first principles for men, unless the Divinity has revealed them."[20] Shakespeare's Berowne, as we shall see, voices a similar scepticism. Where Montaigne pours scorn on the authors of Neoplatonic love treatises like Ficino and

Leon Hebreo, Berowne inverts the Platonic ascent towards ideal Beauty and makes Love a pansexual force living "not alone immured in the brain; / But, with the motion of all elements."[21]

Historically speaking, Montaigne evolved his new concept of the imagination from a double premise. This was by refuting traditional metaphysics and at the same time severing the time-honored alliance between the poet and the speculative philosopher. Renaissance aestheticians, for the most part, saw the poet as, in one way or another, rivaling the metaphysician's pursuit of the ideas or entelechies thought to be superior to reality. The poet's imagination, even his *furor poeticus*, was meant to serve as reason's handmaiden in this endeavor. Poetry, operating in the service of metaphysics, was supposed somehow to show things in their potential perfection. Such perfection – the true aim of the poet – can appear in various guises. To Spenser, "Rapt with the rage of [his] own ravisht thought, / Through contemplation of those goodly sights, / And glorious images in heaven wrought,"[22] they tend to be Platonic. To Sidney, they assume a more earthbound character. But even where Sidney invokes "Nature's child," invention, or tells himself to look in his heart and write,[23] he is hardly in search of a stream-of-consciousness realism. While advocating a poetry written out of a certain "inward touch,"[24] he wholeheartedly subscribes to Aristotle's ruling that poetry is more philosophical than history in that it imitates things, not as they are, but as they ought to be.

The diametrically opposite orientation, as evident in Montaigne, was also pursued by Francis Bacon. The English philosopher in this claimed to have made a radical break with the mainstream Platonic and Aristotelian traditions. These, as he saw it, had confounded philosophy with either theology or logic. "The entire fabric of human reason which we employ in the inquisition of nature" was, to him, "badly put together and built up, and like some magnificent structure without any foundation." What was needed, therefore, was a completely new start: "There remains but one course for the recovery of a sound and healthy condition, – namely that the entire work of the understanding be commenced afresh, and the mind itself be from the very outset not left to take its own course, but guided at every step."[25]

Bacon's well-known Idols, his major contribution towards this recovery, were not as revolutionary as all that. In fact, examples for all four of these "false notions which are . . . in possession of the human understanding"[26] can already be found in Montaigne.[27] Commenting on the first, the Idols of the Tribe, Bacon calls the human mind "an enchanted glass, full of superstition and imposture."[28] In describing man's understanding as "a two-edged and dangerous sword," Montaigne, here, is even more emphatic than Bacon. Even in the hands of a master logician like Socrates, reason, to him, is a "many-ended stick," or "an instrument of lead and of wax, stretchable, pliable, and adaptable to all biases and all measures." In calling reason "that semblance of intellect that each man fabricates in himself,"[29] Montaigne, with equal aptness, characterizes the Idols of the Cave or "false appearances imposed upon us by every man's own individual nature and custom." Concerning his Idols of the Market Place or "false appearances . . . imposed upon us by words,"[30] the English philosopher may even have borrowed one of his examples from the French essayist. "I ask," writes Montaigne, "what is 'nature,' 'pleasure,' 'circle,' 'substitution.' The question is one of words, and is answered in the same way. 'A stone is a body.' But if you pressed on: 'And what is a body?' – 'Substance.' – 'And what is substance?' and so on, you would finally drive the respondent to the end of his lexicon."[31] Bacon simply puts the matter in more abstract terms. Even definitions, he argues, often cannot save us from the inanities of verbal wrangling. For "definitions themselves consist of words, and those words beget others: so that it is necessary to recur to individual instances."[32]

Most notably, the two philosophers joined forces in dismantling the traditional systems of essentialist metaphysics. What to one were the Idols of the Theatre, or mere "play-books of philosophical systems,"[33] was but a kind of "sophisticated poetry"[34] to the other. But in dismissing traditional metaphysics as mere poetic fantasy, neither Bacon nor Montaigne meant to attack poetry as such. Philosophy and poetry were simply separate realms, and traditional philosophy, in its rationalist pursuit of absolute truth, had trespassed onto territories open to the poet and prophet, but not to the metaphysician. For to Bacon "the inquisition of man is not competent to find out *essential forms*,"[35] while to Montaigne "there cannot be first principles for men, unless the Divinity has revealed them, all the rest . . . is nothing but dreams and smoke."[36] In other words, poetry and religion had to be freed from the ill-conceived guardianship of metaphysics. The imagination had to be liberated from its subservience to reason. A two-thousand-year-old misconception about poetry and the imagination had to be jettisoned, and neither Montaigne nor Bacon hesitated to do this.

Of the two, the English philosopher no doubt was more fully aware of the consequences. Montaigne simply argues that man cannot attain final truths unless they be revealed to him by God; and he hints that such revelation can occur through the words of the poet. Bacon, in his usual manner, states the same convictions in more systematic terms. Human knowledge, to him, "admits of two kinds of information; the one inspired by divine revelation, the other arising from the senses." Elsewhere, he makes a tripartite division of human knowledge according to man's threefold mental capacities – reason, memory, imagination – while retaining his basic distinction between revealed and acquired knowledge. The parts of human learning, he writes,

have reference to the three parts of Man's Understanding, which is the seat of learning: History to his Memory, Poesy to his Imagination, and Philosophy to his Reason. Divine learning receiveth the same distribution; for the spirit of man is the same, though the revelation of oracle and sense be diverse: so as theology consisteth also of History of the Church; of Parables, which is divine poesy; and of holy Doctrine or precept.[37]

With the dismantling of traditional metaphysics, poetry and the poetic imagination, then, are freed of their subservience to speculative reason. At the same time poetry, a "philosophical" thing to Aristotle, has become an either playful or religious thing to Bacon and Montaigne. The French philosopher loves "the poetic gait, by leaps and gambols."[38] His British confrère defines poetry as the sport of the human mind. "For as all knowledge is the exercise and work of the mind," he writes, "so poesy may be regarded as its sport. In philosophy the mind is bound to things; in poesy it is released from that bond, and wanders forth, and feigns what it pleases."[39] It is for this reason, that Francis Bacon, in A. S. P. Woodhouse's view, introduced a whole new concept of poetry. Ceasing to be knowledge, poetry has become "fiction and play."[40]

But even more crucial was Bacon's (as well as Montaigne's) tendency to associate poetry with religion and myth. Poetry "was ever thought to have some participation of divineness," writes the English philosopher.[41] "It is the original language of the gods," claims Montaigne.[42] What is more, the poetic imagination, traditionally *ancilla philosophiae*, has become reason's superior, at least in the realm of final truths. Aristotle's opinion that "reason hath over the imagination that commandment which a magistrate hath over a free citizen"[43] is only true in a limited sense. For "in matters of Faith and Religion we raise our Imagination above our Reason; which is the cause why Religion sought ever access to the mind by similitudes, types, parables, visions, dreams."[44] In all this, Bacon shares Montaigne's curiosity for, and indeed appreciation of, imagination's chimeras and monsters, so dreaded by their contemporaries. The Frenchman quotes Horace's image of the beautiful woman tailing off into a hideous fish as an appropriate description of his essays and of the fantasies that inspired them – "grotesques and monstrous bodies, pieced together of divers members, without definite shape, having no order, sequence, or proportion other than accidental."[45] To Bacon, Horace's "desinat in piscem mulier formosa superne" provides an example of how the poet's imagination is privileged to go beyond reason. Poetry, though "in measure of words for the most part restrained," is "in all other points extremely licenced, and doth truly refer to the Imagination; which, being not tied to the laws of matter, may at pleasure join that which nature hath severed, and sever that which nature hath joined, and so make unlawful matches and divorces of things; 'Pictoribus atque poetis, &c.'"[46]

BACON AND MYTH

It was Bacon's distinction to extend these concepts into a theory of myth which, however minimally, may serve as a background to plays like *A Midsummer Night's Dream* and *The Tempest*. Terms like "mythology" or "mythological," of course, were rarely used in Shakespeare's period.[47] Instead, Elizabethans spoke of parables and fables to be "moralized" according to their allegorical meanings. To Thomas Lodge, for instance, our decaying years "are signified" in the person of Saturn, our affections "dissiphered" in the picture of angry Juno, and human knowledge "denotated" in the portraiture of Apollo.[48] Virgil-translator Stanyhurst points out what "deepe and rare poynctes of hydden secrets *Virgil* hath sealde vp in his twelue bookes of *Æneis*."[49] Ariosto-translator Sir John Harington contends that the "ancient Poets haue indeed wrapped as it were in their writings diuers and sundry meanings, which they call the senses or mysteries thereof." The myth of Perseus, son of Jupiter, who, after slaying the Gorgon, flew up to heaven, is taken as an example. In addition to its historical and moral significance, Sir John Harington explicates three of the "infinite Allegories" he could "pike out of" this fable: one, according to which Perseus stands for man vanquishing the earthliness of his "Gorgonicall nature"; a second "more high and heauenly Allegorie, that the heauenly nature, daughter of *Iupiter*, procuring with her continuall motion corruption and mortality in the inferiour bodies, seuered it selfe at last from these earthly bodies, and flew vp on high, and there remaineth for euer"; and a third, "Theological Allegorie: that the angelicall nature, daughter of the most high God the creator of all things, killing & ouercomming all bodily substance, signified by *Gorgon*, ascended into heuen."[50] In such "infinite Allegories" we find the full complexity of the Renaissance allegorical method which Henry Reynolds, drawing on Pico della Mirandola's Neoplatonic and Cabalistic allegorizations of biblical and other texts, was to expand further in his 1632 *Mythomystes*.[51]

But the general method was the same throughout. In the Renaissance it was already commonplace to the point of attracting the ridicule of authors like Rabelais and Montaigne. If his reader believed that Homer, in writing the *Iliad* and *Odyssey*, was thinking of the allegories squeezed out of him by Plutarch, Politian, and others, then he was "not within a hand's or a foot's length" of his opinion, protests the author of *Gargantua*.[52] "Is it possible that Homer meant to say all they make him say, and that he lent himself to so many and such different interpretations," asks Montaigne.[53] It amazed the French philosopher what wonderful correspondences a friend of his drew out of Homer in support of Christian religion.

But for all their irony, even Montaigne and Rabelais left the allegorical approach to myth as such unquestioned. While making fun of the Homer interpreters, Rabelais claims that whoever reads his book as he ought to will be initiated "into certain very high sacraments and dread mysteries."[54] Montaigne, while ridiculing the simple-mindedness of those who think they can explicate Aesop's fables in terms of a single meaning, only favors a more complex mode of interpretation of the same type. For to him, most of these fables

have many meanings and interpretations. Those who take them allegorically choose some aspect that squares with the fable, but for the most part this is only the first and superficial aspect; there are others more living, more essential and internal, to which they have not known how to penetrate; this is how I read them.[55]

Other writers like Sidney defended the primordial quality of myth. Plato to him was wrong in accusing the Greek poets for filling the world with wrong opinions about the gods. For they simply used a body of stories already in existence.[56] Or there are Puttenham's speculations about the earliest poets officiating as lawmakers, inventors, and priests all in one – "they came by instinct diuine, and by deepe meditation, and much abstinence ... to be made apt to receaue visions, both waking and sleeping, which made them vtter prophesies and foretell things to come."[57] But none of these comments questions the basic allegorical assumption that myths, or what the Elizabethans termed fables and parables, were designed to express a meaning. As G. Gregory Smith writes, the "quite contrary position that imagination first constructs the fable, and thereafter the poet or his commentator or his reader finds the moral, could hardly be established until aesthetic criticism had found its axioms."[58]

However, there was at least one exception. In his 1605 *Advancement of Learning*, Francis Bacon took the decisive step beyond his predecessors. Like Sidney, he contends that poets like Homer inherited rather than invented their fables. Like Rabelais and Montaigne, he discredits the various allegorical interpretations which subsequent critics have applied to these myths. Chrysippus, in trying "to fasten the assertions of the Stoics upon the fictions of the ancient poets," for instance, had simply revealed his vanity. But Bacon goes further than all this. As far as he can tell, Homer's fables, for instance, have "no such inwardness in [the poet's] own meaning." Bacon even entertains the possibililty that "all the fables and fictions of the poets were but pleasure and not figure."[59]

But how about the allegorical interpretations of such fables in general? Bacon himself gives three examples in the same context – the stories of the Giants, of Briareus, and of Achilles' education by the centaur Chiron. The first of these – how Earth, upon the defeat of her sons, the Giants, at the hands of the Olympians, brought forth fame – had been said to imply the following: "when princes and monarchs have suppressed actual and open rebels, then the malignity of people (which is the mother of rebellion) doth bring forth libels and slanders." But did this mean that the inventors of these fables had designed them to illustrate such allegorical meanings? Bacon decides that the very opposite is the truth. In many similar instances, he argues, "I do rather think that the fable was first, and the exposition devised, than that the moral was first, and thereupon the fable framed."[60]

How did Bacon arrive at this radical new understanding of myth? Again, the answer is found in his dismantling of essential-ist metaphysics. Bacon's main starting-point, as we recall, is his dissociation of religion from philosophy, of the truth of divine revelation from the truth of scientific enquiry, and of the imagin-ation from reason. In one way, this means going back before Aristotle and Plato to pre-Socratic philosophers like Democritus or, even further, to the mythological insights of pre-philosophical Greek culture, which Bacon deals with in his 1609 *Wisdom of the Ancients*. Both Pentheus and Prometheus, in that study, are said to foreshadow the overweening arrogance of later philosophers who, with no other means than human reason, tried to attain the kind of truths reserved to divine revelation. Prometheus' attempt upon the chastity of Minerva, for instance, appears to Bacon as "no other than that into which men not unfrequently fall when puffed up with arts and much knowledge, – of trying to bring the divine wisdom itself under the dominion of sense and reason . . . [For] men must soberly and modestly distinguish between things divine and human, between the oracles of sense and of faith; unless they mean to have at once a heretical religion and a fabulous philosophy."[61]

For revealing such Baconian insights, fables like those of Prometheus and Pentheus are raised to a level of near-equality with comparable biblical narratives. *The Advancement of Learning* discusses both Greek and Hebrew mythology under the common denominator of "Poesy Parabolical . . . that is when the secrets and mysteries of religion, policy, or philosophy are involved in fables and parables." The enlarged Latin translation of the same work states the basic equality of pagan and biblical mythology in even more unequivocal terms: parabolical poesy is superior to its narrative and dramatic counterpart in that it "appears to be something sacred and venerable; especially as religion itself commonly uses its aid as a means of communication between divinity and humanity." The fact that pagan parabolical poetry was usually left "to boys and grammarians" does not deter Bacon from considering it as "a kind of breath from the traditions of more ancient nations, which fell into the pipes of the Greeks." After all, it represents the most ancient of human writings "next to sacred story." In fact, its underlying fables are even older: "for they are related not as being invented by the writers, but as things believed and received from of old."[62]

Classical myth, then, was to the Greeks what the Bible is to us. In principle, the biblical prophet and ancient poet fulfilled the same function in revealing God's secrets to man. Or put somewhat differently, the delivery "both of prophecies by means of visions and of divine doctrine by parables, partakes of poesy." Bacon even asks himself how this "means of communication between divinity and humanity" operates in psychological terms. Again, the answer is found in an afterthought added to the

Latin edition of *The Advancement of Learning*. In the original English version Bacon had stated that "in matters of Faith and Religion we raise our Imagination above our Reason; which is the cause why Religion sought ever access to the mind by similitudes, types, parables, visions, dreams." In *De Augmentis*, Bacon interpolates several phrases which elucidate the earlier statement:

> For we see that in matters of faith and religion our imagination raises itself above our reason; not that divine illumination resides in the imagination; its seat being rather in the very citadel of the mind and understanding; but that the divine grace uses the motions of the imagination as an instrument of illumination, just as it uses the motions of the will as an instrument of virtue; which is the reason why religion ever sought access to the mind by similitudes, types, parables, visions, dreams.[63]

Read carefully, the interpolated words tone down the radicalness of the previous statement. Though still freed from speculative reason, the imagination has been made subservient to a new guardian, "the very citadel of the mind and understanding." Bacon, as the years went by, was back-tracking in his revolutionary paths.[64] In *The Advancement of Learning*, the "similitudes, types, parables, visions, dreams" are said to be directly prompted by the imagination when it is raised above reason. In *De Augmentis* they have become products of a mental faculty which is inferior to another and, as such, a mere means to the end of illuminating this "citadel of the mind and understanding."[65]

At the same time, Bacon recants what is the most radical contention of his early theorizing about myth – i.e., that in most cases "the fable was first, and the exposition devised, [rather] than that the moral was first, and thereupon the fable framed." The statement was dropped when Bacon translated *The Advancement of Learning* into Latin. Even before that, the philosopher had already reverted to a more allegorical understanding of myth. His preface to *The Wisdom of the Ancients* still entertains the possibility "that always the fable was first and the allegory put in after," concluding that "the wisdom of the primitive ages was either great or lucky; great, if they knew what they were doing and invented the figure to shadow the meaning; lucky, if without meaning or intending it they fell upon matter which gives occasion to such worthy contemplations."[66] But the book itself, an allegorical exegesis of numerous mythological figures from Cassandra to the Sirens, clearly follows the traditional method and, in fact, borrows extensively from older manuals such as Natale Conti's *Mitologia*.[67]

One wonders if Bacon might have retained his earlier notions had he been familiar with Shakespeare's mythopoeic dramas. Would watching *A Midsummer Night's Dream* have confirmed him in his early conviction that the creation of Oberon, Titania, Puck, and the elves came first, and whatever allegorical meanings one might associate with them second? Or might the play have swayed him towards assuming that Shakespeare began with some allegorical "fore-conceite" which he then embodied in these figures? To someone advocating the radically new theory that, in most traditional myths, "the fable was first, and the exposition devised," the answers would have been obvious: Shakespeare was clearly no poet like Spenser, trying to shadow a meaning under a "continued Allegory, or darke conceit."[68] But Bacon, to all evidence, ignored the works of the playwright. "Dramatic Poesy, which has the theatre for its world," he wrote.

would be of excellent use if well directed. For the stage is capable of no small influence both of discipline and of corruption. Now of corruptions in this kind we have enough; but the discipline has in our times been plainly neglected. And though in modern states play-acting is estimated but as a toy, except when it is too satirical and biting; yet among the ancients it was used as a means of educating men's minds to virtue. Nay, it has been regarded by learned men and great philosophers as a kind of musician's bow by which men's minds may be played upon.[69]

Of all of Shakespeare's attitudes which will be shown either to echo or to point towards Bacon's and Montaigne's there remains one, regarding language, which perhaps affected the poet's writing most immediately. Here again, of course, we are not concerned with possible influence. More important, or at least intriguing, is the possible fact of a common attitude towards life which permeated the three men's more specific views on art, imagination, creativity, and language. For good reasons, then, we might for once reverse the approach adopted thus far by letting the poet speak before the philosophers. Just a few words by way of introducing the general problems will have to suffice at this point.

Debates over the function, potential and limitations of language, of course, neither started with the Renaissance nor have ceased to concern us since then. What divides people into, say, Wittgensteinians versus Heideggerians today was discussed under dichotomies such as nominalism versus realism during the Middle Ages. Similar disputes could be traced back to Socrates' quarrel with the Sophists. But what to one age is an erudite debate might turn into an obsession to another, and it is hardly exaggerated to say that this is what happened during the Renaissance. For to the Humanists, to whom language and its study had acquired unprecedented importance, a questioning of this medium's cognitive potential was tied up with most of what either might be or could not be known about all the ultimate issues of metaphysics and religion.

V · The dismantling of essentialist discourse

A S LONG AS man believes in essences – be they Platonic or prelapsarian – language, in one way or another, will be thought to provide access to them.[1] Back in the Middle Ages, John of Salisbury had argued that names were "stamped on all substances"[2] so that there was, at least potentially, a divinely created link between man's language and these final realities. During the Renaissance, such notions were frequently linked to Hermetic and Neoplatonic philosophy. Paracelsus argued, for instance, that "each being should be given the name that belongs to its essence."[3] To Thomas Wilson, author of *The Arte of Rhetorique*, "words that fill the mouth and have a sound with them, set forth a matter very well."[4] On account of such eloquence, man could be "compted for halfe of [the] God" or Logos who created the world. This is particularly true of the poet who, in Scaliger's words, "makes another nature" and at the same time "makes himself another God, as it were."[5] Conversely, the order of God's creatures, as John Hoskyns stood convinced, "is not only admirable and glorious, but eloquent."[6]

But with the belief in transcendental essences questioned, discourse loses this demiurgical potential. What before was geared towards, and ultimately determined by absolutes turns into a tentative medium to communicate what is ever-changing and variable. What ideally would be a statement about immutable truths turns into an ever-insufficient means to express what is mere flux. What previously stood for the transcendent reality of things now at best reflects phenomena as they are. Even worse, language, once reduced to this lowly function, can never equal what it stands for.

As long as a word like "beauty" was believed to denote an essentialist concept, such equation was indeed possible. Even a "tree," for instance, could after all be thought of in terms of the ideal or prelapsarian "Tree." But, with such convictions gone, how can a concept like "beauty" be seen as anything else than an ultimately unverifiable denotation of a finally undefinable human perception? Or how could a word like "tree" be viewed as anything else than a more or less arbitrary label to cover a phenomenon intrinsically eluding such denomination? When does a tree, for instance, cease to be a tree and deserve to be called a bush? In a final sense, then, language, if unrelated to a superior reality, can never equal what it stands for. Where essentialist language finds its fulfillment in articulating absolute truths, its opposite operates from the basic assumption of the intrinsic incommunicability of reality. Its most honest stance, then, is not speech, but silence or speechless wonder; or at least the awareness that discourse, even in its finest achievements, is never more than an approximation to what it tries to capture.

However Wittgensteinian they might appear, such thoughts were not uncommon in Shakespeare's period. It was equally known that language, if placed in such subservience to a constantly changing reality, will never be more than an ever-insufficient approximation to whatever it tries to express. But stronger than all else was the awareness of a collapse of essentialist discourse, which no doubt preceded such linguistic skepticism. Shakespeare himself, whether or not he personally experienced this collapse, made it the central theme of two of his works, *Troilus and Cressida* and the Sonnets.

FROM "TRUTH'S SIMPLICITY" TO SOPHISTRY

Few characters in Shakespeare protest as much as Troilus. "I am as true as truth's simplicity, / And simpler than the infancy of truth" (III, 2). Here as elsewhere, Troilus translates what amounts to a simple vow of faithfulness into high-sounding terms of near-metaphysical abstraction. Constancy becomes the truth, and the words, which tell us so, become truth's perfect medium:

Few words to fair faith: Troilus shall be such to Cressid as what envy can say worst shall be a mock for his truth; and what truth can speak truest not truer than Troilus.　　　　　　　　　　　　　　　　　　　(III, 2)

Whatever truth Troilus thus posits in himself, he demands from Cressida. He hopes that her constancy will outlive "beauty's outward" and that her mind will "renew swifter than blood decays" (III, 2). This, of course, is the familiar language of Petrarchan idealism, a tradition Troilus points at in a prophetic moment. His name, he predicts, will serve as ultimate hyperbole to future poets laboring to express what is noblest in their love. In a historical perspective, Troilus, in this way, assumes the role of "truth's authentic author" to the entire tradition:

> True swains in love shall in the world to come
> Approve their truth by Troilus, when their rhymes,
> Full of protest, of oath, and big compare,
> Want similes, truth tir'd with iteration –
> As true as steel, as plantage to the moon,
> As sun to day, as turtle to her mate,
> As iron to adamant, as earth to th' centre –
> Yet, after all comparisons of truth,
> As truth's authentic author to be cited,
> 'As true as Troilus' shall crown up the verse
> And sanctify the numbers.   (III, 2)

The prophecy, especially when echoed by Pandarus and Cressida, is fraught with dramatic irony. Both now and then, spectators would know that the truth invoked here will be violated. What is meant to celebrate the good and the beautiful is a monument to falsehood and shame. So we are well prepared for Troilus' disillusionment. Nevertheless, Shakespeare explores the collapse of his protagonist's idealism in unusually explicit terms.

We are never allowed to forget that Troilus, at least in his self-esteem, stands for truth and truthful language. As the hero approaches his moment of real truth, his yearning for its idealistic counterpart becomes ever more desperate. At least one character starts to weary of his insistence. "O heavens! 'Be true' again!" (IV, 4), protests Cressida, after Troilus, in their farewell scene, once again exhorts her to be faithful. As far as his own truth is concerned, the hero has fewer doubts than ever:

> Who, I? Alas, it is my vice, my fault!
> Whiles others fish with craft for great opinion,
> I with great truth catch mere simplicity;
> Whilst some with cunning gild their copper crowns,
> With truth and plainness I do wear mine bare.

> Fear not my truth: the moral of my wit
> Is 'plain and true'; there's all the reach of it.   (IV, 4)

Even outside observers reinforce the same impression. In Ulysses' view, Troilus, though "Not yet mature," is "firm of word; / Speaking in deeds and deedless in his tongue" (IV, 5).

An entire scene, and one of the most complex in all of Shakespeare, demonstrates the collapse of this linguistic essentialism.[7] As we watch Thersites watch Troilus and Ulysses watch Cressida's falsity, Troilus' much cherished truth disintegrates into "fragments, scraps . . . and greasy relics" (V, 2). What happens to "truth's authentic author" in the process is explicated with near-emblematic explicitness, complete with motto – "O beauty! where is thy faith?" – as well as with Troilus' and Thersites' commentaries. Initially, Troilus still clings to his idealistic convictions with "An esperance so obstinately strong, / That doth invert th' attest of eyes and ears" (V, 2). But his language at this point shows how self-delusion gradually gives way to total disillusionment. The opening of his monologue was still full of his previous rhetoric:

> This she? No; this is Diomed's Cressida.
> If beauty have a soul, this is not she;
> If souls guide vows, if vows be sanctimonies,
> If sanctimony be the gods' delight,
> If there be rule in unity itself,
> This was not she.   (V, 2)

But such rhetoric, intent on safeguarding the orator's most cherished idealistic values, only convinces him of a general "madness of discourse, / That cause sets up with and against itself!" (V, 2).

Much against his Platonic temperament, reality has taught Troilus a lesson in sophistry. He has learnt to argue *in utramque partem* or on both sides of the question.[8]

> Bifold authority! where reason can revolt
> Without perdition, and loss assume all reason
> Without revolt: this is, and is not, Cressid.   (V, 2)

The sudden distrust of essentialist terms resulting from this "madness of discourse" is brought out with equal explicitness. Truth, once thought "a thing inseparate," has turned into an abyss wider than sky and earth. So enormous is this division that it does not even leave the hero the assurance of a clear dichotomy. Reality's ultimate impenetrability seems to send human cognitive endeavor back into the spiderweb labyrinths of its abstractions:

> Within my soul there doth conduce a fight
> Of this strange nature, that a thing inseparate
> Divides more wider than the sky and earth;
> And yet the spacious breadth of this division
> Admits no orifex for a point as subtle
> As Ariachne's broken woof to enter.   (V, 2)

Whatever rhetoric Troilus has left after this, resembles the "greasy relics" of his lost faith.[9] It simply compounds his confusion. His very "instance[s]" to prove that Cressida is his convince him that the "bonds of heaven are slipp'd, dissolv'd, and loos'd" (V, 2). The only thing emerging intact from all this is his hatred of Diomed. The astute Ulysses is quick to take hold of this emotion in order to pull Troilus out from under the rubble of his broken convictions. From here on, anger and defiance carry Troilus right through to the end of the play. He chides Hector for his "vice of mercy" ("Let's leave the hermit Pity with our mother," V, 3), bids Diomed hold on to his whore Cressida (V, 4), and vows to revenge Hector's death on the "great-siz'd coward" Achilles (V, 10). The previous idealist has learnt his lesson with a vengeance. "Words, words, mere words, no matter from the heart" (V, 3), he exclaims after reading a letter from Cressida. Characteristically, he is also made to complete the prophecies which Cressida and Pandarus unwittingly called upon themselves earlier:

> O Cressid! O false Cressid! false, false, false!
> Let all untruths stand by thy stained name.   (V, 2)

Troilus' similar words about Pandarus are the last he utters in the play:

> Hence, broker-lackey! Ignominy and shame
> Pursue thy life and live aye with thy name!   (V, 10)

THE "MADNESS OF DISCOURSE"

The collapse of Troilus' linguistic essentialism in a "madness of discourse" finds a striking parallel in Shakespeare's Sonnets. Their speaker, alias "Will," protests almost as much as Troilus:

> Therefore my verse, to constancy confin'd,
> One thing expressing, leaves out difference.
> 'Fair, kind, and true' is all my argument.   (105)

There is the same Platonic tendency to speak of the beloved's hoped-for fidelity in terms of metaphysical abstraction: "O, how much more doth beauty beauteous seem / By that sweet ornament which truth doth give!" (54). Like Troilus, Will insists on his truthfulness or on the fact that his language is a direct transcript of his idealistic convictions: "O, let me, true in love, but truly write" (21). What will survive him in his poems, so he assures his lover, is not his body but his soul:

> When thou reviewest this, thou dost review
> The very part was consecrate to thee.
> The earth can have but earth, which is his due;
> My spirit is thine, the better part of me.   (74)

Like Troilus, Will also calls upon the future to bear out his idealistic assertions. Love, to him, should be exempt from all temporal changes and decay of beauty.

> If this be error and upon me prov'd,
> I never writ, nor no man ever lov'd.   (116)[10]

The story of Will's disillusionment differs from Troilus'. But the result – a collapse of his idealistic convictions and language – is near-identical. Like Troilus, Will suffers from the occasional conflict between what reason tells him *ought to be* and what his senses convince him is actually the case. Other sonnets speak in the tones of Troilus' final disillusionment after witnessing Cressida's falsity. What was once associated with truth and constancy has turned into an all-consuming fever robbing the speaker of reason and language:

> My Reason, the physician to my Love,
> Angry that his prescriptions are not kept,
> Hath left me, and I desperate now approve
> Desire is death, which physic did except.
> Past cure I am, now reason is past care,
> And frantic mad with evermore unrest;
> My thoughts and my discourse as mad men's are,
> At random from the truth vainly express'd.   (147)

Here, as in *Troilus and Cressida*, the Horatian *monumentum aere perennius*,[11] dedicated to love and beauty, turns out to be an epitaph on the death of these values.

Yet both Troilus' and Will's idealistic fervor and language appear to us questionable long before we witness their collapse. Troilus, from the start, is a poor advocate of his convictions.[12] Before he pleads for retaining Helen in the name of "honour and renown" (II, 2), he protests that he cannot "fight upon this argument," denouncing the "Fools on both sides" (I, 1). His rhetoric about love and constancy suffers from the strain of what one critic calls his "peculiarly literary concern for words."[13] Troilus often talks in quotations or in terms of what he tells others and others tell him (e.g., I, 1). In a way, he likes to assume the role of his poetic double, invoking future poets and vowing "to weep seas, live in fire, eat rocks, [and] tame tigers" (III, 2). Not surprisingly, such linguistic doublethink can lead to unconscious confusions. In pleading for the retention of Helen, for instance, he associates his prize with soiled silks one would like to return to the merchant and with leftover food the sated palate rejects like garbage (II, 2). Needless to say, such oratory hardly convinces us of what it pleads for. Instead, it reveals some of Troilus' true nature, which Ulysses prophetically describes as immature but "more vindicative than jealous love" (IV, 5) when aroused to action. The fear and violence lurking behind Troilus' Petrarchan clichés is everywhere. Whether he talks about the anticipated delights of sleeping with Cressida or about Pandarus' praises of her beauty, he always ends up invoking open ulcers, knives, and gashes (I, 1) or a "battle, when they charge on heaps / The enemy flying" (III, 2).

This undercutting of Troilus' linguistic essentialism preceding his disillusionment, is brought to even sharper focus by the play as a whole. Here deflation of rhetorical pretense occurs at multiple levels. Much of the very opening scene is taken up with Pandarus' elaborate puns on Troilus' use of the word "tarry." In turn, Pandarus' prosaic cake-baking imagery is thrown back at him when Cressida derides his portrayal of Troilus as the perfect courtier.

Pandarus: . . . Have you any eyes? Do you know what a man is? Is not birth, beauty, good shape, discourse, manhood, learning, gentleness,

virtue, youth, liberality, and such like, the spice and salt that season a
man?
Cressida: Ay, a minc'd man; and then to be bak'd with no date in the pie,
for then the man's date is out.   (I, 2)

From Ajax to Agamemnon, characters are made to speak in a
language at odds with their character, audience, situation, or
topic. A recent critic, adopting Puttenham's terminology, describes these breaches of decorum under categories like bomphiologia or "vsing ... bombasted wordes" (e.g., Hector,
Agamemnon), macrologia "when we use large clauses or sentences more than is requisite to the matter" (e.g., Nestor,
Agamemnon), periergeia or "ouermuch curiositie and studie to
shew himself fine in a light matter" (e.g., Troilus, Aeneas) and
cacozelia or "fonde affectation" (e.g., Troilus, Agamemnon).
Conversely, Ulysses' debunking of Patroclus (I, 3), Patroclus'
caricature of Agamemnon (I, 3), and Thersites' railing on almost
everyone and everything in the play can be classified as Puttenham's tapinosis or "the abbaser."[14] Shakespeare, of course, may
well have ignored this terminology. But some of the rhetorical
vices identified by Puttenham are no doubt the targets of the
elaborate satirical strategies built into the play.

We find similar techniques in the Sonnets. Here again, the
rhetoric of truth and beauty is questioned long before it is brought
to collapse in a "madness of discourse." The speaker's vow that
"Fair, kind, and true" is all his argument (105) is preceded by
statements which seem to answer Troilus' "O beauty! where is
thy faith?" (V, 2) in clearly negative terms. Sonnet 69, while
acknowledging the friend's physical beauty, associates the
"beauty of [his] mind" with "the rank smell of weeds." Before
purporting to disavow all he has written should "the marriage of
true minds" prove an error (116), he admits to both his and his
friend's promiscuity (e.g., 95). Similarly, his avowals of truthfulness, both in language and spirit, are preceded by the admission
that he has "look'd on truth / Askance and strangely" (110). All
this is set against a general backdrop of uncertainty and flux,
which permeate the sequence throughout. S. Booth has argued in
painstaking detail how the Sonnets, on every level of syntax,
prosody, sound patterns, etc., follow a dizzying path of unity

and division, likeness and difference. The reader's mind, almost as if responding to random experience, "is kept in constant motion; it is kept uneasy as it is made constantly aware of relationships among parts of the poem that are clear and firm but in an equally constant state of flux." What we react to is unlike the traditional paradoxes of similar poems. For Shakespeare confronts us not with a literary device, but with the analogue of a truly paradoxical situation. Rather than just amaze us, he throws us off balance.[15]

The same applies to Will's attitude towards language. If he moved from a linguistic idealism to a Wittgensteinian skepticism, we would end up with either a sense of loss or at least the superiority of our cynicism. But the Sonnets give us neither kind of assurance. Although their overall tone darkens towards the end, a clear development is replaced by a see-saw motion covering every possible nuance from naively idealistic affirmation to disillusioned cynicism. The vow to "truly write" as one "true in love" (21), for instance, conflicts with the "madness of discourse" which, like Troilus', sets up causes "with and against itself" (V, 2).

> No more be griev'd at that which thou hast done:
> Roses have thorns, and silver fountains mud;
> Clouds and eclipses stain both moon and sun,
> And loathsome canker lives in sweetest bud.
> All men make faults, and even I in this,
> Authorizing thy trespass with compare,
> Myself corrupting, salving thy amiss,
> Excusing thy sins more than thy sins are.　　　(35; cf. 147)

Troilus uses rhetoric to prove to himself that the unfaithful Cressida before his eyes cannot be the "real" Cressida of his Platonic convictions. Will does the same for the similar purpose of excusing his lover's trespass. Here, as in other sonnets, the speaker has reached a point where anguish has turned into cynical playfulness and deliberate self-deception. But otherwise the lines could be spoken by Troilus, or "truth's authentic author," turned prophet of mendacity. The same techniques of protest, oath, and big compare are transmogrified into an unprecedented art of lying. Even where Will protests his truthfulness after this, he simply gives further instances providing cause with and against himself.

Yet, for all that, an admission such as "Those lines that I before have writ do lie" (115) does not invalidate what preceded it in any absolute sense. Contradictions, and even their open avowal, are part of a rock-bottom authenticity of statement, in which existence prevails over essence, the convictions actually felt at a given moment over what is believed at a more skeptical level. Or as Montaigne said in equally existentialist terms about his essays,

> I do not portray being: I portray passing . . . My history needs to be adapted to the moment. I may presently change, not only by chance, but also by intention. This is a record of various and changeable occurrences, and of irresolute and, when it so befalls, contradictory ideas: whether I am different myself, or whether I take hold of my subjects in different circumstances and aspects. So, all in all, I may indeed contradict myself now and then; but truth . . . I do not contradict.[16]

Several characteristics of the Sonnets – the mention of a three-year period since they were begun (e.g., 104), the occurrences sometimes described as what prompted individual poems (e.g., riding a horse, 50, 51; "my absence," 97), their fiercely introspective bias, etc. – reinforce this diary-like character. At one point, the speaker even advises his friend to keep a book like the one in front of us. The goal proposed is similar to Montaigne's attempt to make his mind ashamed of itself by presenting it with the "many chimeras and fantastic monsters" it "gives birth to."[17] Or, as Shakespeare puts it,

> Look what thy memory cannot contain
> Commit to these waste blanks, and thou shalt find
> Those children nurs'd, deliver'd from thy brain,
> To take a new acquaintance of thy mind.   (77)

THE RELATIVITY OF LANGUAGE

Some of all this sounds familiar enough when we think of Shakespeare's works before the turn of the century. In *Love's Labour's Lost* especially, we already find the critique of linguistic vices at various levels. There is Holofernes' periergeia and Armado's bomphiologia as well as Berowne's and others' tapinosis or deflation of such indecorum. Throughout his early work, Shakespeare also makes his characters voice their struggle with the limitations of language. As Lucrece exclaims,

> Out, idle words, servants to shallow fools!
> Unprofitable sounds, weak arbitrators!
> Busy yourselves in skill-contending schools,
> Debate where leisure serves with dull debaters;
> To trembling clients be you mediators!   (1016–20)

M. M. Mahood has noted "Shakespeare's own linguistic scepticism in the early History plays."[18] This she attributes to the decline of the old feudal order, to Protestant reliance on the word of the Scriptures as against the authority of the Church, and to other religious as well as sociopolitical changes. The *Henriad*, as another critic shows,[19] traces the corruption of public discourse, while *Richard II* documents the fall of both a king and kingly speech. Doll speaks of a similar decline in questioning Pistol's captainship: "A captain! God's light, these villains will make the word as odious as the word 'occupy'; which was an excellent good word before it was ill sorted."[20] Similar changes are implied in Falstaff's comments on the word "honor," with their near-Brechtian tone:

What is honour? A word. What is in that word? Honour. What is that honour? Air. A trim reckoning! Who hath it? He that died o' Wednesday. Doth he feel it? No. Doth he hear it? No, 'Tis insensible, then? Yea, to the dead. But will it not live with the living? No. Why? Detraction will not suffer it. Therefore I'll none of it. Honour is a mere scutcheon. And so ends my catechism.[21]

Of course there is little reason to identify Shakespeare with either Falstaff's attitude or King Richard III's "Conscience is but a word that cowards use" (V, 3). Yet here, as elsewhere, the playwright, to say the least, is as aware of the relativity of language as his characters. A man born blind who suddenly regains his eyesight may be able to distinguish colors but not to name them; that is to say, words are applied to, but not intrinsic to, the phenomena they stand for. This is the gist of a story derived from Hall's chronicle which Shakespeare dramatized in *2 Henry VI*.[22] Simpcox, who claims to have recovered his eyesight by miracle, is proven a fraud by Gloucester, who makes him identify the different colors of his cloak and gown: "If thou hadst been born blind, thou mightst as well have known all our names as thus to name the several colours we do wear. Sight may distinguish colours; but suddenly to nominate them all, it is impossible" (II, 1).

An even deeper skepticism about language is that of Feste, self-styled "corrupter of words." To him "words are grown so false" that he is "loath to prove reason with them." The word "element" is so "overworn" that he prefers to speak of being out of his "welkin" instead. Similarly, a sentence, to Feste, "is but a chev'ril glove to a good wit. How quickly the wrong side may be turn'd outward!" The vagueness of words vis-à-vis a specific meaning is brought out when Touchstone and others express the same thing in several synonyms:

Therefore, you clown, abandon – which is in the vulgar leave – the society – which in the boorish is company – of this female – which in the common is woman – which together is: abandon the society of this female; or, clown, thou perishest; or, to thy better understanding, diest; or, to wit, I kill thee, make thee away, translate thy life into death, thy liberty into bondage.[23]

Equally disconcerting is the William Burroughs-like cut-up method with which Launce and Speed dissect the word "understand." What was taken for granted suddenly strikes us as a strange and alien sound:

Launce: What a block art thou ... My staff understands me....
Speed: It stands under thee, indeed.
Launce: Why, stand-under and under-stand is all one.[24]

Antony's repeated use of the word "honourable" in his speech over Caesar's corpse is essentially an exercise of the same kind (cf. III, 2).

To a playwright thus aware of the arbitrariness of both names and naming, the concept of a thought-transcript beyond language was an equally familiar one. King John, for instance, invokes a language than can "make reply / Without a tongue, using conceit alone, / Without eyes, ears, and harmful sound of words" (III, 3). Will in the Sonnets, as we have seen, suggests as his creative ideal a language of "dumb thoughts, speaking in effect" (85). For the theatre, this means a language richly supplemented by gestures, stage choreography, mere sounds – in short the whole realm of visual and non-visual enactment.

Even Shakespeare's more systematic dismantling of essentialist language in *Troilus and Cressida* has precedents. People in *Romeo and Juliet*, as one critic shows,[25] live in a fake world of names, forms, and rituals. What is worse, they are unable to assess their true values. The protagonists themselves are obsessed with the relationship between essence and name, a concept which reoccurs some thirty times. The anti-Petrarchan Mercutio, of course, acts as a corrective, and in doing so sounds remarkably like some of Shakespeare's dark sonnets. But, with his death, his questioning of the others' false values and language dies too, and tragedy can take over.

Troilus and Cressida, then, only takes Shakespeare's earlier attitudes to language to their *ne plus ultra*. But as such the play, along with the Sonnets, marks an important watershed on the way to the later works. The fact that Edgar, at the conclusion of *King Lear*, for instance, echoes Troilus' "there is no more to say" (V, 10), is no mere coincidence. Edgar's mandate to "Speak what we feel, not what we ought to say" (V, 3) could serve as a motto to the entire tragedy. Truth and love in *King Lear*, writes Anne Barton, "are tongue-tied and silent. The glib and the verbally adroit, the Edmunds, Oswalds, and Regans, are deeply suspect. Only madness and folly are truly articulate, and their speech hovers continually on the edge of the meaningless, the place where words dissolve into pure noise or inarticulate cries."[26] *Coriolanus*, in a similar way, falls victim to a quasi-Marxist politicizing of language out to destroy his aristocratic valuations.

But more interesting in our context is *Antony and Cleopatra*, which, in Terence Hawkes's words, "assigns voice alone to Rome, body alone to Egypt."[27] In this and other ways, the play continues the argument of its titular predecessors, *Troilus and Cressida* and *Romeo and Juliet*. Juliet shows suspicion of Romeo's Petrarchan rhetoric (e.g., II, 6), while Cressida's body language serves as a contrast to Troilus' disembodied Platonic rhetoric. In Ulysses' words,

> There's language in her eye, her cheek, her lip,
> Nay, her foot speaks.   (IV, 5)

Cressida, though negatively, prefigures Cleopatra and Egypt. The Queen's "conversation" is largely a matter of provocation and allurement, of striking her servants, pulling a knife on one of them, or hauling him up and down. Both she and her lover know all too well that their love cannot be expressed in words:

> *Cleopatra:* If it be love indeed, tell me how much.
> *Antony:* There's beggary in the love that can be reckon'd.
> *Cleopatra:* I'll set a bourn how far to be belov'd.
> *Antony:* Then must thou needs find out new heaven, new
> earth.   (I, 1)

As against the "conference harsh" of Rome (I, 1), language in Egypt abounds with physical signs, gestures, and body contact. "The nobleness of life / Is to do thus" (I, 1) – not to talk about love but to make love. Antony's blush speaks volumes (I, 1). Rather than in vows of faithfulness, eternity is in the lovers' "lips and eyes" (I, 3). To Cleopatra, Antony's "mouth-made vows" count but little – they "break themselves in swearing" (I, 3). Even less credit is given to Octavia's "holy, cold, and still conversation" (II, 6) or to Roman language in general: "Sink Rome, and their tongues rot / That speak against us!" (III, 7).

It depends on the critic's temperament how Egypt's language is evaluated against Rome's. T. Hawkes, for one, decides the question in favor of Octavia's "holy, cold, and still conversation"; to him, "a life based on the body alone, on physical love-making, on doing 'thus' as its sole end, finds nothing at its conclusion but a grimmer version of the 'death' it has punningly sought many times."[28] But such an account ignores the play's obvious thrust towards the lovers' "new heaven, new earth" (I, 1) anticipated at the beginning and realized in the end. Antony, falsely assuming that Cleopatra is dead, is the first to imagine this paradise:

> Where souls do couch on flowers, we'll hand in hand,
> And with our sprightly port make the ghosts gaze.   (IV, 14)

A similar mythological world will reoccur in *Cymbeline*, where Jupiter tells the ghosts of Posthumus' relatives – "Poor shadows of Elysium" – to withdraw and "rest / Upon [their] never-withering banks of flow'rs" (V, 4). In *Antony and Cleopatra*, the lovers' paradisal beyond is again invoked shortly before the Queen's suicide. When Antony seems to beckon her, she responds with an unprecedented "Husband, I come!" (V, 2). But her "Immortal longings" to join the dead lover have already put her into a frame of mind in which this transition to the other realm will be an easy one. The Antony she dreamt about has mythic dimensions which seem to translate the language she and her lover stood for into equally universal terms:

> His legs bestrid the ocean; his rear'd arm
> Crested the world. His voice was propertied
> As all the tuned spheres, and that to friends;
> But when he meant to quail and shake the orb,
> He was as rattling thunder.   (V, 2)

Dolabella, who hesitates to grant that there was or ever will be such a man, is called a liar. Cleopatra gives him no chance. The language of myth, she seems to imply, is as incomprehensible to the rationalist as her body language. Whether or not we identify this attitude with the author's, it is unlikely that Shakespeare wants us to see either as an impasse like Troilus's.

CONTEMPORARY ANALOGUES

But perhaps our sense of Shakespeare's attitude towards language springs from Wittgensteinian perspectives simply nonexistent during the playwright's period. This, in fact, has been argued in two recent articles by Margreta de Grazia. To her, the linguistic skepticism other critics have attributed to Shakespeare did not appear until Bacon and Locke questioned the general essentialist assumption that words "*stand also for the reality of things.*" Neither Shakespeare nor his audience, she claims, would have understood this post-Baconian, let alone twentieth-century, antiessentialism. "Sixteenth-century discussions of language provide no evidence of later linguistic skepticism . . . Shakespeare wrote for a period informed by a traditional Christian view of language."[29]

Hence, linguistic failure in Shakespeare is due not to language as such, but to the sinfulness of the speaker who reenacts language's fall from prelapsarian essentialism into Babel-like confusion. Language does not embroil Lear and Coriolanus, but Coriolanus and Lear, through their willfullness, corrupt speech. De Grazia's approach provides some brilliant insights into Shakespeare's Sonnets. Will's desire, for instance, "so thoroughly infiltrates language that acts of speech conflate with acts of love." It is equally perceptive to argue that Will parodies Christian love in his rebaptism, or that he inverts "God's incarnation by making flesh the word." But otherwise de Grazia's perspective proves to be rather narrow especially in the historical sense. Like everything else in Will's language, his self-contradictions are attributed to his sinfulness or lust:

> Language, once appropriated by desire, loses its proper association with reason ... With reason or *logos* gone or on the wane, Will's language cannot be logical. Contradictions crop up within single sonnets. In 139, for example, he begins with the plea, "O Call not me to iustifie the wrong" and continues with, "Let me excuse thee." From sonnet to sonnet, too, he contradicts himself. He announces, "My Mistres eyes are nothing like the Sunne" in 130 but compares them to it in 132. He bids his mistress, "Tell me thou lou'st else-where" in 139 and in the next sonnet forbids her to mention her infidelities. The law of noncontradiction, the basis of Aristotelean logic, clearly is not operating in Will's dialectic.[30]

Judged by their own premises, the conclusions drawn here appear inevitable enough. Will's self-contradictory use of language must indeed be deemed sinful, if measured against a prelapsarian essentialism. It will also be found wanting if judged by the standards of Aristotelian logic. But all this merely presupposes that these were Shakespeare's own standards of judgment as well as the only ones current during his lifetime. A closer look at three thinkers writing during the playwright's lifetime is enough to show the narrowness of such an assumption.

If found wanting in Aristotelian logic, Shakespeare's rhetorical strategies in the Sonnets, for instance, might well have drawn on different forms of "logic" instead. In fact, very few Elizabethan poets, and only the minor ones, seem to have followed the traditional paths in that way. J. Webster's recent "Inquiry into Tudor Conceptions of Poetic Sequence" distinguishes two opposing schools along these lines. One, exemplified by, for instance, Googe's poem "Of Money," affects a plain-spoken directness and logicality of Aristotelian persuasion. The other, represented by Sidney, Spenser, and others, follows a more tortuous path of indirection possibly prompted by the "Prudential Method" proposed by an influential anti-Aristotelian. According to Petrus Ramus, an orator, particularly when faced with a sophisticated audience, should keep his listeners continually off balance in order to maintain their attentiveness. He should "change things, mix things up, make light, feign the contrary, start over again ... rush past things, be irritating, debate, proceed by arrogance." The poet, Ramus adds, "while he excells in all parts of logic, is especially admirable in this one."[31]

But with Shakespeare's Sonnets we obviously move into yet another dimension.[32] Ramus' "Prudential Method" is, in the final analysis, little else than a persuasive ambush to entrap the listener into accepting what, from the orator's point of view, is a preconceived set of communicable facts or "truths." According to Ramus' disciple Abraham Fraunce, it is a "methode of wit and disception"[33] rather than of experimental enquiry. No wonder that Francis Bacon, when reviewing the traditional methods of rhetoric around 1605, found little reason to treat Ramus' "Prudential Method" as an exception.

For all too long, Bacon argues, orators of the mainstream tradition have tried to convey knowledge "in such a way as may be best believed and not as may be best examined." Bacon proposes to reverse this emphasis. The writer should make the reader share in his own search for the truth with all its contradictions and doubts, "and so transplant it into another as it grew in his own mind."[34] In terms of Bacon's own mental habits, that means a rigorous examination of both sides of a question, a thinking in antitheta, first evident in *Colours of Good and Evil*. Bacon was never a Sophist in the negative sense of the word, but his method here and elsewhere closely resembles the *in utramque partem* rhetoric of a Protagoras or Gorgias.

A reasoning in antitheta is central to the aphoristic method, which presents the reader with a "knowledge broken" and invites him "to enquire further." The aim is to launch the reader onto an open-ended and "expectant enquiry" rather than to present him with a preconceived truth. Example VI from *Colours of Good and Evil* shows the degree to which this process amounts to a dismantling of essentialist concepts. Bacon's starting-point is a predicative statement – "That which it is good to be rid of is evil; that which it is evil to be rid of is good" – which in the usual *in utramque partem* method is reduced to a mere relativist assertion:

The reprehension of this colour is, that the good or evil which is removed, may be esteemed good or evil comparatively, and not positively or simply. So that if the privation be good, it follows not the former condition was evil, but less good: for the flower or blossom is a positive good, although the remove of it to give place to the fruit be a comparative good.[35]

Would Shakespeare have been unable to conceive of similar rhetorical strategies? The playwright, we are told, did not write within or for the context of the post-Baconian era. But when did this era begin? Bacon's *Colours of Good and Evil* was published in 1597 and his *Advancement of Learning* in 1605, both during the height of Shakespeare's career. What even if Shakespeare was unaware of these works? Are we therefore supposed to think of Bacon as odd man out ahead of his time, and to group Shakespeare with all his "real" (read "minor") contemporaries instead? Where would we search for Beckett's or Ionesco's philosophical kindred? In Wittgenstein's *Philosophical Investigations* or in the more traditional writings of some obscure linguist? The point, I think, needs little further elaboration.

What is more, Shakespeare had no need of Bacon if indeed he had to borrow others' ideas in conceiving the rhetorical strategies manifest in *Troilus and Cressida* and the Sonnets. As Joel B. Altman has shown, Bacon's way of "representing a knowledge broken" in order to make man "enquire further" is only the culmination of an unbroken tradition reaching from Gorgias and Protagoras right through to More, Sidney, Heywood, Rastell, Lyly, and others. To argue *in utramque partem* was part of Tudor rhetorical training and left its imprint on many literary works of the period before Shakespeare.[36]

The same tendencies were reinforced by Montaigne, who, besides Shakespeare himself, represents the greatest major oversight in de Grazia's distinction between a pre- and a post-Baconian attitude towards language.[37] Neither Bacon's criticism of traditional rhetoric nor his sense of the "false appearances imposed upon us by words"[38] was unknown to the Frenchman. Especially if looked at in a twentieth-century perspective, Montaigne's arguments, in fact, are even more radical and diverse. He not only wants his readers to examine what he says and "to enquire further," but actively seeks "to be contradicted, so as to create doubt and suspension of judgement."[39] Even more incisive, though eclectic, is Montaigne's critique of essentialist language. Bacon's attack on the traditional concepts of language focuses on two major categories: "names of things which do not exist" (like "beauty" and "truth") and "names of things which exist, but yet confused and ill-defined, and hastily and irregularly derived from realities." Moreover, he questions Aristotle's conviction that "words are the signs of cogitations," suggesting that there are many other forms of communication – as manifest, for example, in the conversation of deaf mutes.[40]

Montaigne takes the same notion to the point of challenging the time-honored concept of man as "zoon logon echon." "That we can converse amongst ourselves, and express our thoughts in speech," was to Cicero the main cause of our superiority to animals.[41] Similarly, language, to Ben Jonson, was "the only benefit man hath to expresse his excellencie of mind above other creatures."[42] To Montaigne, this sense of our superiority is simply based on ignorance. In his view, there is full and complete communication of voice and gesture between animals of both identical and diverse species. Montaigne is equally aware of the many non-verbal means of communication, an area which has recently attracted attention in the study of Shakespeare.[43]

Why not; just as well as our mutes dispute, argue, and tell stories by signs? ... What of the hands? We beg, we promise, call, dismiss, threaten, pray, entreat, deny, refuse, question, admire, count, confess, repent, fear, blush, doubt, instruct, command, incite, encourage, swear, testify, accuse, condemn, absolve, insult, despise, defy, vex, flatter, applaud, bless, humiliate, mock, reconcile, commend, exalt, entertain, rejoice, complain, grieve, mope, despair, wonder, exclaim, are silent, and what not, with a variation and multiplication that vie with the tongue. With the head: we invite, send away, avow, disavow, give the lie, welcome, honor, venerate, disdain, demand, show out, cheer, lament, caress, scold, submit, brave, exhort, menace, assure, inquire. What of the eyebrows? What of the shoulders?[44]

No wonder that Montaigne propounds as his ideal the kind of body language Shakespeare gives to Cleopatra. At least meta-phorically speaking, the essayist when writing had a highly physical attitude to his particular subject-matter. Sometimes he proposes "only to lick it, sometimes to brush the surface, some-times to pinch it to the bone." At the same time he draws attention to the genuinely gestural manner of his prose style: "What I cannot express," he writes, "I point to with my finger." Proportionate to Montaigne's preference for such body language is his contempt for essentialist oratory, which his essays seem to repudiate on almost every page. To him, there is hardly an issue that could not be smothered under a maze of "answers, rejoin-ders, replications, triplications, quadruplications." "Our speech," to Montaigne, "has its weaknesses and its defects, like all the rest. Most of the occasions for the troubles of the world are grammatical."[45]

One major defect, as Montaigne realized, in anticipation of F. H. Bradley and Whitehead, is our predominantly predicative and affirmative sentence structure. What would be needed, then, is an entirely new language. The same applies to many of our words such as "truth" and "beauty," "names of things," as Bacon was to put it, "which do not exist."[46] Montaigne's list of some thirty different meanings of the word "soul" speaks for itself.[47] Raymond Sebond could still say "C'est le nom qui represente et signifie *toute* sa chose."[48] But in Montaigne's reductionist adapt-ation of this phrase from the *Theologia Naturalis* words have become mere signifiers: "le nom, c'est une voix qui remerque et signifie la chose:"[49]

There is the name and the thing. The name is a sound which designates and signifies the thing; the name is not a part of the thing or of the substance, it is an extraneous piece attached to the thing, and outside of it.[50]

But how does all this affect the language of the poet and of the writer? Here again, Montaigne provides us with insights that might have a bearing on Shakespeare. As one would expect from his views on language in general, the essayist was averse to a self-reflective use of that medium which imposes itself on what it expresses. Not that the devices of rhetoric, for instance, should be avoided as such; but their use had to be strictly functional in helping communicate a given content. What Montaigne objected to were people who "call judgment language and fine words full conceptions." "When I see these brave forms of expression," he writes, "so alive, so profound, I do not say 'This is well said,' I say 'This is well thought.'"[51] Shakespeare, in Sonnet 85, voices his attitudes towards poetic language in almost identical terms:

> My tongue-tied Muse in manners holds her still,
> While comments on your praise, richly compil'd,
> Reserve their character with golden quill
> And precious phrase by all the Muses fil'd.
> I think good thoughts, whilst other write good words,
> And, like unlettered clerk, still cry 'Amen'
> To every hymn that able spirit affords
> In polish'd form of well-refined pen.
> Hearing you prais'd, I say ''Tis so, 'tis true,'
> And to the most of praise add something more;
> But that is in my thought, whose love to you,
> Though words come hindmost, holds his rank before.
> > Then others for the breath of words respect,
> > Me for my dumb thoughts, speaking in effect.

VI · The language of poetry

L IKE HIS ATTITUDE towards language in general, so Shakespeare's sense of the appropriate language of poetry forms
a major concern of the Sonnets. And here, too, a play will
complement the information gathered from the poems. *Troilus
and Cressida* can be read as a companion piece to the Sonnets, for
dramatizing the collapse of essentialist discourse. Similarly,
Love's Labour's Lost parallels what the poems have to say about a
poetic use of language which, instead of "writ[ing] good words,"
stresses an immediacy of content in which the "words come
hindmost" (85). In turn, both the Sonnets and the comedy can be
seen as documenting the basic attitude behind this and most·
other of the more philosophical aspects of Shakespeare's poetics:
that is to say, the antiessentialism which the poet shared with
Montaigne and Bacon. In *Love's Labour's Lost*, this attitude
emerges against the background of Neoplatonic theorizing as
found in, say, Castiglione's *Book of the Courtier*.

In fact, one incident in the treatise shows remarkable resemblance to a scene in the play. Pietro Bembo has given an account,
derived from Ficino's commentary on the *Symposium*,[1] of love's
ascent from corporeal beauty via universal beauty towards the
vision of divine beauty. Equal to his task, he has talked himself
into what Plato describes as the frenzy of the poet who is "never
able to compose until he has become inspired, and is beside
himself:"[2]

Having spoken thus far with such vehemence that he seemed almost
transported and beside himself, Bembo remained silent and still,
keeping his eyes turned toward heaven, as if in a daze; when signora
Emilia, who with the others had been listening to his discourse most
attentively, plucked him by the hem of his robe and, shaking him a little,
said: "Take care, messer Pietro, that with these thoughts your soul, too,
does not forsake your body."[3]

A similar scene in *Love's Labour's Lost*[4] perhaps echoes this incident directly: "What zeal, what fury hath inspir'd thee now?" exclaims the King after Berowne has burst forth in praise of his beloved Rosaline's heavenly beauty (IV, 3). Berowne, too, orates in praise of love, and both he and Bembo, unlike the homosexually oriented Plato, take female beauty as their starting-point. When the fair aspects of some lady meets the lover's eye, explains Bembo,

his soul begins to take pleasure in contemplating her and to feel an influence within that stirs and warms it little by little; and when those lively spirits which shine forth from her eyes continue to add fresh fuel to the fire – then, at the start, he ought to administer a quick remedy and arouse his reason, and therewith arm the fortress of his heart, and so shut out sense and appetite.[5]

If Shakespeare remembered Bembo's speech when writing Berowne's he must have been aware of how much his lines both echoed and contradicted Castiglione's.[6] Like Bembo, Berowne derives his doctrine from "women's eyes" which will arouse "the nimble spirits in the arteries" (IV, 3) quelled by pedestrian studies. But, unlike Bembo, Berowne does not condemn the arousal of sense and appetite as something to be shunned by reason. To him it is the very mainspring of the activities associated with the lover's sublimest emotions. Speaking in terms of the Platonic ladder, Shakespeare's protagonist, while clearly following Bembo's "divine path of love,"[7] never seems to get beyond the lowest rung. In a way, he even steps down again from that elevation in order to plant his feet all the more firmly on the earthly ground of sensory experience.[8]

Castiglione allows only two of the five senses, sight and hearing, to guide the quester in the early phases of his ascent.[9] And in the end even these "reason's ministers" have to be left behind. The courtier, instead of turning "outside himself in thought," advises Bembo, should "contemplate that beauty which is seen by the eyes of the mind, which begin to be sharp and clear-sighted when those of the body lose the flower of their delight."[10] Shakespeare's emphasis is the entirely opposite one. While to Bembo, love, in its supremest form, is finally realized in the mind alone; to Berowne it only intensifies the senses:

> But love, first learned in a lady's eyes,
> Lives not alone immured in the brain,
> But with the motion of all elements
> Courses as swift as thought in every power,
> And gives to every power a double power,
> Above their functions and their offices.   (IV, 3)

Far from shunning the senses, love acts as their catalyst, and in doing so by no means limits itself to "reason's ministers." Berowne goes out of his way to give examples of such heightened sensory perception, regarding sight and hearing as well as feeling and taste:[11]

> It adds a precious seeing to the eye:
> A lover's eyes will gaze an eagle blind.
> A lover's ear will hear the lowest sound,
> When the suspicious head of theft is stopp'd.
> Love's feeling is more soft and sensible
> Than are the tender horns of cockled snails;
> Love's tongue proves dainty Bacchus gross in taste.   (IV, 3)

Needless to say, the language here perfectly expresses such hypersensitivity above the ordinary functions and offices of the senses. Feeling as delicate as "the tender horns of cockled snails"; hearing which exceeds that of the thief in the act of burglary! What could be further removed from Castiglione's world of disembodied Platonic abstractions? This is what the *Book of the Courtier* tells us about love:

just as from the particular beauty of one body it guides the soul to the universal beauty of all beauties, so in the highest stage of perfection beauty guides it from the particular intellect to the universal intellect.[12]

Not that Berowne's opposite drive away from the universal towards the particular lacks its own kind of transcendence. Shakespeare's protagonist is no mere naturalist of sensory perception. But whatever there is beyond the senses, or "Above their functions and their offices," as Berowne puts it, can only be realized through their quasi-supernatural intensification.[13] From an epistemological point of view, then, Berowne's is a radical empiricism open to another equally empirical, but at the same time, unreal world. Other plays will make clear that this world is one not of metaphysical abstractions, but of imagination, dream and myth.

"APOLLO'S LUTE, STRUNG WITH HIS HAIR"

Although it calls to mind other Renaissance figures, Berowne's empiricism finds few analogues among Shakespeare's contemporaries. Among the authors of Neoplatonic love treatises stemming from Ficino, for instance, Giordano Bruno is probably the only major figure to anticipate Berowne along these lines. The symbol for the philosopher's earth-rooted spirituality – his heroic frenzies which for all their heavenward drive do not deny the body – is the "Annosa quercia" or ancient oak tree in his sonnet of the same title:

Ancient oak, which spreads its branches to the air, and fixes its roots in the earth; neither the trembling earth, nor the powerful spirits which the sky lets loose from the bitter north wind . . . can ever uproot you from the place where you stand firm . . . You demonstrate the true portrait of my faith, which no external accident has ever shaken . . . Upon one single object I have fixed my spirit, my sense and my intellect.[14]

But even a Bruno enthusiast like Frances Yates, who sees Berowne as a partial portrait of the philosopher, stresses the obvious differences between the two. Berowne's Neoplatonic language, in her view, "describes what is, quite frankly, a physical exhilaration. He is not torn between a theoretical belief in the spirituality of matter and a practical difficulty in relating material to spiritual experience, as Bruno was."[15]

Bruno's *Eroici furori* was dedicated to Sir Philip Sidney, and at least one critic has suggested that Sidney's writings, along with Wyatt's, offer another precedent to Berowne's anti-Platonic and anti-Petrarchan love philosophy.[16] Wyatt's Petrarch translations, for instance, frequently de-emphasize the Italian poet's stress on the divine by replacing, for instance, the word "heaven" by "sky."[17] His actual poetry is in much the same key, with an anti-female and frankly sensualist bias not found in the sonnets to Laura. Wyatt's ironic questioning of love's spirituality and his tongue-in-cheek treatment of Petrarchan commonplaces found a successor in Sidney's Astrophil,[18] who, ransacking other sonneteers for their inventions, concludes that it is better to look into one's heart and write.[19]

Sidney's *Apologie for Poetrie* professes a similarly anti-rhetorical confessionalism. In its protests against "a Curtizan-like painted affectation" of poetic diction, it anticipates Berowne's invective against "Taffeta phrases, silken terms precise" (V, 2). But Sidney nowhere advocates an empiricism which, like Berowne's, reaches out beyond the natural boundaries of the senses. For all his emphasis on a historical authenticity of poetry, he retains Aristotle's distinction between the poet and the historiographer as one of his most crucial and often-repeated concepts. Poetry, he paraphrases, "is *Philosophoteron* and *Spoudaioteron*, that is to say, it is more Philosophicall and more studiously serious then history . . . Poesie dealeth with *Katholou*, that is to say, with the vniuersall consideration; and the history with *Kathekaston*, the perticuler."[20]

The same applies to Sidney's claim that the poet, by virtue of his invention, "dooth growe in effect another nature, in making things either better then Nature bringeth forth, or, quite a newe, formes such as neuer were in Nature, as the *Heroes, Demigods, Cyclops, Chimeras, Furies*, and such like."[21] Whatever it may amount to, such "invention" has little in common with the creative faculty evoked by Berowne.[22] For one thing, Sidney talks about a poetry inspired not by the senses, but by wit and imaginative ingenuity.[23] For another, his emphasis on the quasi-surrealist autonomy of invention has to be taken with reservations that also apply to Plato's ironical comments on the poet's mad frenzies.

While paying lip-service to this *furor poeticus*, Sidney is as distrustful of an unbridled imagination as he might have been of an empiricism which, like Berowne's, pushes beyond the ordinary capacity of the senses without ever leaving them behind. "For I will not denie," he concedes, "but that mans wit may make Poesie (which should be *Eikastike*, which some learned haue defined, figuring foorth good things) to be *Phantastike*: which doth, contrariwise, infect the fancie with vnworthy objects." Here, as in most other cases, Sidney links both invention and imagination to Aristotle's claim that the poet, unlike the historian, should show things not as they are, but as they ought to be.[24]

Perhaps the closest antecedent to Berowne's empiricism again comes from Montaigne: "I judge myself only by actual sensation, not by reasoning," the philosopher writes. "I, who operate only close to the ground, hate that inhuman wisdom that would make us disdainful enemies of the cultivation of the body."[25] Reading Montaigne around 1603[26] must have reminded Shakespeare of similar notions he had earlier voiced in *Love's Labour's Lost*. Like Berowne, Montaigne, even in his most ecstatic moments, likes to fly close to the ground. Ficino and Leon Hebreo may talk about love, but the philosopher finds it hard to understand what they are actually saying. "Let us leave Bembo and Equicola alone," he pleads, adding that if he were concerned with their issues, he would try to "naturalize art as much as they artify nature."[27]

Yet even Montaigne's suggestions along these lines take a different slant from Berowne's. Much as he likes to record his sensations and reveries, he is not inclined toward cultivating the love-inspired hypersensitivity advocated by Berowne. Love and sexuality in general have no great spiritual appeal to Montaigne, while the senses, despite his professed empiricism, are to him worthy of being scrutinized for their veracity rather than indulged in for supernatural effects. "As for the error and uncertainty of the operation of the senses," he writes, "each man can furnish himself with as many examples as he pleases, so ordinary are the mistakes and deceptions that they offer us." Nonetheless he wonders about certain "occult" properties of things which are hidden from us merely because we lack the sensory faculties that would enable us to perceive them.[28] Montaigne, in other words, shares some of Berowne's curiosity about the "occult" world of perception beyond our ordinary sensory capacity, but feels less sympathy with his means of realizing this goal.

Berowne's empiricism of heightened sensory perception induced by love, then, seems to be characteristically Shakespearean. Equally original is the theory of artistic creativity associated with these epistemological concerns. "Other slow arts," when compared with the one advocated by the protagonist, "entirely keep the brain" (IV, 3). True poetry, for instance, functions by analogy with the love which inspires it. Love for Bembo, we remember, found its final realization in the mind, after the senses had been extinguished. Not so for Berowne, to whom love "Lives not alone immured in the brain, / But with the motion of all elements" (IV, 3). Poetry's main inspiration, then, is the opposite of Castiglione's chaperone into higher and higher realms of Platonic abstraction – "from the particular intellect to the universal intellect."[29] On the contrary, it "Courses as swift as thought in every power," and, while doubling the capacity of the senses, is the vital force in all we perceive, living "with the motion of all elements" (IV, 3).[30]

Love here is almost synonymous with nature, but hardly in the sense which most Renaissance aestheticians attributed to the word in determining its relationship to art. For all its manifold shades of meaning, as traced by A. O. Lovejoy, H. S. Wilson and others,[31] "nature" usually denoted "a cosmically uniform and regular design from which literature derives its own fixed laws concerning aims, methods, and taste."[32] Everything that Berowne implies about the term seems to contravene such assumptions. Speaking of love in almost synonymous terms with nature, he emphasizes not an order of transcendent abstractions, but a pansexuality immanent in the pulsating flux of phenomena. Rather than talk about the fixed laws which art derives from an equally static cosmos, Berowne proposes an art which reenacts this universal Eros. The image of a lute strung with Apollo's own hair neatly epitomizes this notion of a poetry which, through Nature's means, speaks in Nature's own voice. Love, Berowne explains, is

> as sweet and musical
> As bright Apollo's lute, strung with his hair.
> And when Love speaks, the voice of all the gods
> Make heaven drowsy with the harmony.   (IV, 3)

In Furness's paraphrase, "When love speaks, the responsive harmony of the voice of all the gods makes heaven drowsy."[33] In other words, love unites in itself all other embodiments of the divine and speaks through them just as it speaks through poets. The parallel is once more emphasized in the following lines about the poet who can only write when inspired by love. The Horatian notion of the poet's (alias Orpheus') supernatural powers was a familiar one in Elizabethan England.[34] But Shakespeare, here as elsewhere, insists upon the magically entrancing rather than the verbally persuasive impact of poetry emphasized by Horace. Poetry's influence on the listener is associated with the enchantment of music which ravishes "like enchanting harmony" (I, 1).

> Never durst poet touch a pen to write
> Until his ink were temp'red with Love's sighs;
> O, then his lines would ravish savage ears,
> And plant in tyrants mild humility.   (IV, 3)

Again and again in his work, Shakespeare insists on the powers of poetry evoked here. Had the man who mutilated Lavinia listened to the "heavenly harmony" of her voice, "He would have dropp'd his knife, and fell asleep, / As Cerberus at the Thracian poet's feet," exclaims Marcus in *Titus Andronicus* (II, 4). Music's similar psychological impact is described by Lorenzo in *The Merchant of Venice*.

> Therefore the poet
> Did feign that Orpheus drew trees, stones, and floods;
> Since nought so stockish, hard, and full of rage,
> But music for the time doth change his nature.   (V, 1)

Here, as in Berowne's speech, poetry's impact on man extends to nature in general. *Mutatis mutandis*, poetry realizes itself through the purely natural means of poetry and music. Apollo's lute in *Love's Labour's Lost* is strung with the singer's own hair;[35] Orpheus' in *The Two Gentlemen of Verona* is "strung with poets' sinews" (III, 2). The relationship is a mutual one. Just as nature imparts its own dynamics to poetry, so poetry, as nature's reenactment, can in turn influence nature. The general idea again stems from Horace's *De Arte Poetica*.[36] But Shakespeare clearly puts more emphasis on the magical powers of poetry. Lorenzo goes to great lengths in describing how a wild herd of young colts, when suddenly hearing the sound of a trumpet or a musical air, stop their bellowing, neighing and jumping, "Their savage eyes turn'd to a modest gaze / By the sweet power of music." Proteus, in invoking Orpheus, borrows Horace's notion that the god's songs could tame tigers, just as Amphion's were able to move stones. But Orpheus' lute strung with poets' sinews, as well as another equally striking image documenting poetry's powers to "ravish savage ears," seems to be Shakespeare's additions.

> For Orpheus' lute was strung with poets' sinews,
> Whose golden touch could soften steel and stones,
> Make tigers tame, and huge leviathans
> Forsake unsounded deeps to dance on sands.[37]

SHAKESPEARE'S "INVERTED PLATONISM"

Shakespeare's concern with his art in *Love's Labour's Lost* finds a striking parallel in the Sonnets. To write and criticize sonnets, we remember, is a favorite pastime in *Love's Labour's Lost*. Berowne's own specimen here comes under special scrutiny. Holofernes, as well Rosaline, who attacks it for having a regular prosody with little else to commend itself – "neither savouring of poetry, wit, nor invention" (IV, 2) – is not far off the mark. The poem, while anticipating some of Berowne's subsequent theories of love, certainly lacks the "fiery numbers" advocated there (IV, 3). Such criticism, whether regarding the "new-found methods" of Shakespeare's rivals (76), or concerning his own allegedly more conservative strategies, is equally central to the Sonnets.

But the shared poetological concerns of play and poems go deeper than that. Berowne's theoretical explorations of poetic creativity, as we saw, start off from a clearly Platonic premise, but anticlimactically invert the poet's ascent towards ideational absolutes in favor of a strictly sensory empiricism. A similar tendency is found in what J. B. Leishman calls the "inverted Platonism"[38] of some of the Sonnets. These describe, say, absolute Beauty as actually embodied in the lover rather than in an abstract concept transcending him. In fact, Shakespeare had already explored such inversion in *Venus and Adonis*. In Venus' description, Adonis was made directly from the heavenly molds which Nature stole from the gods.

> Now of this dark night I perceive the reason:
> Cynthia for shame obscures her silver shine,
> Till forging Nature be condemn'd of treason
> For stealing moulds from heaven that were divine,

> Wherein she fram'd thee in high heaven's despite,
> To shame the sun by day and her by night.   (727–32)

At least in Sonnet 53, in which Shakespeare seems to hark back to this description, the same "inverted Platonism" assumes what appear to be deliberately parodistic proportions. Adonis, whom Venus describes as Platonic beauty incarnate, is simply a shadow of such perfection when compared with the lover. The lines here may well allude to Plato's critique of artistic mimesis in the *Republic*:[39] "Describe Adonis, and the counterfeit / is poorly imitated after you." The lover is the "substance" from which the shadows of millions of other phenomena derive their existence. Even spring and autumn are merely manifestations of his essentialist beauty and bounty.

> What is your substance, whereof are you made,
> That millions of strange shadows on you tend?
> Since every one hath, every one, one shade,
> And you, but one, can every shadow lend.
> Describe Adonis, and the counterfeit
> Is poorly imitated after you;
> On Helen's cheek all art of beauty set,
> And you in Grecian tires are painted new.
> Speak of the spring and foison of the year:
> The one doth shadow of your beauty show,
> The other as your bounty doth appear,
> And you in every blessed shape we know.
> > In all external grace you have some part,
> > But you like none, none you, for constant heart.

But parody turns into bitter sarcasm where the poet undercuts such praise of the friend's beauty by drawing attention to his inner corruption:

> But those same tongues that give thee so thine own
> In other accents do this praise confound
> By seeing farther than the eye hath shown.
> They look into the beauty of thy mind,
> And that, in guess, they measure by thy deeds;
> Then, churls, their thoughts, although their eyes were kind,
> To thy fair flower add the rank smell of weeds.   (69)

The "inverted Platonism" or basic antiessentialism, evident in both *Love's Labour's Lost* and the Sonnets,[40] finds its most immediate expression in a poetic language striving towards an utter immediacy of content or, to quote Shakespeare, towards "dumb thoughts, speaking in effect."[41] In this, the poet, like Montaigne before him, seems to oppose not poetic rhetoric as such, but its gratuitous and self-reflective use. Characteristically, Berowne's famous harangue against "Taffeta phrases, silken terms precise, / Three-pil'd hyperboles, spruce affectation" assumes the form of a regular sonnet (V, 2, 402–15). Like some of the Sonnets claiming to contain only "true plain words" by a "true-telling friend" (82), Berowne's words are prima facie reduced to absurdity by the elaborate metaphorical and rhetorical context in which they appear. We sympathize with Rosaline's retort "Sans 'sans,' I pray you" or with a recent critic wondering "what else is 'three-pil'd hyperbole' if not a three-piled hyperbole?"[42] But Berowne's passionate persuasiveness absorbs such strictures. He is glad to admit to a surviving "trick / Of the old rage," and we know he will never lose it. Nor do we think that he ought to.[43] However, the process that will teach him to speak in effect rather than in "painted rhetoric" (IV, 3) is far from over.

"DUMB THOUGHTS, SPEAKING IN EFFECT"

The Sonnets dramatize a similar conflict by opposing the poet's linguistic ideals to those of his rivals. Their poetry amounts to a "gross painting" where no such cosmetics are needed. While "blessing every book" they imitate, they avail themselves of the "strained touches rhetoric can lend" (82). They constantly try to improve on things but, in fact, only make worse "what nature made so clear" (84). "[R]ichly compil'd" from diverse literary sources, their "precious phrase[s] by all the Muses fil'd" reflect upon themselves or "Reserve their character" rather than actualizing their subject-matter. They "write good words" instead of "think[ing] good thoughts" and making the "words come hindmost." Theirs is the mere "breath of words," which, remote from whatever prompted them, are elaborated into the "polish'd form of well-refined pen" (85).

But Will is far from denying the power of the "new-found methods" and "compounds strange" developed by his rival. So forceful is this new style of "variation or quick change" (76), that the speaker's own "gracious numbers" threaten to decay (79), especially at a time when his own style has already found a host of imitators (78). Overawed by "the proud full sail" of his competitor's "great verse" (86), his own muse has fallen sick (79) and became tongue-tied (85). Such words, perhaps directed towards John Donne,[44] are hardly spoken in condemnation or envy. The speaker is glad to acknowledge his rival as a "better spirit" (80) who by "spirits" was "taught to write / Above a mortal pitch" (86). But, however powerful in their impact, the rival's new methods could never become his own.

> Why write I still all one, ever the same,
> And keep invention in a noted weed,
> That every word doth almost tell my name,
> Showing their birth, and where they did proceed? (76)

The question contains its own answer. The speaker's poetic ideal of un-self-conscious poetic expression is strictly incompatible with the rival's deliberate ingenuity. Hence there is admiration for the "new-found methods," but also defiance. The silence and penury of poetic utterance Shakespeare makes so much of in this situation are no mere gesture of defeat. Not unlike more recent proclamations of, say, a poor theatre or a poetics of silence, they merely signal the retreat into a more basic and impregnable position.

In this, Will is only made more aware of what is his fundamental attitude throughout. Even before talking about an actual rival, he distinguishes his "barren rhyme" (16) from that of a poet who, "Stirr'd by a painted beauty to his verse," exhausts his self-conscious efforts in "Making a couplement of proud compare" with whatever his otherwise uninspired muse can find under the sky. "O, let me, true in love, but truly write" (21), he exclaims, and elsewhere anticipates the time when his "poor rude lines" will be "outstripp'd by every pen." Even then, however, he rests assured that while the "better" poets' lines will be read for their style, his will be valued for the emotions which prompted them (32). In other words, his invention, a term then widely used where we would now say imagination, is a direct enactment of his subject-matter:

> How can my Muse want subject to invent,
> While thou dost breathe that pour'st into my verse
> Thine own sweet argument.   (38)

When the imagined rivalry of the earlier poems becomes a real one after Sonnet 76, this basic understanding of his art merely sharpens in focus. Talking about his competitors' new-found methods and strange compounds, the speaker still insists, though with increased intensity, on using his imagination in direct emotional response to the subject – "keep[ing] invention in a noted weed, / That every word doth almost tell my name, / Showing their birth, and where they did proceed" (76). Commenting on his imitators, he draws a similar distinction. Their mere "style," being borrowed from his, is no more than an artificial adjunct to an alien subject-matter. ("In others' works thou dost but mend the style.") This contrasts with his own "art," which does no more than enact what prompts it, a quasi-identification underscored by the wordplay of "But thou art all my art" (78).[45]

Thus threatened from two sides, Will temporarily retreats into a seeming paradox, which is to write poems about a new poetics of silence.[46] Again, the basic notion is not a new or original one. Throughout the sequence, the speaker knew that in order to achieve the experiential authenticity he strove for, his verse had to be somehow barren and crude;[47] but even then it would never be more than an approximation to what he wanted to express. The glaring divisiveness between emotion and expression so openly flaunted by the new-found methods of his competitor only made him more aware of the fact that his own poetic ideal was *de facto* unrealizable. There is no poetry that can ever be a totally unmediated enactment of thought. In an ultimate sense, then, poetry, or the kind advocated in the Sonnets, is condemned to silence. An earlier poem had compared this insufficiency to that of "a tomb / Which hides your life and shows not half your parts" (17). Now the speaker leaves this sepulchral function to his competitors while temporarily withdrawing into his ironically programmatic declarations of silence instead:

> And therefore have I slept in your report,
> That you your self, being extant, well might show
> How far a modern quill doth come too short,

Speaking of worth, what worth in you doth grow.
This silence for my sin you did impute,
Which shall be most my glory, being dumb;
For I impair not beauty, being mute,
When others would give life, and bring a tomb. (83)

For all that, Will, despite some histrionic disclaimers to the contrary, remains fully confident of his artistic achievement. In fact, his new poetics of silence has only increased this confidence. Conceding that his Muse has become tongue-tied, he brags about thinking "good thoughts, whilst other write good words:"

Then others for the breath of words respect,
Me for my dumb thoughts, speaking in effect. (85)

Will acknowledges "the proud full sail" of his rival's "great verse" and grants him victory in the public eye; but he finds the competitor's poetry lacking precisely in the quality which is distinctly his own, its essential silence:

No, neither he, nor his compeers by night
Giving him aid, my verse astonished.
He nor that affable familiar ghost
Which nightly gulls him with intelligence,
As victors, of my silence cannot boast. (86)

Here, as where they explore this poetics into the area of linguistic breakdown –

My thoughts and my discourse as mad men's are,
At random from the truth vainly express'd – (147)

the Sonnets go beyond the position reached in *Love's Labour's Lost*. Berowne, in lambasting "spruce affectation" and praising a language of "Honest plain words" (V, 2), may echo the sonneteer where he advocates "true plain words by [a] true-telling friend" (82). But the silence of poetic discourse proclaimed in the poems remains beyond his reach – or at least it does so in the play itself. The end of *Love's Labour's Lost* merely points in the same direction. Throughout the play the ladies have been the most trustworthy opponents of the "painted" flourishes of poetic rhetoric (II, 1), and particularly of Berowne's language "replete with mocks, / Full of comparisons and wounding flouts" (V, 2).[48] Now Rosaline orders her would-be lover to exercise his "fair tongue, conceit's

expositor" (II, 1) in the company of the speechless and
anguished. His discourse, however ravishing, "sweet and
voluble" (II, 1), will have to absorb an awareness of the unutter-
able, before it can become what it should be:

> To weed this wormwood from your fruitful brain,
> And therewithal to win me, if you please, . . .
> You shall this twelvemonth term from day to day
> Visit the speechless sick, and still converse
> With groaning wretches; and your task shall be,
> With all the fierce endeavour of your wit,
> To enforce the pained impotent to smile.   (V, 2)

THE "TONGUE-TIED MUSE"

How Berowne's poetics will realize itself, then, remains a matter
of speculation. However, Shakespeare gives us another hint in
the right direction. It is contained in the two lyrics which conclude the play like an afterthought.[49] Both *de facto* and symbolically, the songs of Spring and Winter offer examples of a poetry
approximating a silence of discourse. Syntactically, they reduce
rhetoric to the bare minimum of enumeration and temporal
allocation. Each of the four stanzas is structured around a
"When–then" clause, while the simple conjunction "and" serves
as the main link of enumeration. There are no disjunctives like
"although" and "however," while explanatory conjunctions such
as "because" and "therefore" are missing except for the unem-
phatic "for thus sings he." The main gesture is one of pointing
and repetition. Poetic diction, in turn, operates on a minimal
scope. It can be matter-of-fact to the point of triviality ("daisies
pied and violets blue") or graphically descriptive to the degree of
almost hallucinatory precision ("And birds sit brooding in the
snow"). But whatever it is, it neither wastes words nor draws
attention to them. "And Marian's nose looks red and raw." The
facts, no more and no less. For songs supposedly compiled by
Holofernes and Nathaniel, there are surprisingly few latinate
words, while none of them is longer than three syllables.

Yet, for all their seeming simplicity, the songs are deeply
symbolic. What is more, their symbolism makes simplicity programmatic. The four stanzas are crowded with people – maidens

and married men, the parson and his parishioners, shepherds, ploughmen, Dick, Tom, Marian and greasy Joan – enough for the cast of another play. We continually seem to see and hear how they move around or do things – the shepherds piping on oaten straws, the maidens bleaching their summer smocks, Dick the Shepherd blowing his nail, Tom bearing logs into the hall, the milk being carried home frozen in pails, greasy Joan keeling the pot or Marian making the roasted crabs hiss in the bowl – but not a single word from any of them. The only words spoken, those of the parson, are drowned out by the coughing of the parishioners.

Language in the songs is the language of nature. Where the humans remain silent, the cuckoo sings his " 'Cuckoo; / Cuckoo, cuckoo,' " the owl hoots her " 'Tu-who; / Tu-whit, Tu-who,' " the merry larks serve as the ploughmen's clocks and the winter wind blows all aloud. In Milton's "L'Allegro," every shepherd will tell his tale; but in Shakespeare's songs of Winter and Spring they do not utter so much as a single word. Even where they make music, they use the most natural means for doing so. We remember that Apollo's lute in *Love's Labour's Lost* was strung with his own hair, and Orpheus' in *The Two Gentlemen of Verona* with other poets' sinews. The shepherds in the songs use something even more natural, oaten straws.

True poetry, Berowne told us, does not orate in painted rhetoric, but lives with the motion of all the elements. It speaks not about these elements, but through them in their own language. Throughout the play and the Sonnets, Shakespeare seems to criticize a poetry that "paints" or, in other words, imitates things in a self-conscious manner. Her beauty, the Princess tells Boyet, "Needs not the painted flourish of [his] praise" (II, 1). The speaker in the Sonnets defies the gross painting of his competitors. Now, the Spring song of *Love's Labour's Lost* gives us an example of poetic painting in an altogether more satisfactory mode. The flowers here do their own work in "paint[ing] the meadows with delight."[50] Rather than "paint" or imitate nature, poetry simply lets nature reenact itself in her appropriate medium, the language of silence. In similarly symbolic fashion, the speaker in the songs merely sings through his cuckoos, owls, and larks, or at best through the oaten straws of the shepherds.

In letting nature reenact itself through him, the poet, "Cours[ing] as swift as thought in every power,"

> Lives not alone immured in the brain;
> But with the motion of all elements.   (IV, 3)

Almost every word in the songs seems prompted by such empathy with the elemental forces of nature. Growth and decay, sex and jealousy, fire and frost – in short, the ever-recurrent cycles of life and death which the poem also parallels in its structure – the poet makes himself the mouthpiece of all of them. At the same time, he has to go beyond the ordinary limits of perception in doing so. Love, in inspiring the poet, Berowne told us earlier, "gives to every power a double power, / Above their functions and their offices" (IV, 3). The songs again provide examples of all the senses the protagonist has discussed in this context. What, for instance, could be more graphically descriptive than "Dick the shepherd blows his nail"? But at the same time we seem both to hear Dick's blowing and to feel the cold in his fingertips. Such synaesthetic feats, reflecting a simultaneous alertness to multiple levels of sensory experience, abound in the two songs. "When roasted crabs hiss in the bowl" – we seem to smell, see, and hear the apples jump over the fire all in one instant.

Yet, while such empathy spurns self-conscious craftsmanship, there is no attempt to hide craftsmanship as such. A song, after all, is a song, and no "art of hiding art" will make us believe otherwise. Inversions, alliteration, the regular rhyme scheme, fixed stanzaic structure and use of refrain, all contribute to the overall impression of patterned regularity and repetition. Shakespeare, of course, was familiar with the Horatian *ars celare artem*. "In him the painter labour'd with his skill / To hide deceit," he comments with regard to the painting described in *The Rape of Lucrece* (1506–7). But in his own art such concealment must have struck him as an affectation only equal to the self-reflective display of one's craft. Shakespeare, to all evidence, was in sympathy with neither. He attacked the *littérateur*'s "maggot ostentation"[51] with the same sharpness with which he ridiculed those who tried to hide the artefacts of theatrical illusion.

All this has little to do, but is often confused, with the playwright's stance on art versus nature. Even in an early play like *Love's Labour's Lost*, Shakespeare seems to advocate an art in which nature, rather than being imitated, reenacts itself through the poet. But, prompted though it is by nature, such art does not have to hide its artifice. On the contrary, the very attempt to do so would be like a breach of the spontaneity which an "art / That nature makes"[52] commands.

But before turning to this perhaps most comprehensive concern of Shakespeare's poetics, diverse other issues must claim our attention. One of these, to be discussed next, comprises the *furor poeticus*, the poet's imagination, and the act of creativity. Another, again claiming its own chapter, concerns the mythopoeic imagination. Needless to say, all these issues relate back to the larger one of nature, and of how it relates to art. For nature, in the playwright's poetics, is not just poetry's subject-matter; it also denotes the poet's body and mind as involved in the act of creation. As one might expect from his basic antiessentialist orientation, Shakespeare, in either case, stresses the physical and/or psychophysiological aspect of nature. His sense of the poet's fine frenzy is a case in point. Here Shakespeare, like Montaigne before him, takes literally what to others was essentially a metaphor. To Plato and most Renaissance scholars, this fury was almost diametrically opposed to real lunacy. What it meant to them, as we recall, was a hyperintellectual pursuit of ideational absolutes. To Theseus, by contrast, the poet's frenzy is analogous to the hallucinations of the real madman, "who sees more devils than vast hell can hold."[53] Psychology, in a sense, has taken the place of metaphysics.

VII · The poetic imagination

IN CRUCIAL WAYS, Theseus' comments on the lunatic, lover, and poet of imagination all compact, resume some of the issues discussed in *Love's Labour's Lost*. Both plays are informed by their author's antiessentialist bias. But, whereas Berowne argues his inverted Platonism in detail, Theseus more or less takes such inversion for granted; while the former dwells mainly on the outer world of the senses, the latter focuses on the inner world of the mind. Yet both share the common assumption that the power inspiring the poet, to quote Berowne,

> Lives not alone immured in the brain;
> But with the motion of all elements.   (IV, 3)

In this, Theseus differs from most Renaissance critics. Traditional Renaissance poetics of diverse persuasions – Aristotelian, Neoplatonic, or Christian – tends to view the poet's imagination as basically subservient to his reason. Poetry is valued or defended not so much for its imaginative as for its didactic or metaphysical insights. Even the much-acclaimed *furor poeticus*, in this way, was perceived as an ascent to higher metaphysical insights. The imagination, especially when in such frenzy, had to be harnessed to the same pursuit. It was in this sense only that critics would sometimes allow the poet to fly off into phantasmagoric realms peopled with forms, as Sidney puts it, "such as neuer were in Nature, as the *Heroes, Demigods, Cyclops, Chimeras, Furies,* and such like."[1] As for the real "*Chimeres* & monsters in mans imaginations," evoked by Puttenham,[2] neither he nor his numerous British and continental confrères would ultimately allow for them. The well-documented Renaissance distrust of such morbid imaginings was too strong.[3] To some critics like Fracastoro, poets had a right to feign "chimeras, centaurs, gardens, and palaces",[4] but only as long as such phantasizing served their main pursuit of ultimate truth and beauty.

"CHIMERAS AND FANTASTIC MONSTERS"

By equating the poet's imagination with the hallucinations of the lunatic, Shakespeare radically changes this emphasis. In this he resembles Montaigne, who set himself the task of exploring the "chimeras and fantastic monsters" of his mind in essays which, in turn, came to resemble "grotesque and monstrous bodies, pieced together of diverse members."[5] Shakespeare not only makes Theseus stress the semi-psychotic potential of the poet's imagination, but explores this potential in various of his dramatic characters. Most notably, Richard II grows more poetic as he turns frenetic, and at the same time reflects upon these talents. This is also true of Will, the speaker of the Sonnets, who, whether or not he voices Shakespeare's own dilemmas, is poetically at his best, or at least most powerful, when "frantic mad with evermore unrest" (147). As we shall see, then, Shakespeare not only allows us to read Theseus' statement as basically his own, but also ilustrates its tenets in several of his works. But here, to start with, are the Duke's famous lines:

> The lunatic, the lover, and the poet,
> Are of imagination all compact.
> One sees more devils than vast hell can hold:
> That is the madman. The lover, all as frantic,
> Sees Helen's beauty in a brow of Egypt.
> The poet's eye, in a fine frenzy rolling,
> Doth glance from heaven to earth, from earth to heaven;
> And as imagination bodies forth
> The forms of things unknown, the poet's pen
> Turns them to shapes, and gives to airy nothing
> A local habitation and a name.
> Such tricks hath strong imagination
> That, if it would but apprehend some joy,
> It comprehends some bringer of that joy;
> Or in the night, imagining some fear,
> How easy is a bush suppos'd a bear!   (V, 1)

Through use of a multiple irony, Shakespeare makes us affirm what Theseus negates. What the Duke dismisses as these "antique fables" and "fairy toys" is, after all, what we have just seen in the play. What is more, this debunker of myth is a creature of "antique fables" himself. We also know that he is linked with the "fairy toys" of more recent folklore and Shakespeare's own creation. Titania, as Oberon informs us, is or was in love with Theseus and aided him in various adventures (cf. II, 1). But Theseus' very rhetoric makes a mockery of his argument. "Lovers and madmen have such seething brains, / Such shaping fantasies, that apprehend / More than cool reason ever comprehends," he argues at the beginning. Reason comprehends where imagination does no more than apprehend. But only a few lines later, imagination performs both functions in one: "Such tricks hath strong imagination / That, if it would but apprehend some joy, / It comprehends some bringer of that joy." So we are not too surprised to find him announce that "'tis almost fairy time" (V, 1), before Oberon, Titania, Puck, and all their supernatural spirits arrive to bless his house; or to hear him defend the play of the Athenian workmen: "The best in this kind are but shadows; and the worst are no worse, if imagination amend them" (V, 1).

THE POET'S UNPLATONIC FRENZIES

All this, of course, is well known, and most critics would agree with Kenneth Muir that what "Theseus intends as the gibe against poetry is a precise account of Shakespeare's method in this play."[6] But what exactly does this account consist of? The question is surrounded by various textual problems. It has been argued that the mislineation of lines 5–8 and 12–18 in Quarto 1 is due to marginal insertions by Shakespeare in his foul papers. Some editors discount lines 22–3 as interpolations by another, inferior, hand.[7] Would Shakespeare, asks R. G. White, "after thus reaching the climax of his thought, fall to twaddling about bushes and bears? . . . I cannot even bring myself to doubt that these lines are interpolated." Other editors have tried to rescue the lines as Shakespeare's by arguing that they "serve to give character and naturalness to the dialogue" (C. Cowden-Clarke),[8] or that they represent an appeal to proverbial wisdom which "confirms and rounds off Theseus' observations" (H. F. Brooks).[9]

We move on to even unsafer ground in entering the arena of actual exegesis. Here the two words "fine frenzy" have elicited obvious but misleading comments. "The 'fine frenzy' and the rolling eye," writes Kenneth Muir, "recall the divine fury of which Plato, Sidney and others had spoken."[10] Harold F. Brooks seems to agree, arguing that the "fine frenzy" is "the 'furor poeticus' so much honoured in the Renaissance, following Plato and Aristotle, as the mark of true poetic inspiration." In addition to Plato (*Phaedrus*, 245, 249, *Ion*, 533, 534) and Aristotle (*Poetics*, Chapter 17), the editor refers to George Puttenham's mention of "some diuine instinct, the platonicks call it *furor*,"[11] Of course, Puttenham is only one of several English critics who discuss the poet's divine frenzy. Thomas Lodge, for instance, mentions that "Persius was made a poete *Diuino furore percitus*," adding that he will save his readers "a long discourse" he might give them "of Platoes 4 furies."[12] George Chapman praises Homer for his "*Diuine Rapture*,"[13] while the anonymous author of a play entitled *The Return from Parnassus* makes Furor Poeticus appear as a dramatis persona talking in Marlovian bombast.[14]

But such further examples only deepen the somewhat simplistic assumption that Shakespeare's "fine frenzy" is identical with the traditional *furor poeticus*. In fact, there are crucial differences between the two concepts. Theseus links the poet's "fine frenzy" to that of the real lunatic who "sees more devils than vast hell can hold." Plato, by contrast, clearly distinguishes such common lunacy from his four, "heaven-sent," kinds of madness (the prophetic madness, the madness of the sacred ritual, the poetic madness, and the lover's madness).[15] Ficino's influential *Commentarium in Convivium*, while making poetic madness the first of Plato's four frenzies, puts even greater emphasis on the non-pathological nature of the *furor divinus*. "Indeed," Ficino writes, "this is a divine madness of the illumined spirit of reason". ("Est autem furor divinus illustratio rationalis animae.")[16]

Even if Plato and Ficino were unknown to Shakespeare, there were enough others to remind him that Theseus' concept of "fine frenzy" was a rather unconventional concept. Giordano Bruno's *eroici furori*, for instance, are a "rational impetus" freed from all vestiges of the sensual, instinctual, even irrational.[17] In his 1573

De Re Poetica Disputatio, Richard Willis points out that poets possessed by Plato's divine frenzy are distracted, "not because they are out of their minds, but because they so apply their minds to things and assume the emotions they describe, that, as if stimulated by passion or roused by the divine breath, they seem to be transported hither and thither."[18] George Chapman, while praising Homer for his "Diuine Rapture," draws a similar distinction between *insania* and *divinus furor*:

Insania is that which every rank-brained writer and judge of poetical writing is rapt withal, when he presumes either to write or censure the height of Poesy, and that transports him with humour, vain glory, and pride, most profane and sacrilegious; when *divinus furor* makes gentle and noble the never-so-truly inspired writer ... And the mild beams of the most holy inflamer easily and sweetly enter, with all understanding sharpness, the soft and sincerely humane.[19]

The Renaissance consensus, from which Shakespeare's Theseus deviates, is, then, an obvious one. The poet's madness has little, if anything, to do with pathological lunacy. On the contrary, it is a form of hyperintellectuality well in tune with the traditional demand that the poet, following the metaphysician, convey a higher understanding of reality. Thanks to his *"Diuine Rapture,"* Homer, in Chapman's view, portrayed "the vniuersall world."[20] Richard Willis's poet, for all his divine frenzies, imitates things, both existent and non-existent, in good Aristotelian fashion, "as they might be or ought to be."[21]

Theseus' speech is structured clearly enough not to leave doubts as to its almost diametrically opposite orientation. Theseus' madman, compact of imagination with poet and lover, is a real lunatic. The lover, who in Plato ascends from corporeal beauty to the vision of divine beauty – a trajectory previously reversed by Berowne – is simply caught in his own self-delusion. All as frantic as the lunatic, he sees Helen's beauty in the brow of a gypsy. Infatuation, as we might put it, makes him mistake his raven for a swan. Whatever else is said about the imagination of lunatic, lover, and poet is of a similar order. There is no hint of any superior insight into a world of Aristotelian entelechies or Platonic ideas. It is *all* self-delusion: a joy which conjures up the presence of what is absent; or at best, the kind of superstitious projection ridiculed by Shakespeare's contemporary Reginald Scot in *The Discouerie of Witchcraft* (1584).

> Or in the night, imagining some fear,
> How easy is a bush suppos'd a bear!

In sum, Theseus' comments on the poet's imagination, while alluding to the *furor poeticus*, reverse some of the claims traditionally associated with that notion.[22] Whereas writers from Plato to Chapman emphasized its intellectual and basically non-psychological nature, Theseus presents it in primarily psychological terms. The Platonists saw it as an access to higher insight into the universal truths behind reality. To Theseus, by contrast, it is a strictly non-metaphysical process conducive to what rationalists like the Duke himself dismiss as self-delusion and superstition, and others (like the implied author behind Theseus) appreciate as a mythic world of supernatural creatures and events. These, not the abstractions of metaphysical speculation, are the "forms of things unknown" which the poet's pen turns to shapes giving "to airy nothing / A local habitation and a name."

THE CREATIVE PROCESS

Theseus clearly distinguishes two phases in this process. The first is reached when the imagination – the poet's eye, in a fine frenzy rolling and glancing from heaven to earth, from earth to heaven – bodies forth the forms of things unknown through predominantly visual means. Phase two involves the transformation, achieved in the art of writing, of these prelinguistic imaginings into poetic language and its various devices. The deliberateness of this process is stated as explicitly as the simultaneity between imagining and writing. The "poet's pen" "[t]urns ... to shapes" the forms of things unknown "as" imagination bodies them forth. What was vague in the imagination, is made more precise and concrete (given a "local habitation and a name") in language. Yet, whatever else this transformation involves, it is nowhere said to be guided by a "fore-conceite," as stipulated in Sidney's distinction between the poet's inventions and his act of writing.[23] Even Hippolyta, who, in her reply to Theseus, takes up the defence of poetry, makes no such suggestion. The "something of great constancy" she can see in what Theseus dismisses as these "antique fables" and "fairy toys" emerges in the actual telling of the lovers' story and remains ultimately "strange and admirable:"

> But all the story of the night told over,
> And all their minds transfigur'd so together,
> More witnesseth than fancy's images,
> And grows to something of great constancy,
> But howsoever strange and admirable.   (V, 1)[24]

Most remarkable, then, in Theseus' account of the poetic imagination, is his insistence on its psychological functioning and mythopoeic powers. How man's fantasy, if not controlled by reason, produces "terrible" and "monstrous fictions"[25] was, of course, a commonly voiced complaint among Renaissance psychologists and aestheticians. But Theseus' words sound a distinctly new note in this choir. The apologists of poetry tried to dissociate imagination's psychopathological bias from the poetic imagination. By contrast, Theseus simply equates the two, while the playwright, ironically hidden behind his dramatis persona, seems to give his smiling approval. Ronsard, for instance, claims that the poet should invent "great and beautiful things," but be sure to exclude those "fantastic and melancholy inventions which have no more relation the one to another than the disconnected dreams of a lunatic." For the true poet's inventions "will be well ordered and arranged" so that they "can be easily conceived and understood by every one."[26]

Even Puttenham, in his well-known controversy with those who call a poet "a light headed or phantasticall man," follows the same reasoning. As to Ronsard, the poetic imagination to him ought to be well ordered. "For as the euill and vicious disposition of the braine hinders the sounde iudgement and discourse of man with busie & disordered phantasies . . . so is that part, being well affected, not onely nothing disorderly or confused with any monstruous imaginations or conceits, but very formall, and in his much multiformitie *uniforme*, that is well proportioned."[27] Underlying this sense of form or order, as in the case of Sidney's "invention," is the time-honored premise of idealization so clearly absent from the related comments of Theseus and Berowne.

To Puttenham, the poetic imagination should be "a representer of the best, most comely, and bewtifull images or apparances of thinges to the soule and according to their very truth." Like the anatomists of melancholy, he had no good word to say for the "*Chimeres* & monsters in mans imaginations" when in a state of pathological disorder.[28] There was clearly no room in art for the tricks of Theseus' "strong imagination." Despite claims made to the contrary,[29] Puttenham's comments neither anticipate Theseus' nor are unique for their time. Where the critic separates poet from lunatic, Theseus describes both as one. Where Puttenham echoes other Renaissance apologists of poetry in distinguishing men of healthy imagination from mere "*phantastici*,"[30] the Duke simply overrides these carefully worked-out differences.

Here, as elsewhere, Shakespeare displays little interest in such traditional apologies for poetry. To be sure, imagination's mind-destroying influence is often explored in his works. The number of psychopaths and neurotics among his major characters, in fact, is almost endless – Richard II, Lear, Macbeth, Posthumus, to name only some of the more obvious examples. Nearly every other play presents a "mind diseas'd,"[31] and some of the greatest, such as *Hamlet* and *King Lear*, make insanity their central focus. Shakespeare's characters also voice the traditional distrust of the imagination. Hotspur, "with great imagination / Proper to madmen, led his powers to death."[32] Hamlet "waxes desperate with imagination" over his father's ghost (I, 4). "Give me an ounce of civet, good apothecary, to sweeten my imagination," pleads Lear after going insane (IV, 6). But the characters thus afflicted often strike us as the playwright's most poetic. As their imagination plays havoc with their lives, it also enhances their language and creativeness. Lear, his imagination freed from reason's overrule, stages his own courtroom drama or talks about how he will comfort himself with fantasy games when he and Cordelia are taken to prison:

> No, no, no, no! Come, let's away to prison.
> We two alone will sing like birds i' th' cage;
> When thou dost ask me blessing, I'll kneel down
> And ask of thee forgiveness; so we'll live,
> And pray, and sing, and tell old tales . . .
> And take upon's the mystery of things
> As if we were God's spies.   (V, 3)

Lear's profoundest lines, and some of the greatest in all of Shakespeare, strike us, as do these, as "matter and impertinency mix'd! / Reason in madness!" (IV, 6).

The earliest play whose protagonist – as if to illustrate Theseus' argument – is a lunatic and poet in one, may well have been written at the time of *A Midsummer Night's Dream*. *Richard II* shows, on the one hand, what havoc "strong imagination" can play with the human mind. "Sorrow and grief" make the King "speak fondly, like a frantic man" (III, 3) after he has lost his crown to Bolingbroke. But his frenzy also turns him into a poet. Walter Pater even thought it made him an "exquisite poet."[33] W. B. Yeats rose to Richard's defense for similar reasons. To claim that Shakespeare preferred Bolingbroke to Richard, he wrote, "is to suppose that Shakespeare judged men with the eyes of a Municipal Councillor weighing the merits of a Town Clerk; and that had he been by when Verlaine cried out from his bed, 'Sir, you have been made by the stroke of a pen, but I have been made by the breath of God,' he would have thought the Hospital Superintendent the better man."[34]

Be that as it may, the King's poetic urges, as prompted by his crazed mind, are worked out in minute detail. He wants to talk "of graves, of worms and epitaphs," tell "sad stories of the death of kings," and, like Hamlet, have his own tale recounted by a survivor (III, 2; V, 1). Like Lear, he also surrounds himself with a *teatrum mundi* of his own creation, his schizoid self playing all the imagined roles in one (V, 1). As well as a poet and a dreamer, Richard is an actor. He has "a keen sense of theatrical effect," writes Wolfgang Clemen, "each new situation in which he finds himself grows through him into a dramatic performance."[35]

Other characters share some of these characteristics of the poet-lunatic King. Bolingbroke, for instance, is only second to the protagonist in his flair for a timely display of his histrionic talents. "Off goes his bonnet to an oyster-wench; / A brace of draymen bid God speed him well / And had the tribute of his supple knee, / With 'Thanks, my countrymen, my loving friends'" (I, 4), reports the King. Like Richard, who speaks of his "senseless conjuration" (III, 2) or of playing the wanton with his woes (III, 3), Bolingbroke clearly senses the theatricality of certain situations in which he finds himself. "Our scene is alt'red from a serious thing, / And now chang'd to 'The Beggar and the King'" (V, 3), he remarks after the Duchess of York has come to plead for her traitor son. Both Richard and Bolingbroke stage their own scenes, an impression enhanced by York's description of their joint arrival in London:

> As in a theatre the eyes of men
> After a well-grac'd actor leaves the stage
> Are idly bent on him that enters next,
> Thinking his prattle to be tedious;
> Even so, or with much more contempt, men's eyes
> Did scowl on gentle Richard. (V, 2)

Again, Richard is far from the only one whom sorrow or grief cause to feel or speak fondly like a frantic man. How experience is distorted by the tricks of strong imagination is one of the general themes of the play. Theseus describes how man, in apprehending some joy, can sometimes dream up the presence of whoever causes that joy. Similar observations are made by Northumberland: "hope to joy is little less in joy / Than hope enjoy'd" (II, 3), he observes. Joy also seems to shorten our sense of time, while grief "makes one hour ten" (I, 3). Advocates of a more rational imagination are thwarted by either actual events or the empirical astuteness of men like Bolingbroke. John of Gaunt, in trying to comfort his son, advises him to "reason" with his banishment. Imagine, he tells him, that everything the soul holds dear may be found in foreign lands. Imagine the birds there to be musicians, the grass to be the rushes of the royal presence chamber, the flowers fair ladies, and walking a mere dance. But we sympathize with Bolingbroke when he dismisses his father's words as facile make-believe:

> O, who can hold a fire in his hand
> By thinking on the frosty Caucasus?
> Or cloy the hungry edge of appetite
> By bare imagination of a feast?
> Or wallow naked in December snow
> By thinking on fantastic summer's heat? (I, 3).

In denying imagination's customary role as a handmaiden of reason, Bolingbroke, though hardly a man without willpower and rationalist determination himself, reaffirms the autonomous mechanism of his grief-inspired fantasy:

> O, no! the apprehension of the good
> Gives but the greater feeling to the worse.
> Fell sorrow's tooth doth never rankle more
> Than when he bites, but lanceth not the sore.   (I, 3)

Here as elsewhere in *Richard II*, a dramatized debate about the imagination is followed through with startling results. Bolingbroke dismisses the Renaissance consensus that "we should by sway of reason rule over phantasy, and not follow it." In turn, Richard's Queen provides us with living proof against the related argument that the imagination is to be distrusted "unless it be controlled by reason."[36] Puttenham compares such "monstruous imaginations or conceits" with a distorting mirror.[37] Bushy, in trying to dismiss the Queen's evil forebodings upon Richard's departure for Ireland, invokes a similar optical effect:

> Each substance of a grief hath twenty shadows,
> Which shows like grief itself, but is not so;
> For sorrow's eye, glazed with blinding tears,
> Divides one thing entire to many objects,
> Like perspectives which, rightly gaz'd upon.
> Show nothing but confusion – ey'd awry,
> Distinguish form. So your sweet Majesty,
> Looking awry upon your lord's departure,
> Find shapes of grief more than himself to wail;
> Which, look'd on as it is, is nought but shadows
> Of what it is not. Then, thrice-gracious Queen,
> More than your lord's departure weep not – more is not
>   seen;
> Or if it be, 'tis with false sorrow's eye,
> Which for things true weeps things imaginary.   (II, 2)

Shakespeare nowhere voices his age's distrust of the imagination in greater detail; but he does so only to invert the traditional argument. Just after the Queen has reaffirmed her dire premonitions and Bushy once again dismissed them as "nothing but conceit" (II, 2), Green arrives with news of Bolingbroke's rebellion. Bushy's rationalist skepticism is proven wrong, while the

Queen's forebodings have come true. "So, Green," she tells the messenger,

> thou art the midwife to my woe,
> And Bolingbroke my sorrow's dismal heir.
> Now hath my soul brought forth her prodigy.　　　(II, 2)

Along with Richard, there are numerous other characters with an urge to translate the grief-inspired promptings of their imagination into some form of poetic language. The Queen herself, in a later scene (III, 4), wonders if she should tell stories of joy or of sorrow. York telling his wife about Richard's and Bolingbroke's return to London, is moved to tears by his own narrative (V, 2). John of Gaunt, "a prophet new inspir'd" (II, 1) by grief and sickness, hopes that his "death's sad tale" (II, 1), as told by himself, will touch the King's heart. "Too well, too well thou tell'st a tale so ill" (III, 2), comments Richard after Scroop, with "care-tuned tongue" (III, 2), has told him about the people's defection to Bolingbroke. But Scroop has yet "a heavier tale to say" (III, 2), the story of how the King's uncle has joined forces with Bolingbroke. Psychological problems, of course, do not always find such release in language:

> Sometime her grief is dumb and hath no words;
> Sometime 'tis mad and too much talk affords,

we read in an earlier work.[38] It is the same here: where some give voice to their sorrows, others, like Ross, keep it buried in their bursting hearts (II, 1). But all are living examples of how much the imagination can be stirred up by emotional turmoil.

However, only Gaunt, along with Richard, gains the status of a poet in giving voice to his grief-afflicted imagination. In turn, both characters also display some of Theseus' critical faculties in commenting on their creativity. Gaunt presumes that his grief and imminent death will give his language supernatural powers, sufficient to penetrate Richard's hard heart. Though proven wrong with the King, he is certainly right in calling himself a "prophet new inspir'd." Some of the lines he utters in this clairvoyant state no doubt live up to such claims:

> O, but they say the tongues of dying men
> Enforce attention like deep harmony.

> Where words are scarce, they are seldom spent in vain;
> For they breathe truth that breathe their words in pain.
> He that no more must say is listen'd more
> Than they whom youth and ease have taught to glose;
> More are men's ends mark'd than their lives before.
> The setting sun, and music at the close,
> As the last taste of sweets, is sweetest last,
> Writ in remembrance more than things long past.   (II, 1)

But the deepest insights into poetic creativity are Richard's. His great prison speech (V, 5), in this way, appears like a running comment, made in the very process of poeticizing, on how the poet "bodies forth / The forms of things unknown." The King's initial impulse it to express himself through comparison: "I have been studying how I may compare / This prison where I live unto the world." But comparison is impossible for lack of empirical data. So Richard proceeds to create his own world:

> My brain I'll prove the female to my soul,
> My soul the father; and these two beget
> A generation of still-breeding thoughts,
> And these same thoughts people this little world,
> In humours like the people of this world,
> For no thought is contented.   (V, 5)

To be sure, Richard is not a poet with pen in hand writing down his verses; so he fails to distinguish between the forms of things unknown, as conceived by the poet's prelinguistic imagination, and the shapes in which his pen gives these thoughts "A local habitation and a name." But how his imaginings are said to engender a host of concrete images, implies a similar distinction. Uppermost in his mind are "thoughts of things divine," "Thoughts tending to ambition," and "Thoughts tending to content." From these, in turn, arise more detailed imaginings. His thoughts of things divine recall two conflicting passages from Matthew (19:14, 24) as to who will enter the kingdom of heaven. His thoughts of ambition prompt an escapist fantasy in which Richard tries to claw his way through the prison walls with his bare nails. His thoughts of content evolve into the story of beggars in the stocks who take comfort in the thought of others subjected to similar indignity. To speak in T. S. Eliot's well-known terms, the King, in each case, has found "a set of objects, a situation, a chain of events"[39] which act as the formulas of his particular emotions or thoughts. The sum of all these is a proliferating multitude of imagined circumstances and *alter ego* personalities. If Richard had the gifts of his creator, there might be enough here for another tragedy like the one we are watching:

> Thus play I in one person many people,
> And none contented. Sometimes am I king;
> Then treasons make me wish myself a beggar,
> And so I am. Then crushing penury
> Persuades me I was better when a king;
> Then am I king'd again: and by and by
> Think that I am unking'd by Bolingbroke,
> And straight am nothing.   (V, 5)

This is not to say that Richard is a self-portrait of Shakespeare or that the playwright conceived of himself as simply another poet lunatic. Rather, it suggests that the poet sympathized with pathological states of mind in ways which were frowned upon by most of his contemporaries. The apologists of poetry tried to banish the "*Chimeres* & monsters in mans imaginations"[40] from the creative process. Shakespeare, by contrast, not only included such monstrosities in his work, but acknowledged a link between creativity and psychosis. In various of his dramatis personae – Richard II is only the first of them – he also explored possible psychoneurotic elements in the creative process.

We can only guess how far empathy here was deepened by personal experience; nor can we be sure that the Sonnets to the dark lady which abound with such experience tell us anything about Shakespeare himself. But their speaker's complaint that his "thoughts and discourse" are "as mad men's" is no mere rhetorical cliché. As his language fluctuates between sexual obsession and cynical self-analysis, it clearly mirrors a mind "frantic mad with evermore unrest." Many of these sonnets, as Heather Dubrow argues, are "internalized monologues" reflecting the speaker's mental chaos.[41] At the same time, at least one of them tells us how such psychological turmoil can be the very impulse behind the author's creativity:

> My love is as a fever, longing still
> For that which longer nurseth the disease;
> Feeding on that which doth preserve the ill,

> Th' uncertain sickly appetite to please.
> My Reason, the physician to my Love,
> Angry that his prescriptions are not kept,
> Hath left me, and I desperate now approve
> Desire is death, which physic did except.
> Past cure I am, now reason is past care,
> And frantic mad with evermore unrest;
> My thoughts and my discourse as mad men's are,
> At random from the truth vainly express'd.   (147)

As convincingly as a Lear or a Richard, the speaker of these poems, whether haranguing against "lust in action" (129) or parading his self-deceptions, is an embodiment *par excellence* of Theseus' poet lunatic of imagination all compact.

In focusing upon Theseus' poet lunatic and divers of its representatives in the canon, one important aspect of the Duke's speech has been excluded so far. This, of course, was quite deliberate. For the issue – Shakespeare's mythopoetics or, more specifically, his attitude towards dramatizations of the supernatural – is crucial enough to claim its own chapter. Obviously, the Duke is speaking not just of the imagination in general, but of a special kind. What he says about the poet's eye, which, "in a fine frenzy rolling," glances "from heaven to earth, from earth to heaven," shows this special concern. The same is true of the "airy nothing[s]" and "forms of things unknown" bodied forth by the poet's imagination. After all, the whole speech is meant to illustrate the Duke's aversion to the "antique fables" and "fairy toys" he may not believe in. As we recall, this is doubly ironic. For one thing, Theseus himself belongs both to the realm of "antique fables" as a figure from Greek myth and to that of "fairy toys" on account of his amorous links to Titania, Queen of fairyland. For another, he deprecates what is so clearly the outstanding achievement of the play in which he figures. Hippolyta, in replying to his strictures, neatly sums up this strange and admirable feat, of which *A Midsummer Night's Dream* is the first major instance in Shakespeare's work:

> But all the story of the night told over,
> And all their minds transfigur'd so together,
> More witnesseth than fancy's images,
> And grows to something of great constancy,
> But howsoever strange and admirable.   (V, 1)

VIII · Mythopoetics

SHAKESPEARE'S DRAMATIZATIONS of the supernatural
have often been hailed as his greatest achievement. *The
Tempest*, for that reason, was the most striking instance of Shakespeare's creative power to Joseph Warton. To Addison, it showed
far greater genius to have created Caliban than to have drawn
Hotspur or Julius Caesar; for "the one was to be supplied out of
his own imagination, whereas the other might have been formed
upon tradition, history, and observation."[1] Perhaps most
remarkable to critics in all this was how Shakespeare gave his
supernatural agents all the vitality and discreteness of his most
lifelike characters. The playwright, Warburton wrote, "soars
above the bounds of Nature, without forsaking sense."[2] Shakespeare no doubt was the greatest poet of all ages; but it was in his
"fairy way of writing" that he "incomparably excelled" all others
by most powerfully displaying his peculiar talents.[3] Needless to
say, this view, first enunciated in the eighteenth century, has
found numerous followers until the present one.

MYTHOLOGY, WITCHCRAFT, MAGIC

But what more precisely was the nature of this achievement if
viewed from an Elizabethan, or even perhaps the playwright's
own, perspective? The question instantly invites a second. Were
there Renaissance theories of myth that might elucidate Shakespeare's dramatic presentations of the supernatural? The answer
is largely negative. Humanists lacked our present-day terminology of myth, and whatever they had to say about the "ancient
fables" was couched in allegorical rather than symbolic or arche-
typal terms.[4] To a modern reader, Cronus swallowing his children, for instance, might suggest that whoever invented this

ible gave unwitting expression to an equally unconscious
Dedipal emotion. To a Renaissance scholar, the same story
would have a far more explicit meaning. Perhaps the poet who
first told it had tried to signify Time who, like Cronus, destroys
what he engenders. In other words, the story invariably was
thought to have been prompted by the meaning which it illustrated. To ask if perhaps the fable had come first, was tantamount
to challenging an almost unquestioned tradition dating back to
late antiquity. Francis Bacon, who first raised this question, was
well aware that he had taken an unprecedented step. It accounts
for the strength of the tradition he opposed that he finally
returned to it in *The Wisdom of the Ancients* of 1609.[5]

There is a further reason why Renaissance theorizing about
myth is, paradoxically, more of a hindrance than a help in trying
to throw light on Shakespeare's dramatic renderings of the
supernatural. While classical myth is the almost exclusive
concern of Renaissance mythography, it only accounts for part of
the supernatural presentations in Shakespearean drama. The
playwright's more vital portrayals of such forces, as in his
witches, ghosts and general "fairy way of writing," was not
within the purview of such theorizing. Even if Bacon had cared to
watch, say, *A Midsummer Night's Dream* and *Macbeth*, he would
hardly have been tempted to comment on them in his various
discussions of "parabolical" poetry. Granted that Hecate figures
in the tragedy and Theseus as well as Hippolyta in the comedy. As
to the witches and Banquo's ghost in *Macbeth* or Oberon, Titania,
Puck, and all the fairies in *A Midsummer Night's Dream*, they had
little to do with the "wisdom of the ancients," parabolical fables,
or "mitologia" in general. As obviously as a strictly allegorical
interpretation of classical myth is at odds with Shakespeare's
presentations of the supernatural, as little are we invited to
extend such theorizing to this domain.

If, therefore, we turn to more recent theories instead, we are
confronted with similar problems. Modern mythography, of
whatever persuasion, seems to start from the basic assumption
that myths, in one way or another, reflect fundamental human
perceptions or basic patterns and mechanisms of thought. Frazer
might trace them to an obsession with seasonal death and rebirth,

Malinowski to man's role in society, Lévi-Strauss to the basic polarizations of thought, Freud to mass-psyche mechanisms analogous to the Oedipus complex, or Jung to archetypes in the collective unconscious: in each and every case, myth is seen as a projection of the human mind, while the possibility that its supernatural elements might exist as independent forces is either negated or left to occult speculation. Even Jung did not risk the scholarly credit he was left to enjoy by endorsing the reality of ghosts and apparitions. There might have been a time when Jupiter and his retinue were taken to be authentic embodiments of the supernatural; but even the Greeks began to undermine their own beliefs in the supernatural from early on. Already in the fifth century BC Hecataeus called the Greek myths "funny",[6] while Xenophanes argued that men imagine their gods strictly in their own image: "The Ethiopians say that their gods are snub-nosed and black, the Thracians that they have light blue eyes and red hair."[7] More recent mythography may have revalued myth by investing it with various meanings, but hardly by revitalizing our belief in the authenticity of its supernatural elements.

This leads us back to Shakespeare's own time. For where neither modern nor Humanist theories of myth throw much light upon his dramatizations of the supernatural, there is an area of Renaissance religious belief which might. This is the realm of witchcraft and magic, in which the supernatural, contrary to more recent persuasion, was credited with an existence independent to mental projection. Most widespread, of course, was the belief in witchcraft. Human beings were thought to conjure up demons, to copulate with incubi and succubi, or even to fly through the air to their witches' sabbaths. That a great number of people, including scholars, officials, and clergymen, believed such matters to be real, needs little further proof than what is known about the victims. During Shakespeare's lifetime, thousands of them were arraigned, tortured, and executed all over Europe, and many of them in England itself.[8]

Here as elsewhere, belief in witchcraft survived the enlightened skepticism of those who, like Reginald Scot, argued that witches and their victims are possessed by melancholy rather than by the devil. The effects of this mental disease, Scot wrote in

1584, "are almost incredible. For as some of these melancholike persons imagine, they are witches, and by witchcraft can worke wonders, and doo what they list: so doo other, troubled with this disease, imagine manie strange, incredible, and impossible things." But even this additional argument that a belief in witchcraft was "contrarie to reason, scripture, and nature" was lost on most of his contemporaries. Both "old custome" and "yoong ignorance" which he feared proved stronger than reason.[9] As Hunter–Macalpine write, "trials and convictions of witches continued, the greatest number of executions taking place at the turn of the sixteenth and again in the middle of the seventeenth centuries."[10]

Even Scot's more sympathetic readers were unlikely to endorse his arguments completely. What if Scot denied the existence of ghosts? Other Protestants had done so before him, but simply by arguing that what "Popish" writers had misinterpreted as such were either good or evil angels or some other warning sent by God. What if Scot interpreted the phenomena of witchcraft as mere hallucination? The theory, as Lewes Lavater had pointed out before him, was an old one: "There haue ben very many in al ages," we read in his *Of Ghostes and Spirites Walking by Nyght*, "which haue vtterly denied that there be any spirites or straunge sightes." Like these, Lavater grants that the belief of some who claim to see or hear ghosts "proceedeth eyther of melancholie, madnesse, weakness of the senses, feare, or of some other perturbation." Nonetheless he remains convinced "that spirites and straunge sightes doo sometyme appeare."[11]

Others might agree with Scot that witchcraft, by and large, has to be viewed in terms of delusional insanity. But they argued that the disease itself, according to traditional belief, was caused by supernatural agencies. Their model, invoked by Pierre de la Primaudaye, was the New Testament lunatic possessed by the devil. According to his widely read *French Academy*, infernal spirits, through their expert knowledge of the bodily humors, have the power to "trouble the imagination, fantasy, and minds of men."[12] This is precisely the attitude of J. Wier, who, next to Reginald Scot, was most influential in opposing the witchcraft mania of Renaissance Europe. If witches believed they were able to "conjure up ghosts and apparitions" and to "serve the Devil by causing calamities to befall man and beast," it was simply because their imagination was "wounded, troubled and filled with the diverse apparitions of minds confused with melancholy or vapors"; but behind it all was "the Devil who insinuates himself into their imaginations." What is more, Wier distinguished witches from magicians, who, he said, must reap no benefits from his enlightened psychiatric theories. For, as against poor lunatics, magicians were "learned men who curiously seek out their evil knowledge by making long voyages to the ends of the earth, learning about the order of nature so they can then corrupt it."[13]

Yet, for all such reservations, Wier's semi-psychiatric understanding of witchcraft was hardly typical of common opinion. At least as far as the judicial system was concerned, a belief in the supernatural authenticity of witches' sabbaths, ghosts, demonic possession, etc., remained in effect throughout Shakespeare's lifetime. Just a few years before the playwright wrote *Macbeth*, it in fact received a major endorsement.[14] In 1604, shortly after ascending to the English throne, James I introduced a new Witchcraft Act to replace the milder one of 1563. It reintroduced many of the severities of Henry VIII's Act of 1542, and naturally intensified an already powerful witch-hunt mania. The King had well prepared this legal measure by bringing out a new, London edition of his *Daemonologie* in 1603. Here he lashes out against those who describe as mere insanity what he firmly believes to be supernatural intervention by the devil – "against the damnable opinions of two principally in our age, whereof the one called SCOT an Englishman, is not ashamed in publike print to deny, that ther can be such a thing as Witch-craft. . . . The other called WIERVS, a German Phisition." By personally attending some of the trials, the new king made sure that witches, in spite of such theories, would receive "what exact trial and seuere punishment they merite."[15]

None of all this is to suggest that Shakespeare himself agreed with the King or other traditionalist believers in witchcraft. Since no personal records to that effect have survived, the playwright's private opinions on the matter will forever remain a secret. Yet whatever his plays imply regarding the authenticity of witchcraft and related supernatural phenomena no doubt accorded with the convictions of the greater part of his spectators. Most of these had no need of a willful suspension of their disbelief to convince themselves that the witches in *Macbeth* stood for genuinely demonic creatures.[16] Maybe there was a handful of skeptics to whom ghosts, even after seeing *Hamlet*, remained what they initially were to Horatio, that is, mere "fantasy" (I, 1). As for the rest, they might disagree as to whether the apparition in this Shakespeare play was Hamlet's dead father or merely a devil in disguise, but hardly as to whether it stood for a genuine supernatural creature.

SHAKESPEARE'S DRAMATIZATIONS OF THE SUPERNATURAL

But what more precisely is implied about the supernatural if we look at its various dramatizations in the individual plays of the canon? To start with, there are at least two plays which clearly endorse the official attitude towards witchcraft. Joan of Arc in *1 Henry VI* is far more of a "devil's dam," witch, "damned sorceress," hag, and "Foul fiend" than her namesake in Shakespeare's sources. Joan rejects the charge that her feats were accomplished through "baleful sorcery" and "the help of hell." But by the time she claims to have been "chosen from above / By inspiration of celestial grace" and never to have "had to do with wicked spirits," we know that she is lying.[17] Where Holinshed briefly mentions "hir campestrall conversation with wicked spirits,"[18] Shakespeare invents an entire scene in which Joan, before her final arrest, is seen conjuring up her demonic helpmates from hell, offering them her blood, her body, and finally her eternal soul:

> Now help, ye charming spells and periapts;
> And ye choice spirits that admonish me
> And give me signs of future accidents; [*Thunder.*
> You speedy helpers that are substitutes
> Under the lordly monarch of the north,
> Appear and aid me in this enterprise!
>   *Enter* Fiends.
> This speedy and quick appearance argues proof
> Of your accustom'd diligence to me.

> Now, ye familiar spirits that are cull'd
> Out of the powerful regions under earth,
> Help me this once, that France may get the field.
> *They walk and speak not.* (V, 3)

Though unsuccessful on this occasion, Joan of Arc clearly is a witch as much as any who ever suffered the stake. York's words, when Pucelle after bestowing her final curse on England is led away to execution, suggest the attitude which the audience is invited to share with the Duke:

> Break thou in pieces and consume to ashes,
> Thou foul accursed minister of hell! (V, 4)

Equally invented from a casual remark in his immediate source[19] is a second conjuring scene in 2 *Henry VI*. Again we have a witch, Margery Jourdain, who, along with her fellow-wizards, is caught red-handed while communing with an infernal spirit, and thrown into prison, no doubt in expectation of her trial. There the "trinkets" of sorcery found upon the arrest will be used as further evidence against her. Unlike Joan of Arc's taciturn fiends, Margery's spirit, called Asmath, responds to the questions addressed to him. What is more, his prophecies, which prefigure those of the weird sisters in *Macbeth*, will come true at a later point. Other details, which Shakespeare again was to use in later plays, further enliven the presence of Asmath. Like the ghost in Hamlet, the spirit performs his function with a mysterious impatience: "Ask what thou wilt; that I had said and done," he begins, and after barely pronouncing his prophecies, confesses that he cannot endure any further before redescending to "darkness and the burning lake" amidst thunder and lightning. At the same time, Shakespeare surrounds the scene with a general atmosphere prefiguring that of *A Midsummer Night's Dream*. As one of the conjurors points out,

> . . . wizards know their times:
> Deep night, dark night, the silent of the night,
> The time of night when Troy was set on fire;
> The time when screech-owls cry and ban-dogs howl,
> And spirits walk and ghosts break up their graves –
> That time best fits the work we have in hand. (1, 4)

A Midsummer Night's Dream, of course, has little to do with witches and their spirits; but, while dealing with fairies instead,

Shakespeare insists on essential links between the two. Granted that he makes Oberon describe himself and his followers as "spirits of another sort," different from those damned spirits who, "consort with black-brow'd night," break forth from their gaping tombs at nightfall and return to their graveyards before sunrise (III, 2); but, in drawing this distinction, Oberon also emphasizes a common link. Both elvish and demonic spirits form part of the triple team of Hecate, the goddess of heaven, earth, and hell, invoked by Puck:

> Now it is the time of night
> That the graves, all gaping wide,
> Every one lets forth his sprite,
> In the church-way paths to glide.
> And we fairies, that do run
> By the triple Hecate's team
> From the presence of the sun,
> Following darkness like a dream,
> Now are frolic.   (V, 1)

Shakespeare is known to have dissociated his fairies from the demonic allegiances of their folklore prototypes.[20] Hence one of his reasons for stressing the bond with their infernal counterparts may have been his wish to retain for his fairies some of the special credibility Elizabethans reserved for everything supernatural associated with the demonic. Shakespeare was to use similar techniques in *The Tempest*. Here fairyland is shown in direct conflict with the infernal world controlled by Sycorax, "the damn'd witch" (I, 2). After copulating with the devil, this hag was banished from Argier, only to continue her terrible sorceries on the island where she gave birth to the misshapen monster Caliban. As Prospero remembers, she "could control the moon, make flows and ebbs" (V, 1) and, what is more, gain supremacy over Ariel and his fellow-"ministers of Fate" (III, 3). With the help of her "more potent ministers" she imprisoned Ariel in a cloven pine (I, 2), from which only Prospero's magic, even more powerful than Sycorax's, could free him.

For all that, it would be wrong to argue that the attitude which Shakespeare tries to enlist towards fairyland is equal to the assent which a Renaissance audience would have been ready to bestow

on ghosts and witches. No doubt we are meant to smile at
Theseus' incredulity as to the "fairy toys" we have just seen
enacted before us. The Duke, as a figure of classical myth who is
also associated with Titania, ironically forms part both of the
"antique fables" and of the "fairy toys" in which he cannot
believe. Nevertheless, Puck helps to remind us in the Epilogue
that what we have seen is, in one sense, no more than a mere
fantasy:

> If we shadows have offended,
> Think but this, and all is mended,
> That you have but slumb'red here
> While these visions did appear.
> And this weak and idle theme,
> No more yielding but a dream.

After all, the association of fairyland with mere fantasy or
superstition is already found in Shakespeare's works before *A
Midsummer Night's Dream*. The Syracusan Dromio, when
embroiled in the various confusions of identity in *The Comedy of
Errors* wonders "If this is fairy land:"

> O spite of spites!
> We talk with goblins, owls and sprites.
> If we obey them not, this will ensue:
> They'll suck our breath, or pinch us black and blue.   (II, 2)

Another comedy, *The Merry Wives of Windsor*, presents us with
the very counter-image of *A Midsummer Night's Dream*. Where the
latter deals with real fairies, the former turns them into mere
fantasies of "the superstitious idle-headed eld" (IV, 4). The fairies
in *The Merry Wives of Windsor* are commonsense capitalist bour-
geois in disguise playing a prank on the credulous Falstaff. The
joke is on the fat knight, who, after being pinched and burnt by
his elvish persecutors, has some trouble convincing himself of his
error:

And these are not fairies? I was three or four times in the thought they
were not fairies; and yet the guiltiness of my mind, the sudden surprise of my powers, drove the grossness of the foppery into a receiv'd
belief, in despite of the teeth of all rhyme and reason, that they were
fairies.

(V, 5)

THE SUPERNATURAL: HALLUCINATION OR REALITY?

To some extent, this double attitude towards fairyland characterizes Shakespeare's dramatizations of the supernatural in
general. Even where the poet's ghosts, witches, fairies, or
classical divinities appear at their most authentic, there remains a
lingering suspicion that all might be mere fantasy after all. *Julius
Caesar* offers a case in point. Although an Elizabethan audience
no doubt saw Caesar's ghost appear on stage, it would also have
realized that the man to whom it appeared was half insane with
worry and insomnia. The "mad Brutus," as Antony will call
him,[21] is unsure himself as to what to make of the apparition:

> I think it is the weakness of mine eyes
> That shapes this monstrous apparition.
> It comes upon me. Art thou any thing?
> Art thou some god, some angel, or some devil,
> That mak'st my blood cold and my hair to stare?
> Speak to me what thou art.   (IV, 3)

Even after the ghost has spoken to him, Brutus still seems unsure
of its authenticity: "Didst thou see any thing?", "Saw you any
thing?" he asks his bewildered servants who were asleep during
the visitation (IV, 3).

Hamlet is full of even greater ambivalence. While dramatizing
most major Renaissance attitudes towards apparitions, it
commits itself to none of them. Horatio's response when told that
a ghost has appeared to the sentinels is to deny its authenticity:

> *Marcellus*: Horatio says 'tis but our fantasy,
> And will not let belief take hold of him
> Touching this dreaded sight, twice seen of us;
> Therefore I have entreated him along
> With us to watch the minutes of this night,
> That, if again this apparition come,
> He may approve our eyes and speak to it.
> *Horatio*: Tush, tush, 'twill not appear.   (I, 1)

If someone needed converting from such Reginald Scot-type
skepticism, there could be no better exemplum than the opening
scene of this play. No doubt the audience was meant to react with
some of the "fear and wonder" harrowing Horatio when the

ghost makes his first appearance on stage. The skeptic is taught a lesson, much to the satisfaction of those he discredited:

> *Bernardo*: How now, Horatio! You tremble and look pale.
> Is not this something more than fantasy?
> What think you on't?
> *Horatio*: Before my God, I might not this believe
> Without the sensible and true avouch
> Of mine own eyes.   (I, 1)

Hamlet himself, whom Horatio, now thoroughly convinced, assures of the truth of what appears "strange" to the protagonist (I, 2), has his own problematic responses to the apparition.[22] Though never a renegade like Scot, he wavers between the Catholic versus the Protestant interpretation of apparitions, as current during the Renaissance. Even before he encounters the ghost, he responds like a Protestant demonologist such as Lewes Lavater or James I. To these there was no purgatory. What Catholics had misinterpreted as emissaries from thence, had to be devils, or less likely angels, in disguise. "If it assume my noble father's person," Hamlet protests, "I'll speak to it, though hell itself should gape" (I, 2). The fear that the apparition might be a "goblin damn'd" or perhaps "spirit of health" (I, 4), but not the ghost of his deceased father, haunts the protagonist until the staging of "The Mouse-trap." Although the ghost is seen by several, Hamlet even suspects that it might be an illusion put into his mind by Satan. Wier's and others' theory to that effect was well known to Shakespeare: "what devil suggests this imagination?" exclaims one of his characters.[23] Hamlet even relates this possibility to his melancholic condition:

> The spirit that I have seen
> May be a devil; and the devil hath power
> T' assume a pleasing shape; yea, and perhaps
> Out of my weakness and my melancholy,
> As he is very potent with such spirits,
> Abuses me to damn me.   (II, 2)[24]

By catching the conscience of the King with "The Mouse-trap," Hamlet manages to assuage these fears. To all evidence, the apparition is not "a damned ghost," his imaginations not "as foul / As Vulcan's stithy" (III, 2). But where Hamlet's doubts are

resolved, the audience's trust in the authenticity of the ghost, so
carefully built up at first, is suddenly thrown into jeopardy in the
closet scene. Though the ghost appears to speak to the protagonist, he remains invisible to Gertrude. What is more, Hamlet's
demeanor, at least in his mother's graphic description – his hair
standing on end and his spirits wildly peeping through his eyes –
clearly shows him to be in the "heat and flame" of his self-
avowed melancholic distemper. As if to reinforce her point,
Gertrude is made to articulate another, Reginald Scot-like explanation of her son's visitation:

> This is the very coinage of your brain.
> This bodily creation ecstasy
> Is very cunning in.   (III, 4)

Characteristically, this is the last major comment on the ghost in
the play, which to some degree returns us to Horatio's initial
skepticism. Since the ghost *de facto* appears on stage, few, of
course, would attribute its visual and vocal presence to Hamlet's
hallucinatory fantasies alone. However, we are left with a strong
feeling of ambivalence which persists to the end of the play. What
in one sense is real is hallucination in another, neither possibility
cancelling out the other.

Just as Shakespeare allowed himself to give voice to all major
Renaissance theories of the supernatural, equally freely he mixed
and transformed the traditional prototypes of ghosts, witches,
fairies, and demons. In *Macbeth* he does both. The ghost of
Banquo, like that of Hamlet's father, only appears to the protagonist, while Lady Macbeth, like Gertrude, provides us with a
Reginald Scot-like commentary. From the time of his murder of
Duncan, we know about the protagonist's susceptibility to both
visual and auditory hallucination, and so does his wife. What she
explains as a "momentary fit" to her guests, she puts down to
mere fear in talking to her husband:

> This is the very painting of your fear;
> This is the air-drawn dagger which you said
> Led you to Duncan. O, these flaws and starts –
> Impostors to true fear – would well become
> A woman's story at a winter's fire,
> Authoriz'd by her grandam. Shame itself!
> Why do you make such faces? When all's done,
> You look but on a stool.   (III, 4)

Banquo voices similar incredulity regarding the witches, wondering if they are "fantastical, or that indeed / Which outwardly [they] show." Even after conversing with them, he is full of doubt:

> Were such things here as we do speak about?
> Or have we eaten of the insane root
> That takes the reason prisoner? (I, 3)

As the first dramatis personae to appear in the play, the witches, unlike the ghost in *Hamlet*, never come in for the kind of skepticism some Jacobean spectators might share with Horatio. Nonetheless, there is little in their hybrid nature to allow for an identification with any well-known and believed-in supernatural prototype. Are they the spirits of the "master conjurer" Macbeth? Or infernal demons? Or Norns? Or perhaps just vulgar witches?[25] These and further identifications have been attempted by modern critics, and they no doubt echo the similarly varied response of the more educated members of Shakespeare's audience. But more than all else they simply suggest that the playwright drew on every possible source and convention while letting them coalesce in the quick forge and working-house of his mythopoeic imagination.

This, of course, is even truer of his greatest mythopoeic creation, *The Tempest*. Fascinating, though ultimately frustrating, is the endeavor to try to search out the literary and folklore antecedents of Caliban, Ariel, or even Prospero himself. The protagonist may be said to be a sorcerer, whose magic, according to traditional distinctions, "is the antithesis of the black magic of Sycorax."[26] But the mage himself confesses to having practiced necromancy, while his general practices contravene a crucial claim made by contemporary demonologists. According to James I and others, the distinction between witches who are "servantes onelie ... to the Devil" and magicians who are "his maisters and commanders" is essentially delusory.[27] But in *The Tempest*, as R. H. West points out, it has become real.[28] Prospero may not command the devil, but he controls a host of elves and spirits.

Equally unconventional is Shakespeare's portrayal of Ariel. Though this spirit often behaves like a native English fairy, he has distinctly demonic allegiances. One of his duties is to do "business in the veins o' th' earth" (I, 2), recalling Agrippa's description of him as the presiding spirit of the earth and "evil demon."[29] Traces of black magic appear in his pact with Prospero, recalling Mephistopheles' with Dr Faustus in Marlowe's play. Cleaving to Prospero's thoughts and arriving "with a thought" (IV, 1) when bidden to do so, he also acts like a conjuror's "familiar spirit."[30] His ability to cause tempests, thunder, and lightning is shared by Burton's air-spirits, discussed in *The Anatomy of Melancholy*.

Even more numerous precedents than for Ariel have been found for Caliban – from folklore, demonology, travellers' tales about primitive men, Spenser's *Faerie Queene*, Montaigne's *Essays*, and many other sources. But what is true of the play as a whole is even more so of Caliban and its other mythic characters. "No specific source has been found," writes Geoffrey Bullough, "so we must content ourselves with analogues."[31] Modern scholarship thus makes us quibble with Addison's view that Shakespeare, in creating Caliban, did not rely upon "tradition, history, and observation." Undoubtedly the playwright took many hints from such sources. But that Caliban, like other of the play's supernatural creations, ultimately had to be "supplied out of his own imagination"[32] is as true today as it was when Addison said so.

MYTHOPOEIC CREATIVITY

What finally, then, can be said about this process of mythopoeic creativity as such? As we have seen, the answer is hardly to be found in an investigation of Shakespeare's sources. By contrast, the poet's attitude towards the supernatural, as far as it is manifest in his plays, might throw at least *some* light on the issue. This is true in the most general terms. It is one thing to create supernatural figures for a public like Shelley's, which may have witnessed the rise of modern mythological theorizing but had lost most of its belief in the authenticity of the supernatural; it is quite another to do the same for an audience, which, like Shakespeare's, still believed that there were genuine witches and ghosts. To say that the "weird sisters" in *Macbeth* are as alive and real as the human characters in this play, while Shelley's "Furies" in *Prometheus Unbound* strike one as rather lifeless though highly symbolic abstractions, is not just a value judgment. To a large extent, it is a result of cultural demand and supply.

Given the basic beliefs of his spectators, Shakespeare would best fulfill his audience's expectations by creating supernatural figures at their most realistically compelling. And, of course, so he did. But similar efforts would have been lost on Shelley's readers with their more abstract religious sentiments and metaphysically minded aspirations. It is no surprise that most nineteenth-century critics read Shakespeare's mythic plays as strictly subjective, if not allegorical, creations.[33] Prospero, for instance, might stand for the imagination, Ariel for fancy, and Caliban for brute understanding. Since then we may have learned to add further matrices derived from modern mythography to our reading of the same play; yet we have lost an appreciation of what Shakespeare's spectators, or most of them, would have demanded above all else in representations of the supernatural – that is, the realistic persuasiveness which Shakespeare gave them so superbly. And there are many reasons why this should be so and not otherwise. But even where we no longer share the beliefs of Shakespeare's time, we can hardly ignore them in trying to assess the process that engendered the playwright's mythopoeic creations.

But does all this apply to *The Tempest*? Most critics even today would probably argue that this play, along with its alleged companion-piece, *A Midsummer Night's Dream*, is hardly a serious dramatization of supernatural events, even if judged by Renaissance standards. And this indeed may be partly true of the earlier comedy. As Reginald Scot points out, belief in fairies was rapidly declining in Queen Elizabeth's England,[34] and Shakespeare, as we have seen, was not averse to exploiting the resultant ambivalence in at least two of his other plays. But *The Tempest* is not just about folklore fairies and elves. Its proper realm is Renaissance magic, which to some was invested with even greater awesomeness than witchcraft. J. Wier, for instance, while defending witches as victims of melancholy, invoked the full rigor of the law against magicians.[35] Here even his arch-opponent James I was to agree with him. To the King, all magic was of the devil, who alone could engineer feats like the following, reminiscent of *The Tempest*: "Yea, he will . . . make them to please Princes, by faire banquets and daintie dishes . . . Such-like, he will guard his schollers with faire armies of horsemen and foote-men in appearance, castles and fortes: Which all are but impressiones in the aire, easilie gathered by a sprite."[36]

Needless to say, apologists of magic were hardly less convinced of the reality of what they advocated. One of them in real life was Cornelius Agrippa, in his own words a "*divinorum cultor & interpres*, a studious observer and expounder of divine things," whose art was "the absolute perfection of Natural Philosophy."[37]

> 'Tis known I ever
> Have studied physic, through which secret art,
> By turning o'er authorities, I have,
> Together with my practice, made familiar
> To me and to my aid the blest infusions
> That dwell in vegetives, in metals, stones;
> And I can speak of the disturbances
> That nature works, and of her cures,

proclaims Prospero's fellow-magician Cerimon in *Pericles* (III, 2). This is just before he resurrects the dead Thaisa with the help of music and the knowledge derived from some Egyptian books,[38] perhaps the widely known *Corpus Hermeticum*. In Thaisa's and Pericles' view, "The gods can have no mortal officer / More like a god" than Lord Cerimon, "Through whom the gods have shown their power" (V, 3). In Cerimon as in Prospero, we find Shakespeare raising the Renaissance mage to the stature of a demi-god such as, in Agrippa's view, gains his power not by a pact with the devil, but by ascending to "the Maker of all things, and First Cause, from whence all things are, and proceed."[39] How else could Prospero set roaring war "'twixt the green sea and the azur'd vault," resurrect the dead, or rive "Jove's stout oak / With his own bolt" (V, 1)?

Except for the occasional cynic like Reginald Scot, Shakespeare's contemporaries, then, no doubt found magic to be as supernaturally authentic as witchcraft. In turn, the poet's basic endeavor in dealing with either was to cater to this basic belief rather than to ensure the proverbial suspension of the opposite. Shakespeare's unsurpassed realization of this task – the way in which he gives his supernatural figures and events all the visual, audible, and dynamic vitality of live ones – though obvious at every turn, remains largely unanalyzed. Specific techniques to that effect, such as Ariel's onomatopoeic feats or the witches' numerologically determined prosody, syntax, and semantics, would claim a separate chapter. Here we can only point to the way in which Shakespeare, though indirectly through his characters, seems to comment on his general mythopoeic approach.

A case in point occurs when Prospero, controller of natural and supernatural elements, uses his magic to play the creator of mythical art himself. This is, of course, where he presents his daughter and her prospective husband with "Some vanity of [his] art" (IV, 1). The subject-matter of his wedding masque for the young couple is derived from classical mythology. But Shakespeare is at obvious pains to make clear that the agencies which enact it are part of a magic most of his spectators would consider as more authentic than the ancient fables. Ariel is sent offstage to allow for a rather superfluous harangue in which Prospero, once again, warns Ferdinand not to give way to his lust with Miranda: "Do not approach / Till thou dost hear me call." Then, only a few lines later, Ariel is called back to act as *metteur en scène*: "Now come, my Ariel, bring a corollary, / Rather than want a spirit; appear, and pertly." Being enacted by magical agents a Jacobean audience could believe in, classical myth is given back some of the vitality it once possessed in antiquity.

Needless to say after what has been said already, this is typical of Shakespeare's method in general. Where fairyland, for instance, was about to become a mere superstition of the "idle-headed eld,"[40] he revitalized the tradition, partly by making it partake of the surviving belief in the demonic. Whatever classical mythology appears in *A Midsummer Night's Dream* and *The Tempest* was affected in a similar way. The main impulse in all this was towards a concretely lifelike and convincing dramatization of the supernatural. Even in a spectacle as unusually didactic and allegorical as the wedding masque in *The Tempest*, we are primarily called upon to abandon ourselves to the actual spectacle. The instructions which poet–presenter Prospero gives Ferdinand and Miranda to that effect are no doubt directed toward the audience

as well: "No tongue! All eyes! Be silent." "*Soft music*," which
seldom fails to accompany epiphanous events in Shakespeare,
will help put us into the appropriate state of mind.

At the same time, Ferdinand, while watching the masque, is
made to raise a question central to the present argument. Are
Shakespeare's dramatizations of the supernatural to be taken as
presentations of fact or of fantasy? Or, as Ferdinand wonders,
"May I be bold / To think these spirits?" In reply, Prospero, once
again, sums up an attitude implied by Shakespeare's plays as a
whole. Where most of his more erudite contemporaries were
probably either skeptics or believers, the playwright presents us
with a paradox. No doubt the ghost appearing at the beginning of
Hamlet, for instance, is real. But what are we to make of him in the
closet scene, where he appears to the obviously hallucinating
protagonist while remaining invisible to his mother? Here as
elsewhere, Shakespeare juxtaposes contradictory views of the
supernatural in unresolved contrast. Was his attitude towards
mythopoeic creativity a similar one?

His poet–presenter's mysterious reply to Ferdinand suggests
that it might have been. The mythological figures in the wedding
masque are genuine "spirits." At the same time, they are there
only by virtue of their creator's imaginative efforts, and there to
enact his imaginings:

> Spirits, which by mine art
> I have from their confines call'd to enact
> My present fancies.

Prospero reacts with some impatience to Ferdinand's questioning attitude. Even his creations seem unable to bear much more of
the same. They have started to whisper to each other – one more
interruption might totally disrupt Prospero's mythopoeic
creation:

> Sweet now, silence;
> Juno and Ceres whisper seriously.
> There's something else to do; hush, and be mute,
> Or else our spell is marr'd.   (IV, 1)

Characteristically, it is the creator's own mind which finally
brings about this disruption. The poet–presenter suddenly
remembers something which mars his fantasies and, along with

them, their mythopoeic correlatives. Once again, Shakespeare seems to stress the paradoxical simultaneity of fact and fantasy, suggesting that what so clearly proceeds from the poet's mind yet has its authentic, autonomous reality; or *mutatis mutandis*, that what possesses an independent existence once it is created yet remains inextricably linked to its source in the creator's imagination.

Prospero himself seems surprised that, while he was talking to Ferdinand, Juno and Ceres started to whisper to each other in words apparently inaudible to him as much as to us. Conversely, the mythological creatures suddenly vanish when the fancies which they enact and whence they proceed are disrupted. This intricate interrelationship is emphasized in both the stage directions and the commentaries spoken by Ferdinand, Miranda, and Prospero himself. Before the reapers and nymphs have concluded their dance, Prospero suddenly remembers the plot against his life planned by Caliban and his confederates. He "*starts suddenly,*" mumbling to himself in an aside – "*after which, to a strange, hollow, and confused noise,*" the figures "*heavily vanish.*" His worries do not allow him to conclude his creation with the harmoniousness which Ferdinand noted earlier: "avoid; no more!" he orders the spirits. Both Ferdinand and Miranda remark upon Prospero's strange distemper, before the protagonist finally explains to them the sudden disappearance of his mythopoeic creations. Prospero again emphasizes the paradoxical simultaneity of fact and fantasy, but adds an important afterthought.

On the one hand, the mythic phenomena we see are presentations of supernatural fact, not mere fiction – "These our actors, / As I foretold you, were all spirits, and / Are melted into air, into thin air." On the other, they are no more than the "baseless fabric of this vision." At the same time, the "insubstantial pageant," that has just vanished in front of our eyes, is no different from the daytime world on whose reality we rely so unquestioningly. Neither of them is any more real than a dream:

> And, like the baseless fabric of this vision,
> The cloud-capp'd towers, the gorgeous palaces,
> The solemn temples, the great globe itself,

> Yea, all which it inherit, shall dissolve,
> And, like this insubstantial pageant faded,
> Leave not a rack behind. We are such stuff
> As dreams are made on; and our little life
> Is rounded with a sleep.   (IV, 1)

That life is a dream, was a commonplace in both Shakespeare and Renaissance literature generally, of course. Also well known was the association of actors with the dissolving pageant of dreams,[41] and even the notion that supernatural creatures often reveal themselves to human beings in sleep. Shakespeare himself has shown how Diana appeared to Pericles (V, 1), and Jupiter, "*in thunder and lightning, sitting upon an eagle*" and throwing "*a thunderbolt,*" to Posthumus,[42] as both lie sleeping on stage. Conversely, we are asked by Puck to look back upon the supernatural phantasmagoria we have seen enacted in *A Midsummer Night's Dream* as "visions" we saw while asleep (V, 1). What is so extraordinary about Prospero's famous speech, then, is not its rather commonplace ingredients, but the way in which they interconnect to sum up most of what has been said about Shakespeare's mythopoetics so far. The supernatural spectacle which Prospero, in the role of the mythmaker poet, has created is neither mere fact nor mere fantasy. Rather, it is both at the same time. It is like a dream, but only if we grant that even this daytime world of concrete reality is no more. The same, in turn, applies to the mythopoeic creative process. The supernatural world created by the poet is like a dream dreamt by his imagination, but only if we concede that dreams have many of the characteristics of reality.

The crucial statement to that effect is Theseus' about "antique fables" and "fairy toys" in *A Midsummer Night's Dream* (V, 1). As we have seen in the preceding chapter, the lunatic, whom Theseus makes the poet's double, is no mere Platonist involved in hyperintellectual pursuits. In turn, the "fine frenzy" which makes roll the poet's eye may partake of semi-psychotic experience. Like Macbeth, who sees a ghost where others see none, this poet lunatic might see "more devils than vast hell can hold." Most of the remaining lines of Theseus' speech illustrate these hypnagogic resources of the poet's imagination. The Duke calls them "tricks:" the power to evoke a concrete figure from a positive emotion which that figure comes to embody, and, more simply, the tendency to turn a neutral object into a representation of what one is afraid of:

> Such tricks hath strong imagination
> That, if it would but apprehend some joy,
> It comprehends some bringer of that joy;
> Or in the night, imagining some fear,
> How easy is a bush suppos'd a bear? (V, 1)

At the same time, none of this hypnagogic experience precludes conscious craftsmanship, once the poet expresses it in words. Just as Theseus stresses the elusiveness of the poet's imaginings, he emphasizes equally strongly the discrete deliberateness with which the poet "Turns them to shapes." The mythic contents gathered in ranging from "heaven to earth, from earth to heaven," the "airy nothing" and "forms of things unknown," in this way, contrast with how the poet, pen in hand, gives these mysterious fantasies concrete "shapes" as well as "A local habitation and a name." The poet, and especially the playwright, works as a highly conscious craftsman when bodying forth his mythopoeic fantasies, even though they may derive from hallucination or dream.

Cleopatra, telling her dream of Antony, stresses the same point in pitting herself against Dolabella's incredulity. Her lover, as he appeared to her while asleep, has truly mythic dimensions:

> His legs bestrid the ocean; his rear'd arm
> Crested the world. His voice was propertied
> As all the tuned spheres, and that to friends;
> But when he meant to quail and shake the orb,
> He was as rattling thunder. (V, 2)

Dolabella, who denies that such a creature can be real, is characteristically charged with lying "up to the hearing of the gods." As Cleopatra explains to him, there is more to her nocturnal vision than either reality or dream. What invaded her while asleep was clearly larger than a mere dream: "But if there be nor ever were one such, / It's past the size of dreaming." In turn, nothing in conscious reality can match her vision, however hard one might strain one's combinatory capacities. We should never be able to reproduce what she saw by piecing together fragments from everyday experience: "Nature wants stuff / To vie strange forms with fancy." But what thus transcends nature in the sense of both conscious and unconscious experience can be created, or at least visualized, by man's imagination. The paradox is a simple but complex one. Nature, through this channel, creates a world beyond ordinary nature, or myth. But only if the imagination remains rooted in nature, or in man's whole psychological being, will this supernatural world be more than mere fantasy.

> Nature wants stuff
> To vie strange forms with fancy; yet t' imagine
> An Antony were nature's piece 'gainst fancy,
> Condemning shadows quite.

This brings us back to the starting-point of this book, and also to the, in many ways, most central issue in Shakespeare's poetics, the relationship between art and nature. Few other concerns – the imagination, the poet's language, his readers or audience – are as frequently discussed in the canon. None, to the playwright's contemporaries, was as intrinsically Shakespearean. To them, for better or worse, he was the poet of nature, a view which his own implied comments seem to endorse. Even where these echo the commonplace of art's superiority over nature, we are made aware that art, by reason of its basic artificiality and lifelessness, can never outdo nature; at best, it can try to reenact life.

But what in all this is meant by nature? Nature, as embodying some higher teleological or providential scheme, or nature as simple flux? Reality, to be understood according to some essentialist matrix, or simply according to what can be known of it empirically? The former view, as we know, more or less represented the Renaissance consensus; the latter was advocated by Montaigne and Bacon. To all evidence, it was also favored by Shakespeare. We have already seen it emerge in various aspects of his poetics. Berowne, in taking a first step up the Platonic ladder, quickly reverses this trajectory towards ideational absolutes and opts for a total commitment to sensual experience instead. The poet's fine frenzy, which traditionally denotes a strictly intellectual pursuit, is redefined in genuinely psychological, and potentially pathological, terms. Language, rather than providing us with ideational absolutes, proves to be an ever-insufficient means of reflecting concrete reality. These and other issues impinge upon the art–nature relationship *per se*, and Shakespeare reveals an antiessentialist bias towards all of them. But what about art in relation to nature itself? Shakespeare, as our first chapter showed, broached the issue in several of his works; but naturally it was only in one of his later plays that he revealed his final attitude on the matter. This was in *The Winter's Tale* which, along with *The Tempest*, contains Shakespeare's testament as to what he has to tell us about the art he mastered so superbly.

IX · Time's argument, or art and nature

"THE WINTER'S TALE" affords one of the rare occasions on
which Shakespeare seems to address us more or less
directly. About to break the unity of time by leaving a gap of
sixteen years between Acts III and IV, the playwright assumes
the mask of Time to defend his dramaturgy:

> I, that please some, try all, both joy and terror
> Of good and bad, that makes and unfolds error,
> Now take upon me, in the name of Time,
> To use my wings. Impute it not a crime
> To me or my swift passage that I slide
> O'er sixteen years, and leave the growth untried
> Of that wide gap, since it is in my pow'r
> To o'erthrow law, and in one self-born hour
> To plant and o'erwhelm custom.   (IV, 1)

No doubt, the Chorus, however cryptically, speaks for the playwright himself. Time is not an objective personification, but the
author flying over sixteen years "in the name of Time." He also
refers to his "tale" as well as to the "scene" and reminds his
"Gentle spectators" of a previous scene (I, 2), in which he
"mentioned a son o' th' King's, which Florizel / I now name to
you." He gives an authorial forecast of the ensuing action while
explicitly withholding enough to create suspense. Time concludes with a convoluted *captatio benevolentiae* to the audience.[1]

CYCLICAL TIME AND TIMELESSNESS

Of course, such self-defense for breaking the unity of time is
nothing new in Shakespeare's oeuvre – we have already noticed
similar apologies in, for instance, *Henry V* and *Pericles*.[2] What is
more, it is not even at the heart of Time's argument. "Time's

news" and "th' argument of Time" are about to be revealed to us, not what we have seen already. Regarding this first part of the play, Time plays the role of a creator who deliberately disrupts his own creation – making "stale / The glistering of this present, as my tale / Now seems to it." Time's tale, to quote Frank Kermode's paraphrase, "seems stale compared with the play it interrupts."[3] The Chorus justifies such disruption by claiming the "pow'r / To o'erthrow law, and in one self-born hour / To plant and o'er-whelm custom." At the same time he purports to return to a primordial state "ere ancient'st order was / Or what is now receiv'd." This time before historical time, as one might put it, is characterized by two major attributes, its cyclical returns as well as its role of creator and destroyer in one.

To the Elizabethans, Father Time, equipped with scythe and hour-glass, was primarily the destroyer and truth-revealer, as portrayed, for instance, in *The Rape of Lucrece* (939–44).[4] Here "Time's glory" is said "To unmask falsehood and bring truth to light" as well as "To ruinate proud buildings with [his] hours, / And smear with dust their glitt'ring golden tow'rs." Shake-speare's Chorus, even where he alludes to these traditions, modifies them considerably. Time not only unfolds but also creates error. Instead of destroying the lawless, it overthrows ancient laws and customs. Its trials, which affect everyone, simply unfold "Time's news" rather than lead to a triumph revealing the truth, as in Shakespeare's major source, Robert Greene's *Pandosto*. In assuming Time as his mask, the author strips this personification of some of its traditional moralistic trappings. Time has become an amoral force beyond good and evil. It is like Nature herself, creator of both "good and bad," "joy and terror." It is able to "plant and o'erwhelm" in "one self-born hour," to "make stale" "freshest things now reigning" while giving growth to others.

Little, then, in Time's soliloquy recalls the "blending of the Platonic sense of sublunary imperfection and mutability with the Christian teleology" which a study of *Shakespeare and the Nature of Time* describes as the mainstream Renaissance tradition.[5] Rather, the Chorus evokes a primordial sense of time previous to "what is now receiv'd."[6] Time's dualities of planting and overwhelming, as well as the Chorus' insistence on change, recall Heraclitus, whom Shakespeare may have known through Montaigne. Thoroughly Heraclitean, for instance, are some of the final paragraphs of the essayist's "Apology for Raymond Sebond": "not only . . . is the death of fire the generation of air, and the death of air the generation of water; but even more obviously we can see it in ourselves. Our prime dies and passes when old age comes along, and youth ends in the prime of the grown man, childhood in youth, and infancy in childhood. And yesterday dies in today, and today will die in tomorrow; and there is nothing that abides and is always the same."[7] Time, as we read in the first of Shakespeare's romances, is

> the king of men;
> He's both their parent, and he is their grave,
> And gives them what he will, not what they crave.[8]

This goes hand in hand with a sense of eternity as timelessness, contrary to our mainstream teleological sense of life of either classical or Christian derivation. Aristotelian drama is a case in point here. Being geared towards things not as they are, but as they ought to be, it is concerned with the journey towards that goal rather than with cyclical repetition or moments of a timeless here and now. The same applies to the orthodox Christian eschatalogical understanding of life. St Augustine, like other Church Fathers, was aghast at the pagan notion, current in the Mediterranean world of his time, of a cyclical return of history. "For Christ died once for our sins, and, rising again, dies no more."[9] Even the notion of eternity, as Thomas Aquinas determined, had to be reached through time: "In cognitionem aeternitatis, oportet nos venire per tempus."[10] Montaigne, in affirming an eternity of the "here and now," which he identifies with God, sounds a clearly heretical note in this tradition. Nature to him, however it is regarded, shows no progression. In one sense, "the birth, nourishment, and growth of each thing is the alteration and corruption of another." Or looked at from a more positive angle, "Death is the origin of another life." In turn, eternity is not what we arrive at through linear time, but "one single *now*" that "fills the *ever*."[11]

Shakespeare, in *The Winter's Tale* and the romances in general, seems to draw the same "most religious conclusion of a pagan" reached in Montaigne's "Apology for Raymond Sebond."[12] A cyclical sense of time corresponds to a sense of timelessness in the here and now. The supreme poetic achievement in capturing this mystical *"ever"* in "one single *now*" is found in Florizel's words about Perdita, which, in one critic's words, are "formulated as a desire to arrest time, to achieve permanence outside the flux of time."[13] There is syntactical repetition, climaxing in the metaphor of a wave, which the verse seems to enact rhythmically ("move still, still so"). This prepares us for a more abstract statement about a transcendence reached in the here and now of a specific experience:

> When you speak, sweet,
> I'd have you do it ever. When you sing,
> I'd have you buy and sell so; so give alms;
> Pray so; and, for the ord'ring your affairs,
> To sing them too. When you do dance, I wish you
> A wave o' th' sea, that you might ever do
> Nothing but that; move still, still so,
> And own no other function. Each your doing,
> So singular in each particular,
> Crowns what you are doing in the present deeds,
> That all your acts are queens.   (IV, 4)

Shakespeare's deliberate use of anachronisms, as demonstrated by S. L. Bethell, creates a similar impression of timelessness.[14] Or there is the recurrent image of nature reprinting a copy of the parent in the child. In a Proustian flash, the perception of such resemblance can raise dramatis persona and audience to a level where two moments, divided by a wide gap, unite in a sudden sense of atemporality:

> *Leontes:* . . . Looking on the lines
> Of my boy's face, methoughts I did recoil
> Twenty-three years; and saw myself unbreech'd,
> In my green velvet coat.   (I, 2)[15]

Similarly, there is Time, the Chorus, who, abandoning "what is now receiv'd" (IV, 1) for a primordial sense of nature, is yet behind or beyond the cyclical understanding of nature he may advocate. His very language, with its dichotomies of joy and terror, planting and overwhelming, point to an ultimate force beyond and inherent in these cycles. Here and elsewhere, the author tells us more or less directly how his art enacts this cyclical vision of nature.

FROM TRAGEDY TO ROMANCE

All this is thrown into even sharper relief when considered in the light of the play's opening parts. As has often been noted, this first half of *The Winter's Tale* is a tragedy in miniature. Even Barbara Mowat, while questioning this assumption, admits that "the Leontes story presents a potentially tragic plot, along with many tragic accoutrements: noble figures, intense passions, deaths."[16] In addition, there is the more specifically tragic sense "of something decisively accomplished"[17] through the suffering we have witnessed. Hegel's "insistence on the need for some element of reconciliation in the tragic castastrophe," as reiterated by A. C. Bradley,[18] is fully satisfied by the wisdom Leontes learns through repentance.

Needless to say, there are critics who disagree with this general sense of the tragic, and no doubt there will be more to do so in the future. Be that as it may, there are numerous plays for which the "tragic" à la Hegel or Bradley provides the appropriate description. What is more, this tradition reaches back to the play traditionally identified with the very origins of the genre. Aeschylus' *Oresteia*, as I have tried to show elsewhere,[19] offers the archetype for plays in which something decisive is accomplished through human suffering. A seemingly endless chain of crime, revenge, and death is finally broken by human endeavor. The ordeals of Orestes, along with the deaths of those before him, are presented as serving the inexorable dialectics of progress.

At least in one play, Shakespeare is found to be working in similar patterns. Although Romeo and Juliet suffer and die, their pitiful ordeals bring about the reconciliation of their families. The play's Prologue announces this "tragic" theme in unmistakable terms:

> Two housholds, both alike in dignity,
> In fair Verona, where we lay our scene,
> From ancient grudge break to new mutiny,

> Where civil blood makes civil hands unclean.
> From forth the fatal loins of these two foes
> A pair of star-cross'd lovers take their life;
> Whose misadventur'd piteous overthrows
> Doth with their death bury their parents' strife.

Leontes' tragedy is of a somewhat different kind. The progress achieved through his suffering concerns his own life rather than the public welfare. But at least his suffering has taught the protagonist repentance. In this way, his final words, like those of many tragic heroes before him, round off a tragedy which, however short, forms a self-contained unity:

> Prithee, bring me
> To the dead bodies of my queen and son.
> One grave shall be for both. Upon them shall
> The causes of their death appear, unto
> Our shame perpetual. Once a day I'll visit
> The chapel where they lie; and tears shed there
> Shall be my recreation. So long as nature
> Will bear up with this exercise, so long
> I daily vow to use it. Come, and lead me
> To these sorrows. (III, 2)

Furthermore, there is nothing here to make us surmise that Hermione, the tragic victim of Leontes' jealousy, is still alive.

A look at *Pandosto* suggests that Shakespeare, while stressing what amounts to a fake tragic conclusion in III, 2, eliminated the final tragic ending of his main source. Greene's King of Bohemia, whose unjustified jealousy leads to the death of his queen and the exposure of his daughter, incurs an Oedipus-like end. Unwittingly reunited with his daughter, he falls in love with her and tyrannically pursues her with his lust. When finally made aware of his incestuous urges, and "calling to mind how . . . contrarie to the law of nature he had lusted after his own daughter . . . he fell into a melancholie fit, and to close up the Comedie with a Tragicall stratageme, he slewe himselfe."[20] Needless to say, Shakespeare avoids this incest tragedy of Oedipal self-destruction, and changes the tragic into a happy ending by resurrecting Hermione. The tragedy of the first part of *The Winter's Tale* is turned into romance in the second part.

At the same time, the second half of *The Winter's Tale* avoids the overt Christian references of the first. Here Polixenes, when suspected of treason, sees himself linked with Judas "that did betray the Best" (I, 2). Earlier on, he remembers his childhood, when neither he nor Leontes knew

> The doctrine of ill-doing, nor dream'd
> That any did. Had we pursu'd that life,
> And our weak spirits ne'er been higher rear'd
> With stronger blood, we should have answer'd heaven
> Boldly 'Not guilty,' the imposition clear'd
> Hereditary ours.   (I, 2)

Yet for all that, there is little reason to claim that the entire play bears out "the Christian view of the historical redemption of the human race" (J. A. Bryant)[21] or corroborates, "without copying, the Christian revelation" (G. Wilson Knight).[22] For Christian elements, like tragic ones, are conspicuously absent from the second part of *The Winter's Tale*. Instead, we find a proliferating host of pagan divinities in a world in which Apollo's oracle, rather than Christian providence, guides men's destinies. The one person to think of a Christian concept, "the life to come," decides to "sleep out the thought of it" (IV, 3).

In invoking his power "To o'erthrow law and in one self-born hour / To plant and o'erwhelm custom," Time, then, clearly refers to the general transition from tragedy to romance as much as to the author's breach of the unities. How otherwise could the tale he is about to unfold "make stale / The glistering of this present" or, in other words, disrupt what we have seen already? A breach of the unities was nothing new in Shakespeare's oeuvre, and even the fourteen-year gap between Acts III and IV of *Pericles* had not elicited similar comments. Gower, in his Prologue, no more than refers to "our fast-growing scene." Time's statements about planting and overwhelming custom in one self-born hour to all evidence refer to structural and thematic changes in *The Winter's Tale*, of which the sixteen-year lapse between Acts III and IV is only a signal. On the one hand, there is the teleological pattern – both tragic and Christian – in part one; on the other, "Time's news" or "th' argument of Time," in part two. If the first half is ruled by what is traditional, then the second will revert to a sense of things "ere ancient'st order was / Or what is now receiv'd."[23]

With his emphasis on contraries such as "please" and "try," "joy" and "terror," "good" and "bad," "make" and "unfold," "plant" and "o'erwhelm," all perpetrated in the name of this primordial time, the Chorus implies what will replace the traditional order of tragic and Christian teleology. In fact, the scene just preceding the Chorus already prepared us for this transition. Here Antigonus and the sailors incur death, while Perdita, though abandoned to die, survives. Nevill Coghill aptly calls the scene "a kind of dramaturgical hinge, a moment of planned structural antithesis"[24] which seems to sum up the entire play in miniature. There is death and life, with a separate on-stage spectator reporting on each spectacle. The Clown tells the Shepherd of Antigonus' and the sailors' death, the Shepherd the Clown of the little foundling. Shakespeare, in the Shepherd's words, suggests the cyclical sense of life that is about to replace the teleological thrust of what we have seen so far:

Now bless thyself: thou met'st with things dying, I with things new-born.   (III, 3)

THE POETICS OF CYCLICAL RETURN

Throughout the second part of *The Winter's Tale*, the rebirth theme is emphasized with all the new symbolist techniques Shakespeare first developed in *Pericles*. Everywhere in the earlier play, as discussed in a previous study,[25] we find the imagery of seasonal change: flowers on tombs, things dying, and things new-born intertwine with equally numerous shipwrecks, seeming deaths, and resurrection ceremonies, along with the attendant paraphernalia of tombstones, corpses, and magic. The death and rebirth symbolism in the second part of *The Winter's Tale* is less contrived but equally insistent. As in *Pericles*, the playwright rarely misses an opportunity to express his cyclical sense of life. When Perdita, at the sheepshearing feast, wishes to strew Florizel "o'er and o'er" with flowers, her lover half-jokingly asks "What, like a corse?", eliciting the appropriately symbolist reply from Perdita:

No; like a bank for love to lie and play on;
Not like a corse; or if – not to be buried,
But quick, and in mine arms.   (IV, 4)

Particularly emphasized in a winter's tale about rebirth is the imagery of seasonal change, and of life and death in general. Camillo, to give only a few examples, desires to lay his bones in Sicily (IV, 2). Perdita, in Florizel's view, is given a life by her Flora costume (IV, 4). Paulina, in remembering the "dead" Hermione, talks of the life–death dichotomy in terms of its eternal return.

> As every present time doth boast itself
> Above a better gone, so must thy grave
> Give way to what's seen now!   (V, 1)

To Leontes, the arrival of Florizel and his bride is as welcome as "the spring to th' earth" (V, 1). Perdita, in associating the ages of her unknown guests "With flow'rs of winter," relates the seasons to the notions of life and death:

> Sir, the year growing ancient,
> Not yet on summer's death nor on the birth
> Of trembling winter, the fairest flow'rs o' th' season
> Are our carnations and streak'd gillyvors.   (IV, 4)

As in *Pericles*, these life–death cycles in *The Winter's Tale* are connected with various classical divinities centered round "great creating nature."[26] Nature, Lucina, goddess of childbirth, and Diana, "goddess argentine," preside over the various birth, death, and rebirth rituals of the earlier play.[27] In *The Winter's Tale*, the mythological backdrop to the rebirth theme has simply become more complex and diversified. The oracle of Apollo, whose isle is called fertile (III, 1), prophesies that Leontes "shall live without an heir, if that which is lost be not found" (III, 2). Apollo, Neptune, and Jupiter, though immortal, nonetheless undergo metamorphoses into various beasts (IV, 4). Perdita, dressed up as Flora, also invokes the goddess who more than all others symbolized the eternal rhythms of life and death to classical antiquity:

> O Proserpina,
> For the flowers now that, frighted, thou let'st fall
> From Dis's waggon!   (IV, 4)

Perdita does not tell the rest of the story. Here Proserpine is abducted by Dis, alias Pluto, to the underworld, but finally, upon her mother Ceres' intercession with Jupiter, is allowed to return to the upper world for six months each year. However, Shakespeare no doubt was familiar with the full myth from reading Ovid's *Metamorphoses* (v, 487–502). In fact, he returned to it in *The Tempest*, where Ceres, in the wedding masque for Ferdinand and Miranda, explains how "dusky Dis [her] daughter got" (IV, 1).

The endless cycles of life and death, which Proserpine stands for, are spoken of in another part of Ovid's *Metamorphoses*:

> Nothing remains the same: the great renewer,
> Nature, makes form from form, and, oh, believe me
> That nothing ever dies. What we call birth
> Is the beginning of a difference,
> No more than that, the death is only ceasing
> Of what had been before. The parts may vary
> Shifting from here to there, hither and yon,
> And back again, but that great sum is constant. (XV, 251–8)[28]

Other sources available to Shakespeare and his audience linked Proserpine directly with cyclical rebirth. A 1584 interpretation of Ovid's fables makes it clear that "Proserpina foecunditatem seminum significat."[29] Another handbook of classical myth, Francis Bacon's *De Sapientia Veterum*, which appeared in 1609 (that is, shortly before the writing of *The Winter's Tale*), relates Proserpine "to Nature, and explains the source of that rich and fruitful supply of active power subsisting in the under-world, from which all the growths of our upper world spring, and into which they again return and are resolved."[30] To be sure, such interpretations are not directly echoed in Shakespeare's mention of Proserpine and Dis; but they sum up the main theme of the play, as climactically embodied in the last scene. Polixenes, shortly after Hermione's "rebirth," wonders "where she has liv'd, / Or how stol'n from the dead" (V, 3) like a second Proserpine.

Looking back from here over the play in its entirety, we realize that the transition from part one to part two – from tragedy to romance, from a teleological to a cyclical sense of life – is one of careful integration rather than contrast. The imagery of death and rebirth, though initially used with anticlimactic effect, is there from the very beginning. The friendship between Leontes and Polixenes, which, Camillo thinks, "cannot choose but branch now" (I, 1), is to die in the very next scene. Mamillius, in Archidamus' eyes "a gentleman of the greatest promise that ever came into [his] note," is to suffer real death shortly afterwards. On the other hand, the two courtiers are made to utter truths on a level they are not even aware of. In evoking the coming summer or in talking about things rooted that are about to branch, they weave the opening patterns of a finely knit symbolist tapestry spreading over the entire play.

In turn, Mamillius, who in the courtiers' view "physics the subject," making "old hearts fresh" so that those "that went on crutches ere he was born desire yet their life to see him a man," is made to appear as an oracle of his own death. At the same time, he unwittingly weaves further configurations of the rebirth theme. This happens in a scene which also presents the theme in more concrete fashion. Hermione, pregnant with the future Perdita, has of late, as one of her ladies remarks, spread into "a goodly bulk" (II, 1). Mamillius is adept at frightening his mother with his ghostly tales, and when Hermione asks him to tell a tale "As merry as [he] will," he characteristically proposes to deliver one of his specialties instead. "A sad tale's best for winter," he says, "I have one / Of sprites and goblins." But, with the jealous Leontes storming into this wintry idyll, Mamillius never gets beyond his opening lines, which, if read at their deeper symbolic level, forebode his imminent death. "There was a man . . . Dwelt by a churchyard – I will tell it softly; / Yond crickets shall not hear it" (II, 1). In a play whose title derives from his last words, Mamillius will not speak again, and the winter's tale about a rebirth in spring, which the opening scene misleadingly invests in his person, will find its fulfillment in others. Tragedy will turn to romance, but in a way which, however devious, is prepared from the beginning. In other words, the tragic as well as Christian patterns are absorbed into the new ones.

There are other themes in this first part of *The Winter's Tale* which, in retrospect, help subsume the teleological first half of the play within an overall cyclical structure. The fertility associated with Apollo and his oracle points beyond death towards rebirth. More importantly, "great creating nature" (IV, 4), who presides over the rebirth cycles of the second part, is twice introduced in the first half. Linked to Perdita's birth in both cases, nature appears as a force independent of, as well as contrary to, the tragic destiny of Leontes. "This child," as Paulina explains to the jailor,

> was prisoner to the womb, and is
> By law and process of great Nature thence
> Freed and enfranchis'd – not a party to
> The anger of the King, nor guilty of,
> If any be, the trespass of the Queen.   (II, 2)

By law and process of great nature, the newborn, at least as far as the sins of its parents are concerned, is cleared of the "doctrine of ill-doing . . . Hereditary ours" (I, 2). In fact, Polixenes' words to that effect now sound like a similar refutation of hereditary sin. For if a child can be thought to be free of it, then such collective guilt has obviously ceased to exist in the strictly hereditary sense. At the same time, the law and process of great Nature, where they first emerge in *The Winter's Tale*, are associated with a cyclical rather than teleological order of time. Paulina, Shakespeare's main agent in leading the play from its first to its second part, here again is made to advocate this new sense of nature while Leontes negates it. Leontes' own daughter, a mere copy of himself engendered by the "good goddess Nature," remains unrecognizable to the King in his tragic blindness.

> *Paulina*:   It is yours.
> And, might we lay th' old proverb to your charge,
> So like you 'tis the worse. Behold, my lords,
> Although the print be little, the whole matter
> And copy of the father – eye, nose, lip,
> The trick of 's frown, his forehead; nay, the valley,
> The pretty dimples of his chin and cheek; his smiles;
> The very mould and frame of hand, nail, finger.
> And thou, good goddess Nature, which hast made it
> So like to him that got it, if thou hast
> The ordering of the mind too, 'mongst all colours
> No yellow in 't, lest she suspect, as he does,
> Her children not her husband's!   (II, 3)

Again, there are multiple elements in both plot and characterization in the first half of *The Winter's Tale* which, in retrospect, feed into the cyclical structure of the entire play. As E. Schanzer and others have shown, a startling number of incidents, scenic constellations, etc., in part one are paralleled, almost repeated, in part two.[31] To name some of the more obvious instances: Polixenes, towards the end, displays a tyranny comparable to Leontes' in the beginning; Camillo, having saved Polixenes from Leontes' fury, later saves Florizel from Polixenes'. The principal effect of these repetitions, as another critic writes, "is not of a circle but of a spiral."[32] In other words, human life, however cyclically we may experience it, never repeats itself completely. "Plus ça change, plus c'est la même chose." Even the ending of *The Winter's Tale*, in recalling an earlier scene, simply points beyond the play to another "conclusion" of similar kind that might follow it. There is nothing "decisively accomplished" in a teleological sense. Symbolically speaking, the wheel of life has come full circle. But, as in other Shakespearean romances, we know that it will keep on revolving beyond the somewhat artificially tagged-on "happy ending." We are never left without a reminder that whatever rebirth is finally achieved is a rebirth into mortal life and not into immortality. While surprised to see how closely the statue resembles his former wife, Leontes notes that "Hermione was not so much wrinkled, nothing / So aged as this seems";[33] and just after Hermione's "resurrection" Paulina reminds the King of his wife's ever-imminent mortality:

> Do not shun her
> Until you see her die again; for then
> You kill her double.   (V, 3)

Teleology, or the fall and tragedy of Leontes in the first part, then, is subsumed within the cyclical sense of life in the second. Linear time pointing toward the future is absorbed into circular time drawing us in on the present.

The Winter's Tale seems to comment on some of these facts in its very title. Instead of the generic terms we expect – a tragedy, comedy, or history – we are told that what we are to see is a tale. What is more, it is not a tale of people and human events, but a winter's tale. Jacobeans probably associated the phrase with little else than "an old trivial tale ... to while away a winter evening."[34] Still, they would have been quick to realize that such proverbial legerdemain is gradually charged with deeper meaning as the play unfolds before our eyes. An actual "winter's tale" told by Mamillius is interrupted by a force which will cause the storyteller's death. This tragedy concludes with Paulina telling the protagonist that even ten thousand years of repentance "Upon a barren mountain, and still winter / In storm perpetual, could not move the gods" to forgive him for his misdeeds (III, 2). It is disrupted by Time's "tale" about a revival of the life forces which winter only put into a slumber. Autolycus' song leading up to the sheepshearing feast with its multiple symbolism of rebirth and seasonal change, introduces the new theme in its first stanza:

> When daffodils begin to peer,
>   With heigh! the doxy over the dale,
> Why, then comes in the sweet o' the year,
>   For the red blood reigns in the winter's pale.   (IV, 3)

At the same time, Autolycus' song makes a statement about the art of poetry familiar from the Winter and Spring songs in *Love's Labour's Lost*. These two lyrics are crowded with people whom we all seem to see and hear move around and do things. But not a single word is spoken by any of them. Instead we hear the singing of the cuckoo, the hooting of the owl, and the blowing of the winter wind. Language, in these songs, is the language of nature. This is also true of Autolycus' song, which amounts to an even more explicit comment on an "art / That nature makes." There are the sounds of the birds – "O, how they sing!" Their twitterings are "songs" to Autolycus. Moreover, they act as aphrodisiacs when he and his beggar-woman lady friends play the beast with two backs in some haystack:

> The lark, that tirra-lirra chants,
>   With heigh! with heigh! the thrush and the jay,
> Are summer songs for me and my aunts,
>   While we lie tumbling in the hay.   (IV, 3)

AN "ART THAT NATURE MAKES"

What finally, if looked at afresh in the light of what has been said so far, is this "art / That nature makes"? The words, of course, are from the Perdita–Polixenes debate, whose basic argument is well known. Perdita trying to relate her flowers to both the annual seasons and the ages of man, apologizes for lacking the kind of flowers which would best befit the time of year as well as the age of her older guests.[35] For to her the "carnations and streak'd gillyvors" most suited for this purpose are products of a grafting process and hence deserve to be called "nature's bastards." There is obvious irony when Polixenes, who is about to disrupt the matching of his "bud of nobler race" to "a bark of baser kind," opposes Perdita's attitude:

> *Polixenes*:   Wherefore, gentle maiden,
>   Do you neglect them?
> *Perdita*:   For I have heard it said
>   There is an art which in their piedness shares
>   With great creating nature.
> *Polixenes*:   Say there be;
>   Yet nature is made better by no mean
>   But nature makes that mean; so over that art,
>   Which you say adds to nature, is an art
>   That nature makes. You see, sweet maid, we marry
>   A gentler scion to the wildest stock,
>   And make conceive a bark of baser kind
>   By bud of nobler race. This is an art
>   Which does mend nature – change it rather; but
>   The art itself is nature.   (IV, 4)

It is customary to treat Perdita's and Polixenes' attitudes as two conflicting viewpoints, one advocating a primitivist view of art as a completely unadulterated enactment of nature, the other defending "the distinctive human power to improve and civilize the environment."[36] In this way, Perdita is said to reflect Montaigne's attack on the grafting process in "Of Cannibals," while Polixenes' side of the argument is associated with Puttenham's use of horticultural imagery in *The Arte of English Poesie*.[37] And indeed the resemblances are striking enough to invite such conjecture. As Montaigne writes,

we call wild the fruits that Nature has produced by herself and in her normal course; whereas really it is those that we have changed artificially and led astray from the common order, that we should rather call wild. The former retain alive and vigorous their genuine, their most useful and natural, virtues and properties, which we have debased in the latter in adapting them to gratify our corrupted taste ... It is not reasonable that art should win the place of honor over our great and powerful mother

Nature. We have so overloaded the beauty and richness of her works by our inventions that we have quite smothered her.[38]

Even closer to Shakespeare is Puttenham's analogy of the artist with the gardener, in which the critic even mentions Perdita's "gillyvors." Discussing various relations between art and nature, Puttenham considers the case in which

arte is not only an aide and coadiutor to nature in all her actions but an alterer of them, and in some sort a surmounter of her skill, so as by meanes of it her owne effects shall appeare more beautifull or straunge and miraculous. . . . And the Gardiner by his arte will not onely make an herbe or flowr, or fruite, come forth in his season without impediment, but also will embellish the same in vertue, shape, odour, and taste, that nature of her selfe woulde neuer haue done, as to make single gillifloure, or marigold, or daisie, double . . . any of which things nature could not doe without mans help and arte.[39]

After setting up this dichotomy, one is tempted to conclude with Lovejoy and Boas that Shakespeare, favoring the Polixenes–Puttenham side of the argument, intended the whole debate as a "devastating comment upon the primitivism of Montaigne."[40]

But the dichotomy itself is a false one. For one thing, Perdita and Polixenes never really take opposite sides. After listening to the King's argument, Perdita, though refusing to make her garden rich in gillyvors, replies "So it is." It is also erroneous to see Polixenes' attitude in direct analogy to Puttenham's. Though the King may echo the critic's words, his argument is clearly different. To Puttenham, art, like the gardener's grafting process, works toward a definite improvement of nature. Polixenes, though seemingly geared toward the same conclusion, corrects himself in midline – "This is an art / Which does mend nature – change it rather" – adding "but / The art itself is nature." Perdita and Polixenes, then, are in basic agreement concerning an art "That nature makes." Their main difference is that Polixenes allows for the use of artifice in this process while Perdita opposes it, though in rather half-hearted fashion.

It is equally misleading to maintain that Polixenes' "an art / That nature makes" merely repeats a commonplace. As a book on *Nature and Art in Renaissance Literature* tries to convince us, the King's argument, though it "may appear sophistical," "is in fact an orthodox statement of the 'real' significance of the ancient opposition:"

Aristotle had argued in the *Physics* that when we claim that Art perfects Nature we do in fact mean in the last analysis that Nature perfects herself: "The best illustration is a doctor doctoring himself: nature is like that." And Plato in the tenth book of the *Laws* had maintained that the good legislator "ought to support the law and also art, and acknowledge that both alike exist by nature, and no less than nature."[41]

Such analogies simply presume that *The Winter's Tale* shares its basic concept of nature with Aristotle's *Physics* and Plato's *Laws*. They tacitly imply that Perdita's and Polixenes' use of the word points to an either teleological or ideational notion rather than to, say, a Heraclitean understanding of life. This also is the conclusion drawn by Harold S. Wilson after exploring the concept of nature in Renaissance literary theory. It was the age's controlling assumption, Wilson writes, "that literary art is an organic part of a cosmically uniform and regular design from which literature derives its own fixed laws concerning aims, methods, and taste." The conviction, ultimately derived from antiquity, but more directly from the Middle Ages, is based on "the symbolic conception of *Natura* as the creative and administrative agent of the divine purposes in all things, *ministra et factura dei*." Polixenes' comments on the "art / That nature makes," in H. S. Wilson's view, then, simply reiterate the traditional idea of cosmic nature as "exercising some kind of normative control upon literary art."[42]

But little in *The Winter's Tale* seems to bear out this supposition. The play, on the contrary, seems to offer a critique of the idea. Teleological time, as manifest in the fall and tragedy of Leontes, is disrupted and gradually subsumed by a sense of cyclical return, as manifest in the imagery, structure, and plot of the play as a whole. The "art / That nature makes" exemplified by *The Winter's Tale* is prompted, not by *Natura* as "the creative and administrative agent of the divine purposes," but by Time, who causes things to be born, destroyed, and reborn in endless cycles. Even Leontes' "tragedy," which, with the protagonist breaking down in repentance, gives us the sense of "something decisively accomplished" through suffering, is simply caught up in a revo-

lution of this ever-turning wheel. It is true that Hermione invokes
divine providence:

> if pow'rs divine
> Behold our human actions, as they do,
> I doubt not then but innocence shall make
> False accusation blush, and tyranny
> Tremble at patience –   (III, 2)

And she is proven right regarding herself.

But how about Mamillius, Antigonus and the drowned sailors?
Did the divine powers allow innocence to prevail in their case?
Similarly, Apollo's oracle may be fulfilled in the end; but, in a
final sense, even Apollo and all the other gods either enact the
endless cycles of death and rebirth like Proserpine or are subject
to the metamorphoses of Time's argument. Apollo, Neptune,
and Jupiter all assumed the shape of beasts, "Humbling their
deities to love" (IV, 4). As in Homer, where the Olympians are
filled with horror at the hateful chambers of decay, there is an
ultimate force stronger even than the gods.[43] While Ovid's *Metamorphoses* gives Shakespeare his mythology, the *Corpus Hermeticum* may have reinforced him in this more general sense of life
surrounding it. Here the energy animating the "great and perfect
Animal the World" in endless cycles of "making" and "unmak-
ing" even governs the destiny of the gods:

And every generation of animated flesh, and of the fruit of seed, and of
all art energy; those which are diminished, shall be renewed by necessity, and by renewal of Gods, and by course of periodical circle of Nature.
For Divine is the whole cosmical composition renovated by Nature.[44]

In sum, Shakespeare's "art / That nature makes" in *The Winter's
Tale* seems to reverse rather than follow the mainstream Renaissance notion about the interrelationship of nature to art. Most
aestheticians then thought that art, as Aristotle put it, "partly
completes what nature cannot bring to a finish" and fills out "the
deficiencies of nature."[45] Art, as Sir Hugh Plat wrote in 1602,
"might helpe where Nature made a faile."[46] Even aestheticians
who, like Daniel, protested that "Nature . . . is aboue all Arte"[47]
can hardly be said to anticipate what Shakespeare seems to imply
through Perdita and Polixenes. For almost all of them associated

nature with a telelogical or ideational order of things of which art becomes the direct expression. There are exceptions, of course, but hardly among the aestheticians themselves. When Montaigne exclaims that he "would naturalize art as much as they artify nature,"[48] we find one, and when Bacon protests that "nature ... governs everthing"[49] including human artifice, another. But their concept of nature was the result of an unprecedented dismantling of essentialist metaphysics which few contemporaries, and least of all the tradition-bound critics, had the intellectual daring to equal or even to follow.

The final scene of *The Winter's Tale*, in which Shakespeare's "art / That nature makes" receives its emblematic *coup de théâtre* enactment, presents us with similar reversals of Renaissance aesthetics.[50] To be sure, comments on the statue and its creator are in a way traditional enough. "But here it is," announces Paulina, "Prepare / To see the life as lively mock'd as ever / Still sleep mock'd death." "Masterly done!" confirms Polixenes. "The very life seems warm upon her lip." To Leontes, "The fixure of her eye has motion in't, / As we are mock'd with art" (V, 3). This terminology of primitive *trompe l'oeil* illusionism can be traced back to Pliny's mention of Zeuxis' painted grapes, which were pecked at by living crows, and to even earlier sources. It counts among the stock-in-trade of Renaissance art criticism which Shakespeare had drawn on in earlier works, most notably in Bassanio's description of Portia's counterfeit in *The Merchant of Venice* (III, 2).

Even here, however, Shakespeare avoids the notion of an ideational or teleological improvement upon nature which customarily went along with this *ars simia naturae* concept during the Renaissance.[51] This is most obvious in the extended comment on Julio Romano "who, had he himself eternity and could put breath into his work, would beguile Nature of her custom, so perfectly he is her ape" (V, 2). The artist, it is suggested here, *would have* been able to equal the feats of nature if he had been eternal and had owned the power to bring his creations alive. But those precisely are the powers he lacked. By contrast, Julio Romano's epitaph, reported by Vasari, and Shakespeare's possible source here, conveys an altogether Neoplatonic understanding of art.

There the artist is credited with the divine powers denied him in
The Winter's Tale: "Jupiter saw sculpted and painted bodies
breathe and the homes of mortals made equal to those in heaven
through the skill of Giulio Romano. Thus angered he summoned
a council of all the gods, and he removed that man from the earth,
lest he be exposed, conquered, or equalled by an earth-born
man."[52]

But the traditional fondness for a *trompe l'oeil* verisimilitude of
art to life is most drastically undercut when Hermione is
"reborn." In this sense, it is somewhat pointless to trace the
whole "history of statues coming to life"[53] as a background to the
Shakespearean scene. For Hermione, who only pretends to be a
statue, is the very opposite of Pygmalion's statue. Hence, the
audience, misled by the playwright, is suddenly made to realize
that what was thought to be art is really nature. Shakespeare, as
Jean H. Hagstrum puts it, "has reversed the situation that usually
prevails in the art epigram. Art has not defeated nature; nature
has defeated art."[54]

In turn, it seems misleading to claim that this final symbolic
gesture for an "art / That nature makes" turns *The Winter's Tale*
into a negation of art. "The Shakespeare of this play," as the same
critic concludes,

finds only temporary and limited value in art. It is nature and reality that
finally satisfy ... *The Winter's Tale* is a negation of one element in the
pictorialist and iconic tradition. The birds in the trees, even though they
are dying generations, are preferable to the birds of hammered gold and
gold enameling set upon a golden bough to keep an emperor awake.[55]

Shakespeare's art indeed avoids the idealization of Yeats's
Byzantium poems and instead reenacts the dying generations of
nature's rhythms. But this by no means amounts to a denial of art
as such. Polixenes' "art / That nature makes," as we have seen,
makes full allowance for artifice. And that, again, is the message
conveyed by *The Winter's Tale* as a whole.

It is hard to think of another work by Shakespeare in which the
theme of art's fictionality in general is pursued with similar
insistence. The comments on Autolycus' ballads to this effect are,
of course, as satirical as Shakespeare's implied depiction of the
mountebank's audience. Despite Autolycus' outrageously facile

tricks of make-believe, "all men's ears" are said to grow "to his tunes" (IV, 4):

Clown: What hast here? Ballads?
Mopsa: Pray now, buy some. I love a ballad in print a-life, for then we are sure they are true.
Autolycus: Here's one to a very doleful tune: how a usurer's wife was brought to bed of twenty money-bags at a burden, and how she long'd to eat adders' heads and toads carbonado'd.
Mopsa: Is it true, think you?
Autolycus: Very true, and but a month old . . . Here's another ballad, of a fish that appeared upon the coast on Wednesday the fourscore of April, forty thousand fathom above water, and sung this ballad against the hard hearts of maids. It was thought she was a woman, and was turn'd into a cold fish for she would not exchange flesh with one that lov'd her. The ballad is very pitiful, and as true.
Dorcas: Is it true too, think you?
Autolycus: Five justices' hands at it; and witnesses more than my pack will hold.   (IV, 4)

But what is satire here merely enhances a deeply ironical sense of fictionality which permeates the entire play.

From the start, Jacobeans, not unlike us, would associate a "winter's tale" with something trivial and untrue. This sense is reinforced by Mamillius' fragmentary "winter's tale" about sprites and goblins. Time's "argument," "news," and "tale," then, finally turn out to be what we are somehow made to expect from the start. They are "so like an old tale that the verity of it is in strong suspicion" (V, 2). The words here apply to how the oracle was fulfilled and the King's daughter found. They are repeated almost verbatim when someone tells the story of Antigonus' death – "Like an old tale still, which will have matter to rehearse, though credit be asleep and not an ear open" (V, 2). They are heard once again when Paulina comments on Hermione's rebirth: "That she is living, / Were it but told you, should be hooted at / Like an old tale" (V, 3).[56]

Three separate tales, then, by way of summing up the play in miniature, once more take us through a full cycle of birth, death, and rebirth. Time's argument, however unbelievable, is one of life and death, "joy and terror," a duality which, along with the fictionality of what we witness, is repeatedly stressed in the narratives themselves. In the way these refer, for instance, to the "dignity of this act" full of pretty touches and worth "the audience of kings and princes," they seem to report stage events rather than real ones. Hermione's "rebirth," as we have seen, symbolically inverts the Renaissance commonplace of the statue that comes alive. In turn, the play's narrators seem to reverse this reversal by petrifying the living persons they talk about in the artifice of their storytelling:

> there was speech in their dumbness, language in their very gesture; they look'd as they had heard of a world ransom'd, or one destroyed. A notable passion of wonder appeared in them; but the wisest beholder that knew no more but seeing could not say if th' importance were joy or sorrow.   (V, 2)

If *The Winter's Tale* embodies the "art / That nature makes," then artifice, so Shakespeare seems to insist, is clearly part of such an art, however natural. So in one sense the playwright might have agreed with Montaigne in his endeavor to naturalize art where others artify nature. An art prompted by nature, in other words, should be free from the teleological preconceptions of both Christian and classical aesthetics. Life is mere flux, and art tries to enact this flux without subjecting it to forms that imply such "fore-conceite[s]" or ideas. But this does not mean that art should or can dispense with the artifice of its medium.

Here again, as in Theseus' discussion of the imagination, Shakespeare, for all his insistence on a lifelike openness of art's contents, stresses both the need for conscious craftsmanship in the creative process and the inescapable artificiality of art's products. Art, in other words, can never be life, nor life art, and the pretense that they might only spoils the genuineness of an art that, as Polixenes puts it, is nature itself. For except where it reflects our metaphysical fantasies about nature rather than nature itself, even artifice is ultimately part of the natural process:[57]

> so over that art,
> Which you say adds to nature, is an art
> That nature makes.   (IV, 4)

As far as I can tell, only one of Shakespeare's contemporaries parallels this theory in all its complexity; but when he did so the playwright had long departed from life. To Sir Francis Bacon, writing in 1623, it was an error to assume that art "is something different from nature, and things artificial different from things natural."

But there is likewise another and more subtle error which has crept into the human mind; namely, that of considering art as merely an assistant to nature, having the power indeed to finish what nature has begun, to correct her when lapsing into error, or to set her free when in bondage, but by no means to change, transmute, or fundamentally alter nature . . . Whereas men ought on the contrary to be surely persuaded of this, that the artificial does not differ from the natural in form or essence, but only in the efficient . . . Still therefore it is nature which governs everything; but under nature are included these three: the *course* of nature, the *wanderings* of nature, and *art* or nature with man to help.[58]

In sum, Shakespeare, like Bacon and Montaigne, dissolves the traditional dichotomy between art and nature.[59] And once again, this joint impulse derives from the three authors' common anti-essentialist bias. Art and nature: regardless of which of the two was thought to be superior to the other in more traditional Renaissance theorizing, there was the basic assumption of a higher order behind the flux of phenomena which art could or ought to reveal to us. If art was superior to nature, it was because nature was identified with this world of phenomena rather than with the "real," that is to say essentialist, world. If nature was superior to art, it was because nature was identified with the higher order of the cosmos, which simply communicated its laws to those of art. But to the antiessentialist, higher orders of this kind have ceased to exist. There is only one nature, the world of flux and cyclical return, of which human artistic endeavor is as much a part as any "natural" process. Far from revealing the truth *behind* things, art can at best try to capture the mystery of what *is*. In that sense, art is like nature, and nature, to quote Montaigne, is "nothing but an enigmatic poem . . . [or] a veiled and shadowy picture, shining through here and there with an infinite variety of false lights to exercise our conjectures."[60]

Shakespeare, speaking through the veiled and shadowy picture of *The Winter's Tale*, expresses himself in more tentative manner. At the same time, his concept of an "art / That nature makes" nowhere negates the element of artifice. Here he differs from Montaigne with his consistent appeal to "naturalize art as much as they artify nature."[61] As a *tour de force* illustration of Polixenes' doctrine, *The Winter's Tale*, like no other work by Shakespeare, also stresses this message regarding the artificiality of its medium. A play, after all, is a play, and no amount of talk about an "art / That nature makes" will teach us otherwise. However, it is obviously a special kind of play, and what the title suggests about that is three times repeated in the final act. A "winter's tale" is not like a drama, with the usual teleological build-up and conclusion, but more like an improbable old story which could somehow go on forever.[62] What is more, it is a tale about what one critic calls "the life-death-life pattern of nature, and of human existence."[63] "Spring," as another puts it, "must inevitably turn to summer, summer to autumn, and autumn to winter."[64] There is death and rebirth, but only into another life on the way to death.[65]

Conclusion

The Winter's Tale, by either chance or intention, also reflects back upon the course which Shakespeare's poetics underwent between the great tragedies and the romances. The play's division into a tragic first and a romance-like second part has often been noted. More specifically, the first half is absorbed, or made to disappear, in an open cyclical structure that gradually overwhelms the closed, teleological thrust of Leontes' tragedy. The central symbol of this transformation, here and elsewhere in the romances, is "great creating nature" (IV, 4) in her dual aspect of life and death. Shakespeare, like Montaigne, increasingly turned towards this principle as he grew older.[1] But neither writer forgot that "the birth, nourishment, and growth of each thing," as the French philosopher wrote, "is the alteration and corruption of another."[2] Or, as Shakespeare's Shepherd puts it at the crucial point where tragedy turns romance in *The Winter's Tale*, "thou met'st with things dying, I with things new-born' (III, 3).

This present study has made no attempt to explore the growth of Shakespeare's views on his craft and creativity throughout his career. Perhaps, too, it would be more accurate to speak of a maturing process, rather than of an actual development along these lines. The diverse aspects of the playwright's poetics discussed in this volume – his attitude toward the arts of language in general, his ideas about the theatre and about acting, his treatment of the unities and of the audience, his concept of language generally and of poetic language in particular, his notions about the imagination and mythopoeic creativity, and finally his view of art in relation to nature – all these and other issues, however complex, show a remarkable interconnectedness in general orientation. In all of these aspects Shakespeare stands revealed as the "poet of nature." This is how he was seen by his contemporaries, and this, too, is how he seems to have viewed his own craft and creativity. Needless to say, the playwright was not a systematic philosopher, not even in the sense of being at least consistently inconsistent like Montaigne. However, all his implied and more direct comments on his poetics have a general tone or flavor that is recognizable in, for instance, the ironic dismissal of the "Sweet smoke of rhetoric"[3] as much as in the invocation of "a Muse of fire, that would ascend / The brightest heaven of invention."[4]

What at first sight, then, might seem to be a radically new and suddenly emerging idea is often revealed in retrospect as a mere change of emphasis. Shakespeare's attitude toward his audience is a case in point. Where critics like Castelvetro and Piccolomini worked out irreconcilable dichotomies of how the spectators would either identify themselves with or detach themselves from the dramatic illusion, Shakespeare asks them to range freely from one to the other. This demand for a protean audience participation was first given full articulation in the choruses of *Henry V*. But it is already summed up *in nuce* in what Shakespeare, in *The Rape of Lucrece* and again in *The Taming of the Shrew*, has to say about a spectator's imaginative collaboration with the artist in viewing a painting. Or take the playwright's attitude toward language. Different critics have tried to show how Shakespeare, at this or that point in his career, went through a sudden phase of doubt regarding his basic medium; but when all their arguments are added up, then such a crisis seems to have been a more or less lifelong affair.

No doubt there was a phase when Shakespeare, perhaps while "in a temporary disillusionment with the stage,"[5] made more explicit what at other times was merely taken for granted. It was then that his basic antiessentialism and linguistic skepticism may have gained in intensity. This is obvious from *Troilus and Cressida*, a play remarkable for its near theorematic dismantling of essentialist discourse and its underlying metaphysic. But, then, how about *Love's Labour's Lost*, a much earlier play, which, though in a more cheerful vein, shows a comparably antiessentialist bias while deflating similar linguistic pretense? Not to speak of the

Sonnets, which show even stronger parallels to *Troilus* in the way in which Will's idealistic claims are brought to collapse in a "madness of discourse."[6] We simply do not know when precisely before 1609 most of these poems were written, although at least one of them (138), which stands out for such linguistic skepticism, was already pirated by 1599. There is equal uncertainty as to when precisely Shakespeare evolved the mythopoetics which is most fully articulated in Prospero's wedding masque for Ferdinand and Miranda. For most of what is implied there is already summed up in Theseus' comments on the imagination, whose inverted Platonism in turn finds a precedent in Berowne's speech about the true poet's "fiery numbers."[7]

The most common background informing these various attitudes toward his audience, his medium, his imagination, and other aspects of his poetics – Shakespeare's antiessentialist bias – again by no means emerged suddenly at a specific point in the poet's life. Granted that *The Winter's Tale*, as it overtly moves from a teleological towards a cyclical view of life, is the clearest statement to that effect. Equally radical is how the play accounts for this transformation in terms of an art prompted by the same cyclical understanding of nature. But the transcendence of teleology is already a major theme in *Troilus*, while a basic antiessentialism appears as early as in *Love's Labour's Lost* and *Venus and Adonis*. Also in the latter poem, the playwright first inverts the traditional concept whereby art either imposes its essentialist matrix upon nature or derives such a matrix from the laws inherent in nature itself. In sum, even in matters revealing his most radical dissent from the Renaissance consensus, Shakespeare, as he grew older, simply spelt out more clearly what in principle was there from the beginning.

Notes

Shakespeare quotations are from Peter Alexander's edition of *The Complete Works* (London and Glasgow: Collins, 1973). They are identified in the text (by act and scene) wherever the title of the individual work is either named or otherwise self-evident (from, say, the mention of Romeo or Lucrece). Else, they are listed (by act, scene, and line numbers) in the annotations. Other references in the annotations are given in abbreviations (author's name plus short title of book or of journal with volume number and year) throughout. For full references see Bibliography.

Notes to Introduction

1 Ben Jonson, [*Works*], VIII, 583–4 (*Discoveries*); I, 133 (*Conversations with Drummond*); VIII, 391 [Poem to the memory of Shakespeare]; VIII, 633, 586 (*Discoveries*). For a general, though somewhat one-sidedly Ben Jonsonian, discussion of Jonson's relationship to Shakespeare, see S. Musgrove, *Shakespeare and Jonson, passim*. For recent discussions of Jonson's 1623 poem to the memory of Shakespeare, see F. M. Fetrow, *EL* 2 (1975), 24–31; and S. van den Berg, *SSt* 11 (1978), 207–18.

2 Ben Jonson, [*Works*], VIII, 392. As Sara van den Berg writes, Jonson's poem for Shakespeare "may suggest something of the pressure he felt to reconcile his own poetics to Shakespeare's . . . By the end of the poem, Shakespeare also becomes the norm for critics, looking down from the heavens as a very Jonsonian critic" (*SSt* 11 (1978), 213, 214).

3 F. Beaumont, "To Mr. B. J.," quoted in E. K. Chambers, *Shakespeare*, II, 224.

4 J. Denham, "Upon Mr. *John Fletcher's* Playes," in F. Beaumont and J. Fletcher, *Works*, I, xxiii.

5 W. Cartwright (Commendatory Poem) (F. Beaumont and J. Fletcher, *Works*, I, xl).

6 R. Flecknoe, *Discourse*, n.p. See also L. Digges's "Next Nature onely helpt him" [commendatory verses to Shakespeare's *Poems* 1640], quoted in E. K. Chambers, *Shakespeare*, II, 232.

7 There are, of course, several works on Renaissance music in general. See bibliography for those by (or edited by) Paula Johnson, Elise B. Jorgens, Gustave Reese, and F. W. Sternfeld. A host of scholars (see Nan C. Carpenter, G. H. Cowling, John P. Cutts, John H. Long, A. H. Moncur-Sime, Edward W. Naylor, Richmond Noble, J. H. P. Pafford,

Peter J. Seng, F. W. Sternfeld) have dealt with Shakespeare and music, music on the Shakespearean stage, and the playwright's use of song; others (see Sir Frederick Bridge, Louis C. Elson, Phyllis Hartnoll) with Shakespearean music in the plays and early operas, as well as with Shakespeare's works in musical adaptation generally. Other studies (e.g., by J. B. Cutts, C. M. Dunn, R. W. Ingram, J. M. Nosworthy) deal with the function of music in the structure of Shakespeare's plays. See also S. K. Heninger, Jr, *Touches of Sweet Harmony*, pp. 4f. *et passim*.

8 Arthur H. R. Fairchild's *Shakespeare and the Art of Design* is one of the most comprehensive attempts along these lines. W. M. Merchant's *Shakespeare and the Artist* (1959), after an opening chapter about "The Elizabethan Theatre and the Visual Arts," deals primarily with the changing stage settings, etc., of Shakespearean theatrical productions through the centuries. William S. Heckscher's "Shakespeare in His Relationship to the Visual Arts ...," *RORD* 13–14 (1970–1), after an introductory survey of references revealing "Shakespeare's awareness of the fine arts" (pp. 8ff.) and "references to works of art explicit and oblique" (pp. 24ff.), focuses on the playwright's use of the figure of Patience. See also S. C. Hulse's erudite discussion of Shakespeare's over 200-line-long description of a painting or tapestry of Troy in *The Rape of Lucrece*, *SS* 31 (1978), 13–22.

9 See primarily J. H. Hagstrum's *Sister Arts*, pp. 79–80, 85–8, *et passim*. The connections between emblems and Elizabethan dramatic writings have been explored by D. Mehl, *RD* n.s. 2 (1969), 39–57, and others (cf. R. Juneja, *RR* n.s. 4 (1980), 86, note 8). R. M. Frye has written on "Ways of Seeing in Shakespearean Drama and Elizabethan Painting," *SQ* 31 (1980), 323–42, and promises further work along similar lines.

10 The standard work here is Sister Miriam Joseph's *Shakespeare's Use of the Arts of Language* (1947). See also V. K. Whitaker, *Shakespeare*, pp. 14ff. Brian Vickers gives a more recent survey of "Shakespeare's Use of Rhetoric," in *New Companion*, ed. K. Muir *et al.*, pp. 83–98. See also T. O. Sloan *et al.*, eds., *Rhetoric of Renaissance Poetry* (especially R. B. Waddington's "Shakespeare's Sonnet 15 and the Art of Memory," pp. 96–122), as well as R. A. Lanham, *Motives of Eloquence*, especially pp. 83–94 (on *Venus and Adonis*), 94–110 (on *The Rape of Lucrece*), 115–28 (on the Sonnets), 129–43 (on *Hamlet*) and 190–209 (on the *Henriad*). For a recent, structuralist account of "Rhetorical Norms in Renaissance Literature," see W. J. Kennedy's 1978 study of that title.

11 G. L. Brook's *Language of Shakespeare* (1976) gives a useful survey of the subject in general. See also M. M. Mahood's *Shakespeare's Wordplay*, especially pp. 164–88. Several recent studies by J. L. Donawerth (Ph.D. 1976), M. de Grazia, (*SQ* 29 (1978), 374–88), J. P. Hammersmith (Ph.D. 1977), *et al.*, deal specifically with Shakespeare's concepts of language. A. Barton (*SS* 24 (1971), 19–30), (I. Ewbank, *SS* 24 (1971), 13–18), T. R. Waldo, (*Shakespeare's "More*

than Words Can Witness," ed. S. Homan, pp. 160–77), and others, discuss Shakespeare's awareness of the limitations of language. Shakespeare's use and understanding of language in individual works have been studied by A. Barton, *Shakespeare's Styles*, ed. P. Edwards *et al.*, pp. 131–50 (Last Plays), M. de Grazia, *SpS* 1 (1980), 121–34 (Sonnets), G. J. Greene, *SEL* 21 (1981), 271–85 (*Troilus and Cressida*), G. J. Greene, Ph.D. 1977 (*Julius Caesar*), Z. Jagendorf, *E* 27 (1978), 121–8 (*Hamlet*); R. C. Johnson, *AJES* 5 (1980), 190–210 (*Coriolanus*), T. McAlindon, *PMLA* 84 (1969), 29–43 (*Troilus and Cressida*), M. Sacharoff, *PMLA* 87 (1972), 90–3 (*Troilus and Cressida*), C. M. Sicherman, *ELH* 39 (1972), 189–207 (*Coriolanus*), S. P Zitner, in *"King Lear,"* ed. R. L. Colie *et al.*, pp. 3–22 (*King Lear*). See also the recent studies by J. L. Calderwood, *Metadrama in Shakespeare's Henriad*, and J. A. Porter, *Drama of Speech Acts* (on Shakespeare's Lancastrian tetralogy).

12 Since the pioneer studies of C. Spurgeon and W. Clemen, there have been several book-length studies of Shakespeare's imagery. See especially R. Berry's recent *Shakespearean Metaphor* (1978). More specific aspects of the subject, such as Shakespeare's "stage imagery," "visual and rhetorical imagery," as well as "iconic imagery," are dealt with by C. Lyons, in *Essays . . . in Honor of Hardin Craig*, ed. R. Hosley, pp. 261–74; D. Mehl, *ES* n.s. 25 (1972), 83–100; and J. Doebler, *Shakespeare's Speaking Pictures*.

13 E.g., E. A. Armstrong, *Shakespeare's Imagination*, and N. Holland, *Shakespearean Imagination*. However, both these studies deal with their subject in a twentieth-century psychoanalytic rather than an Elizabethan context. See also W. Carroll, *SP* 74 (1977), 186–215 (on imagination in *The Merry Wives of Windsor*) and D. P. Young, *Art of "A Midsummer Night's Dream,"* pp. 111ff., as well as I. B. McElveen's Ph.D. thesis on Shakespeare and Renaissance concepts of the imagination.

14 T. W. Baldwin's *Shakespeare's Five-Act Structure*.

15 T. McAlindon's *Shakespeare and Decorum*.

16 E. C. Pettet, *ES* n.s. 3 (1950), 29–46.

17 K. Muir, *Shakespeare the Professional*, pp. 22–40.

18 J. W. H. Atkins, *English Literary Criticism*, pp. 246–54.

19 L. Abel, *Metatheatre*, p. 60.

20 J. L. Calderwood, *Shakespearean Metadrama*, p. 6.

21 S. Homan, *When the Theater Turns to Itself*, pp. 10–11: "The term 'Aesthetic Metaphor' in the title of this book refers not just to theatrical references in the text itself but to metaphors based on all the components of the theater: the act of creation on the playwright's part, the resulting text, the techniques of acting and the delivery of that text, and the presence and function of the audience."

22 M. Shapiro, *RD* n.s. 12 (1981), p. 155.

23 *Ibid.*, p. 152. The works referred to are D. Fenton's 1930 study of *The Extra-Dramatic Moment in Elizabethan Plays Before 1616*, M. Mack's essay on "Engagement and Detachment in Shakespeare's Plays,"

and E. P. Nassar's "Shakespeare's Games with His Audience," in *The Rape of Cinderella*, pp. 100–19. One might add E. A. J. Honigmann's *Shakespeare*, especially pp. viii, 194, and three recent essays, by M. Garber (*RD* n.s. 9 (1978), 71–89) and J. Howard (*SQ* 30 (1979), 343–57; *SEL* 20 (1980), 185–99).

24 M. Shapiro, *RD* n.s. 12 (1981), 152.

25 *Ibid.*, p. 153. Here M. Shapiro refers to W. H. Matchett's articles on certain dramatic techniques in *King Lear* and *The Winter's Tale*, as well as to Stephen Booth's "Speculations on Doubling in Shakespeare's Plays."

26 M. Shapiro, *RD* n.s. 12 (1981), 154. This category largely concerns itself with the various forms of role-playing, as analyzed by T. F. van Laan, and the *teatrum mundi* and "life's a dream" topoi in their influence on dramatic form, as studied in T. B. Stroup's *Microcosmos*, and J. I. Cope's *Theater and the Dream*.

27 M. Shapiro, *RD* n.s. 12 (1981), 155ff. One might add R. Fly's *Shakespeare's Mediated World*, which follows the thesis that certain of Shakespeare's plays "arise out of a growing conviction – expressed in varying degrees of intensity – that poetic drama, although wide reaching, is not always answerable either to the complexities of human existence or to the art that tries to mirror it. If occasionally his plays fail to satisfy our expectations, it may be because they are about the artist's inability to create a meaningful order out of hostile and intractable materials – a general sense of failure that encompasses both their substance and structure" (p. x).

28 See, e.g., R. Abrams, *ELR* 8 (1978), 43–66; S. R. Homan, *SSt* 5 (1969), 141–8; S. E. Hyman, *Sh*, 21:2 (Winter 1970), 18–42.

29 This has been done, and on the whole with good commonsense, in D. Klein's *Elizabethan Dramatists*, to which I am indebted for several useful points of information.

30 M. de Grazia, *SpS* 1 (1980), 121–34, *passim*.

31 R. A. Lanham, *Motives of Eloquence*, pp. 111–28, *passim*.

32 *A Midsummer Night's Dream*, V, 1, 12–17.

33 D. P. Young, *Art of "A Midsummer Night's Dream,"* p. 139.

34 K. Muir, *Shakespeare the Professional*, p. 27. See also H. F. Brooks, ed., *A Midsummer Night's Dream*, p. cxl.

35 W. C. Booth, *Rhetoric of Fiction*, pp. 73–4. For a general discussion of the problem, see E. Faas, *Anglia* 87 (1969), 338–66.

36 *The Winter's Tale*, IV, 4, 86ff.

37 E. C. Pettet, *ES*, n.s. 3 (1950), 35.

38 K. Muir, *Shakespeare the Professional*, p. 38; see also G. Bullough, ed., *Sources*, VI, 225 and H. J. Oliver, ed., *Timon of Athens*, pp. xiiiff.

39 R. Battenhouse, in *Essays for Leicester Bradner*, ed. E. M. Blistein, p. 3. For a more recent example, see R. Egan, *Drama Within Drama*, p. 11: "Mimesis, then, the ability to reflect reality in an effective image that codifies and communicates the artist's vision: this is what Shakespeare defines as the utmost power of drama in *Hamlet*."

40 S. L. Bethell, *Shakespeare*, p. 147. For an even earlier warning to

similar effect, see A. Harbage, *Shakespeare's Audience*, p. 129: "We should be placed on our guard against taking Hamlet's dramatic pronouncements as literally Shakespeare's."

41 See, e.g., R. Battenhouse, in *Essays for Leicester Bradner*, ed. E. M. Blistein, pp. 8–9, and H. Felperin, *Shakespearean Representation*, p. 50.

42 D. Seltzer, in *New Companion*, ed. K. Muir *et al.*, pp. 36–7.

43 B. Mowat, *RP* (1970) 41–54. See also A. C. Dessen's various studies: "Elizabethan Audiences and the Open Stage . . .," *YES* 10 (1980), 1–20; "The Logic of Elizabethan Stage Violence," *RD* 9 (1978), 39–69; and *Elizabethan Drama*, especially pp. 7ff. See also the earlier studies by A. Gerstner-Hirzel, *Action and Word, passim*; R. Hapgood, *DS* 5 (1966–7), 162–70; and W. D. Smith, *SQ* 4 (1953), 311–16. David Bevington's recent *Action is Eloquence: Shakespeare's Language of Gesture*, came too late to my attention to be discussed in the above chapter.

44 For this and the following, see above, pp. 28ff.

45 As J. L. Calderwood wrote in 1971, "The big set-piece speeches like Jaques's 'All the world's a stage' and Prospero's 'Our revels now are ended' are familiar but less common than the transient appearances of such terms as act, play the part, counterfeit, shadow, stage, cast, plot, quality, scene, and pageant, each of which momentarily sets the world in the focus of art" (*Shakespearean Metadrama*, p. 5). More recently, see P. Berek's interesting analysis of Leontes' "we are mock'd with art" in *The Winter's Tale* (V, 3) against the background of Shakespeare's use of the word "mock" at large (*SEL* 18 (1978), 289–305, *passim*).

46 For this and the following, see above, pp. 47ff.

47 M. Palingenius, *Zodiake of Life*, p. 217.

48 E. C. Pettet, *ES* n.s. 3 (1950), 46.

49 J. Huarte, *Examination of Mens Wits*, p. 19.

50 Montaigne, *Essays*, p. 369 (II, 12).

51 F. Bacon, *Works*, III, 355.

52 Montaigne, *Essays*, p. 404 (II, 12).

53 *The Two Noble Kinsmen*, V, 4, 144–95.

54 *Love's Labour's Lost*, IV, 3, 331–2.

55 *A Midsummer Night's Dream*, V, 1, 3.

56 Quoted by G. Castor, *Pléiade Poetics*, p. 30. See also B. Hathaway, *Age of Criticism*, pp. 415, 421, *et passim*.

57 Cf. M. W. Bundy, *PQ* 23 (1941), pp. 239, 245.

58 Cf. B. Hathaway, *Age of Criticism*, pp. 404, 445, *et passim*.

59 See above, p. vii.

60 Montaigne, *Essays*, p. 21 (I, 8).

61 *A Midsummer Night's Dream*, V, 1, 9.

62 See above, pp. 139ff.

63 Montaigne, *Essays*, p. 135 (I, 28).

64 See, e.g., M. W. Bundy, *SP* 27 (1930), 244–64, *passim*.

65 See Horace, *Ars Poetica*, lines 7ff., *Satires, Epistles, Ars Poetica*, p. 450; and above, p. 82, n. 9.

66 F. Bacon, *Works*, III, 343; V, 503.

67 A. S. P. Woodhouse, *Princeton Encyclopedia*, p. 372; see also Philip Edwards, *Shakespeare*, pp. 9, 55, *et passim*.

68 F. Bacon, *Works*, III, 382. As P. Rossi writes, Bacon, with such ideas, foreshadowed "a notion that was to become a turning point in the development of European thought: the notion that religion stems from fantasy" (*Francis Bacon*, p. 87).

Notes to Chapter I

1 *Timon of Athens*, I, 1, 40–1; 33–5. For more detailed discussions of the Poet–Painter *paragone* from *Timon of Athens*, see M. Doran, *Endeavors of Art*, pp. 72–3; J. H. Hagstrum, *The Sister Arts*, pp. 69–70; and K. Muir, *Shakespeare the Professional*, pp. 36ff.

2 *Pericles*, V, 1, 6–7.

3 *Cymbeline*, II, 4, 82–5.

4 *The Winter's Tale*, V, 2, 94–5, V, 3, 18–20.

5 *The Winter's Tale*, IV, 4, 91–2; *Timon of Athens*, I, 1, 40.

6 *Love's Labour's Lost*, IV, 2, 63–9.

7 *King John*, III, 1, 53; *Twelfth Night*, I, 3, 27; *Macbeth*, III, 1, 97.

8 For the following, see R. L. Anderson, *Elizabethan Psychology*, pp. 16–17.

9 See, e.g., *Twelfth Night*, I, 5, 108; *Troilus and Cressida*, II, 1, 69. Concerning the division of the brain according to medieval and Renaissance psychology, see, e.g., M. W. Bundy, *JEGP* 29 (1930), 537, who, however, is corrected by M. Kemp, *V* 8 (1977), 361, for falsely allocating "fantasy" to the second ventricle.

10 Charron's phrase, quoted by R. L. Anderson, *Elizabethan Psychology*, p. 17.

11 R. Burton, *Anatomy of Melancholy*, p. 160.

12 *The Merchant of Venice*, III, 5, 57–8.

13 *Love's Labour's Lost*, V, I, 35; IV, 2, 47, 57.

14 Cf. M. Joseph, *Arts of Language*, p. 51.

15 *Love's Labour's Lost*, IV, 2, 54–9.

16 *Essays*, ed. G. G. Smith, II, 94–95.

17 *Love's Labour's Lost*, IV, 2, 115–19.

18 *Ibid.*, V, 2, 34–6. For a study of Shakespeare's actual metrics, see D. L. Sipe's work on that subject.

19 Cf. Gower's "Only I carry winged time / Post on the lame feet of my rhyme," *Pericles*, IV, 48–9.

20 *As You Like It*, III, 2, 103.

21 *Much Ado About Nothing*, V, 2, 31; cf. *Hamlet*, II, 2, 323.

22 For a more recent account of Shakespeare's use of verse versus prose in the plays, see G. L. Brook, *Language of Shakespeare*, pp. 160–1.

23 G. Chapman, "Epistle Dedicatory: *The Iliads*" (*Poems*, p. 387).

24 Sonnet 79; *Love's Labour's Lost*, IV, 3, 51, 53.

25 G. G. Smith, ed., *Essays*, I, xlvi.

26 *As You Like It*, II, 5, 16–17.
27 *Love's Labour's Lost*, IV, 2, 99, 114–15.
28 Cf. *A Midsummer Night's Dream*, III, 1, 21–2.
29 Cf. F. W. Ness, "Shakespeare and the Contemporary Attitude Toward Rhyme," in *Use of Rhyme*, pp. 8–20.
30 *Much Ado About Nothing*, V, 2, 31–7.
31 *Romeo and Juliet*, II, 1, 9–10.
32 *As You Like It*, III, 2, 86–8.
33 Sonnets, 16, 107.
34 *Hamlet*, II, 2, 95.
35 *Love's Labour's Lost*, V, 2, 407, 408, 741.
36 1 *Henry IV*, II, 4, 234–40, 243.
37 1 *Henry IV*, I, 2, 77–9.
38 *Troilus and Cressida*, I, 3, 194.
39 *Venus and Adonis*, 8.
40 *Love's Labour's Lost*, V, 2, 37.
41 *A Midsummer Night's Dream*, III, 2, 138–9.
42 *Ibid.*, V, I, 17. *Edward III*, Act II, which some critics trust is Shakespeare's, contains a scene dealing largely with the nature of poetic comparison. The King has asked a poet, called Lodowick, to write a poem which will help him seduce the Countess, but Lodowick preserves his integrity. For a detailed analysis, see K. Muir, *Shakespeare the Professional*, pp. 28ff., and especially pp. 29–30:

> Lodowick's first line –
> More faire and chast then is the Queen of Shades –
is criticized by the King on two grounds: that his love should not be compared to "the pale Queene of night" and for the epithet *chaste*:
> I did not bid thee talke of chastitie,
> To ransack so the treasure of her minde, ...
> Out with the moone line, I wil none of it;
> And let me have hir likened to the sun.
> Lodowick continues:
> More bould in constancie ... than Iudith was.
The King naturally objects to this line, as he remembers the fate of Holofernes.

It can hardly be doubted that Lodowick's lines were written deliberately to remind the King that he is proposing to commit a sin. . . . If Lodowick was Shakespeare's creation he is the only one of his poets who emerges with much credit.

43 *A Lover's Complaint*, 16.
44 *Love's Labour's Lost*, II, 1, 72.
45 *The Merchant of Venice*, III, 5, 50–7.
46 W. Webbe, in *Essays*, ed. G. G. Smith, I, 236.
47 As P. Edwards points out, "Juliet's nervousness that words might tamper with love seems justified. Juliet, Perdita, Cordelia – and

Cressida too – are front-line troops in a campaign to deflate a rotundity of language which seems to characterise even the best people when they try to voice their feelings of love" (*Shakespeare's Styles*, ed. P. Edwards *et al.*, p. 50).

48 *Love's Labour's Lost*, III, 1, 58.

49 *As You Like It*, V, 1, 38, 39–40.

50 Cf. *All's Well That Ends Well*, V, 2, 11; *Twelfth Night*, I, 3, 67.

51 *Twelfth Night*, I, 5, 44–8.

52 *Love's Labour's Lost*, V, 2, 407.

53 *Troilus and Cressida*, I, 3, 158–61.

54 *All's Well That Ends Well*, V, 2, 24; *Othello*, I, 1, 14: *Love's Labour's Lost*, IV, 2, 7; V, 1, 14; *The Taming of the Shrew*, V, 2, 54; *1 Henry IV*, I, 2, 77.

55 *Love's Labour's Lost*, I, 1, 163.

56 *Henry V*, III, 6, 74; *The Merry Wives of Windsor*, II, 1, 10; II, 2, 28; *Love's Labour's Lost*, V, 2, 406; *Romeo and Juliet*, I, 4, 37; *2 Henry IV*, III, 2, 70; *Hamlet*, I, 3, 108; *Troilus and Cressida*, III, 1, 40; *Hamlet*, II, 2, 110.

57 Sonnet 85.

58 See, e.g., G. Gascoigne, *The Steel Glas, Glasse of Government* (*Complete Works*, II, 169): "That *Grammer* grudge not at our english tong, / Bycause it stands by *Monosyllaba*"; T. Nashe, *Summer's Last Will* (*Works*, III, 234): "Ile shewe you what a scuruy *Prologue* he had made me, in an old vayne of similitudes."

59 Cf. *Essays*, ed. G. G. Smith, II, 160, 169, 184 *et passim*.

60 Cf. *1 Henry IV*, II, 4, 386ff. See also G. L. Brook, *Language of Shakespeare*, pp. 200–1.

61 M. Joseph, *Arts of Language*, pp. 288–9.

62 Montaigne, *Essays*, p. 223 (I, 51). At the same time, literate Elizabethans were no doubt far more aware of rhetorical figures than we are. "One thing is certain," Brian Vickers writes, "that every person who had a grammar-school education in Europe between Ovid and Pope knew by heart, familiarly, up to a hundred figures, by their right names" (*New Companion*, ed. K. Muir *et al.*, p. 86).

63 Regarding Renaissance critics' relative unconcern with questions of poetic structure, see M. Trousdale, *ELH* 40 (1973), 198 *et passim*. As M. Doran, *Endeavors of Art*, p. 61, points out, the interest of Renaissance theorizers went "to style rather than to structural form."

64 R. Flecknoe, *Discourse*, n.p.

65 J. Fletcher, *Works*, VIII, 2.

66 W. Cartwright, "In the memory of the most Worthy Beniamin Iohnson" (Ben Jonson, [*Works*], XI, 456).

67 T. Jay, "To his friend the Author" (P. Massinger, *Plays and Poems*, II, 296).

68 C. Tourneur, *Works*, p. 204.

69 J. Lyly, *Complete Works*, II, 416.

70 J. Webster, *Works*, I, 112.

71 Ben Jonson, [*Works*], VI, 527; VIII, 647.

72 For this and the following, see *Troilus and Cressida*, Prologue 28; *Love's Labour's Lost*, V, 2, 863; *A Midsummer Night's Dream*, III, 2, 461.

73 *2 Henry VI*, V, 2, 28.

74 *Troilus and Cressida*, IV, 5, 224–6.

75 *King Lear*, I, 2, 128.

76 *Love's Labour's Lost*, IV, 1, 70, 72.

77 *Othello*, II, 1, 160, 137.

78 *Richard II*, II, 1, 12–13.

79 *Henry V*, I, 2, 181–2.

80 Shakespeare's use of the word here and elsewhere is discussed by R. Abrams, *ELR* 8 (1978), 45: "The dual meaning of 'plot' – the plotting of a historical action and the plotting of a story – is common in the Renaissance and in Shakespeare. Humphrey, Duke of Gloucester, speaks of a 'plotted tragedy,' meaning a bloodbath plotted like a stageplay (*2H6*, III.i.153). In *Twelfth Night* the 'plot' against Malvolio is literally Shakespeare's subplot, an 'interlude' devised by a group of 'authors' or plotting collaborators (II.v.70; V. 1. 362, 343). In *Richard III*, to take an extended example, Richard's plot is, until the final act, virtually congruent with Shakespeare's own."

81 The phrase "prologues vilely penn'd" is from *Love's Labour's Lost*, V, 2, 305.

82 *Hamlet*, II, 2, 392–5.

83 J. Lyly, *Complete Works*, III, 20.

84 T. Dekker, *The Guls Horn-Booke*, p. 53.

85 *A Midsummer Night's Dream*, I, 2, 10, 5; V, I, 56, 57. See also *The Taming of the Shrew*, Induction, 2, 131 ff.

86 J. Marston, *What You Will*, Induction (*Works*, II, 324).

87 J. W. H. Atkins, *English Literary Criticism*, p. 248.

88 See J. Bartlett, *Complete Concordance*, pp. 77, 198, 202, 376, 386, 427, 476, 780, 997, 1102, 1134, 1233, 1305, 1320, 1324–5.

89 See *OED*, s. vv. Concerning "romance," see also Sir John Suckling, *The Goblins*, Epilogue (*Works*, p. 215): "Romances, cries easy souls, / And then they swear / The play's well writ, though scarce a good line's there." Also J. Shirley, *Cardinal*, Prologue (*Dramatic Works and Poems*, p. 275): "Whether the comic Muse, or ladies' love, / Romance, or direful tragedy it prove, / The bill determines not." Concerning "tragicomedy," see also J. Fletcher, *The Faithful Shepherdess*, Preface (*Works*, II, 522).

90 G. Puttenham, in *Essays*, ed. G. G. Smith, II, 27.

91 T. Lodge, *ibid.*, I, 80.

92 G. Puttenham, *ibid.*, II, 36.

93 See, e.g., *Richard III*, III, 2, 59.

94 *Richard III*, IV, 4, 7; *2 Henry VI*, IV, 1, 4; *Richard III*, II, 2, 39.

95 See, e.g., *A Midsummer Night's Dream*, V, 1, 57, 66; *Hamlet*, III, 2, 144. See also *Titus Andronicus*, IV, 1, 48; *The Phoenix and the Turtle*, 52.

96 *The Phoenix and the Turtle*, 52; *2 Henry IV*, I, 1, 61. As an exception,

see the reference to "the tragic tale of Philomel" in *Titus Andronicus*, IV, 1, 48.

97 *The Rape of Lucrece*, 766.

98 *All's Well That Ends Well*, IV, 3, 247; *Richard III*, III, 5, 5–8.

99 *Titus Andronicus*, IV, 1, 59–60.

100 T. Tomkis, *Albumazar*, IV, 2. See also Sidney, in *Essays*, ed. G. G. Smith, I, 199; *ibid.*, I, xliv; J. W. H. Atkins, *English Literary Criticism*, p. 243.

101 See above, p. 36, and *The Taming of the Shrew*, Induction, 2, 135, 132.

102 *Twelfth Night*, I, 5, 167.

103 For the following, see S. K. Heninger, Jr, *Touches of Sweet Harmony*, pp. 294ff. During the Renaissance, "invention" would often be identified with either "imitation" or "imagination." For instance, A. Lionardi writes that "essendo lo scriuere poeticamente null'altro, che imitare le attioni de gli huomini, se il Poeta non si servisse ancora di questa guisa di parlare, sarebbe imperfetta la inuentione, ò imitatione" (quoted by August Buck, Preface to J. C. Scaliger, *Poetices Libri Septem*, p. x). For identifications of "invention" with "imagination," see M. W. Bundy, *JEGP* 29 (1930), p. 542 *et passim*; M. Kemp, *V* 8 (1977), 364, 378–9.

104 G. Gascoigne, in *Essays*, ed. G. G. Smith, I, 47.

105 Sidney, *ibid.*, I, 157.

106 Ben Jonson, [*Works*], VIII, 635.

107 Sidney, in *Essays*, ed. G. G. Smith, I, 156.

108 Ben Jonson, [*Works*], VIII, 89.

109 *Hamlet*, III, 2, 135, 225; 1 *Henry IV*, II, 4, 271–2. See also 2 *Henry IV*, IV, 5, 198–9: "For all my reign hath been but a scene / Acting that argument."

110 *Much Ado About Nothing*, V, 1, 269, 270; *As You Like It*, II, 5, 42–3; IV, 3, 35, 31, 34; *Twelfth Night*, III, 2, 40; *Othello*, II, 1, 125–6.

111 According to C. S. Lewis, *Discarded Image*, p. 163, medieval and Renaissance theorists "would have used *invention* where we use *imagination*."

112 Ben Jonson, [*Works*], III, 285 (*Every Man in His Humour*, V, 3).

113 G. Puttenham, in *Essays*, ed. G. G. Smith, II, 3, 191.

114 Cf. E. N. Tigerstedt, *CLS* 5 (1968), 456ff.

115 G. Puttenham, in *Essays*, ed. G. G. Smith, II, 3, 191–2.

116 Sidney, *ibid.*, I, 156.

117 Ben Jonson, [*Works*], VIII, 637 (*Discoveries*). Also compare "E. K.'s" similar comments concerning the "rakehellye route of our ragged rymers" who write "as if some instinct of Poeticall spirite had newly rauished them aboue the meanenesse of commen capacitie" (*Essays*, ed. G. G. Smith, I, 131.)

118 As M. Kemp, *V* 8 (1977), 357, points out, the distinction was a common one during the Renaissance. Originally derived from rhetoric, it increasingly fused with the notion of poetic creativity, particularly when conceived of in terms of divine inspiration. "The

two traditions, the rhetorical and poetic – the one stipulating a division of labor between invention of content and composition of form, the other interpreting invention in terms of divine inspiration – became increasingly inseparable in Renaissance discussions of the poetic faculty. This process is well under way in Salutati's *De laboribus Herculis* and is fully realized in Landino's introduction to his Dante commentary." In painting, this went to the point of an actual division of labor between "inventor" and craftsman. While theorizers often vied with each other in advocating bizarre flights of infinite inventiveness or "inexcogitable" inventions (cf. *ibid.*, pp. 365, 396), they also felt "that subject matter and meaning were too important to be left to the painter or sculptor. Thus it was that Leonardo Bruni, a master of rhetoric who was professionally skilled in *invenzione*, sought to provide a program for Ghiberti's second set of Baptistry Doors. Such situations would inevitably persist when erudite patrons like Leonello d'Este continued to make (according to Angelo Decembrio's credible account) a sharp division between the cerebral qualities of the writer's *ingenium* and the limited mimetic powers of the painter's hand . . . Few such programs drawn up by the patron or his humanist advisers have survived, but the practise of presenting the artist with a cut-and-dried *invenzione* was probably the general rule in the case of new or difficult subjects, particularly those of a classical nature" (*ibid.*, p. 358).

119 G. Puttenham, in *Essays*, ed. G. G. Smith, II, 191.
120 Sidney, *ibid.*, I, 157. For more detailed discussions of Sidney's concept of the "fore-conceite" in relation to the actual process of composition, see F. G. Robinson, "Sidney's *Apology*: From Fore-conceit to Ground-plot," in *Shape of Things Known*, pp. 97–136, especially pp. 131–2; and, more recently, L. C. Wolfley, *JMRS* 6 (1976), 217–41 (pp. 224ff.). According to M. N. Raitiere, *SEL* 21 (1981), 56, the distinction is also borne out by Sidney's own works: "Thus although the Icarean voice celebrates the poet's creation of 'forms such as never were in Nature, as the Heroes, Demigods, Cyclops, Chimeras, Furies, and such like' . . . it is significant that Sidney in his own *Arcadias* elaborates a 'realistic' or verisimilar narrative with a carefully defined causal structure that (with very few exceptions) eschews supernatural actors such as 'Cyclops, Chimeras . . . and such like.' Similarly, it would be easy to show that the two *Arcadias* bear little relation to the kind of 'golden' or wish-fulfillment poetic universe prescribed by the Icarean voice of the *Apology*." See also D. H. Craig, *ELR* 10 (1980), 184: "The notion of the poet as the creator of a rival world to Nature's is not as audacious as it seems, Sidney says, since the achievement of the artificer lies in 'that *Idea* or fore-conceit of the work' and not in its execution . . ."
121 See, e.g., M. W. Bundy, *JEGP* 29 (1930), 535–45.
122 G. Fracastoro, *Navgerivs*, p. 65. See also B. Hathaway, *Age of Criticism*, pp. 405–6; also M. Doran, *Endeavors of Art*, p. 58: "To Shake-

speare's age man is by his essence a rational being, and if poetic inspiration comes to him as a divine gift, it must yet be exercised through the medium of an exact discipline elaborated by reason."

123 An alternative to the teleological thrust of the Chorus is contained in the Friar's long speech in II, 3, 7–22 (especially lines 9–10: "The earth that's nature's mother is her tomb; / What is her burying grave, that is her womb"), which suggests the spirit of Shakespearean romance rather than of tragedy. For a discussion of this paradox, see R. Grudin, *Shakespeare and Renaissance Contrariety*, p. 36, which shows the Friar's speech to be "conspicuously Paracelsian."

124 Ben Jonson, [*Works*], VIII, 584 (*Discoveries*).

125 *1 Henry VI*, III, 1, 1–2, 5–6.

126 *Timon of Athens*, I, 1, 22–6.

127 *Love's Labour's Lost*, IV, 2, 119, 118, 117.

128 Sidney, in *Essays*, ed. G. G. Smith, I, 185.

129 E. C. Pettet, *ES* n.s. 3 (1950), 35.

Notes to Chapter II

1 See especially R. W. Battenhouse, in *Essays for Leicester Bradner*, ed. E. M. Blistein, pp. 3–26.

2 For this and the following, see G. G. Smith, ed., *Essays*, I, 369; W. A. Ringler, Jr, in *Essays . . . in Honor of Hardin Craig*, ed. R. Hosley, p. 204; J. W. H. Atkins, *English Literary Criticism*, p. 226 (concerning Gosson's retort to Lodge's Ciceronian argument in *Plays Confuted in Five Actions*, Action II.) In H. Felperin's view, Hamlet's "to hold, as 'twere, the mirror up to nature" fuses "two distinct notions of drama, each with a long tradition and each in some degree antagonistic to the other in aim and method. The former, the view of the play as moral vision, transcends by its very nature considerations of time and place, associates drama with theology or moral philosophy, and is identifiable in Hamlet's account with medieval and Tudor allegorical theater – note the vestiges of personification in the phrases, 'virtue *her own feature*, scorn *her own image*.' The latter, the view of the play as lifelike illusion, is by its very nature timebound and localized, associates drama with historiography, and is identifiable in Hamlet's account with the more or less naturalistic theatre of classical Rome and Renaissance Italy. Taken as a whole, Hamlet's speech is predominantly a plea for the new doctrine of dramatic illusionism and falls in line with the special pleading of such Elizabethan classicists as Sidney and Jonson" (*Shakespearean Representation*, pp. 45–6).

3 Ben Jonson, [*Works*], III, 427, 515.

4 Ben Jonson, [*Works*], III, 432; VI, 545; VII, 735. See also A. Leggatt, *Ben Jonson*, pp. 258–9.

5 R. Juneja, *RR* n.s. 4:1 (1980), 74.

6 S. L. Bethell, *Shakespeare*, p. 148.

7 Ben Jonson, [*Works*], III, 479; VI, 527 (*The Magnetic Lady*, I, 7, Chorus);

VIII, 643 (*Discoveries*). For an interesting discussion of Ben Jonson's concepts in the context of Renaissance views of form generally, see M. Trousdale, *ELH* 40 (1973), 195 *et passim*. Trousdale's general conclusion, which draws on Roland Barthes for some of its terminology, is that the typical Elizabethan play "is a structure *created* to generate meanings" (p. 203) rather than to contain them.

8 For a general acount of the "Elizabethan Distrust of the Effects of Drama," see S. S. Hilliard, *ELR* 9 (1979), 234ff.

9 Ben Jonson, [*Works*], VI, 351–2 (*The Staple of News*, IV, 2).

10 *Ibid.*, VI, 509 (*The Magnetic Lady*, Induction); III, 137 (*The Case is Altered*, II, 7); VI, 283, 282 (*The Staple of News*, Prologue). See also A. C. Dessen, *Elizabethan Drama*, p. 12.

11 Ben Jonson, [*Works*], VI, 283 (*The Staple of News*, Prologue); IV, 324.

12 Cf. R. W. Battenhouse, in *Essays for Leicester Bradner*, ed. E. M. Blistein, p. 17.

13 T. Tomkis, *Lingua*, facs. H 3.

14 T. Dekker, *Dramatic Works*, I, 369.

15 P. Massinger, *Plays and Poems*, III, 488 (*The Emperor of the East*, Epilogue.)

16 Ben Jonson, [*Works*], VIII, 587 (*Discoveries*); III, 353.

17 *Ibid.*, III, 515 (*Every Man Out of His Humor*, III, 6).

18 S. L. Bethell, *Shakespeare*, p. 145. There is also W. A. Ringler, Jr's interesting suggestion that Shakespeare may have used Hamlet for a defense of the theatre in neoclassical terms after the stage had come under attack from various sides (*Essays . . . in Honor of Hardin Craig*, ed. R. Hosley, p. 207 *et passim*).

19 See my *Tragedy and After*, pp. 111–28.

20 R. Ascham, in *Essays*, ed. G. G. Smith, I, 7. See also M. T. Herrick, *Poetics of Aristotle in England*, pp. 18ff.

21 Sidney, in *Essays*, ed. G. G. Smith, I, 158.

22 *Troilus and Cressida*, I, 3, 149–58.

23 *Love's Labour's Lost*, IV, 2, 129. See also *Julius Caesar*, IV, 1, 36–7: "one that feeds / On abjects, orts, and imitations."

24 *3 Henry VI*, II, 3, 25–8.

25 *The Winter's Tale*, V, 3, 68. For a recent view of "The Mockery of Art in *The Winter's Tale*," see A. A. Ansari, *AJES* 4 (1979), 124–41.

26 For a more recent discussion of such matters, see E. Jones, *Scenic Form in Shakespeare*.

27 Cf. K. Farrell's interesting discussion of Berowne's comments in *Shakespeare's Creation*, p. 5: "In a sense Berowne is disowning the literally 'art-ful' behavior of the characters up to this point, welcoming uncomfortably spontaneous life into the play. What follows, he implies, will be more authentic – indeed more real – than what is past. At the same time on another level Shakespeare seems to be suggesting that his play itself is closer to life than conventional, pat comedy can be."

28 *Romeo and Juliet*, Prologue, 12.

29 *Henry V*, I, Prologue, 30–1; II, Prologue, 32.
30 *Troilus and Cressida*, Prologue, 28–9. Concerning *in medias res* and related techniques in Renaissance neoclassical criticism, see D. Riggs, *RD* 6 (1973), 156–7 *et passim*.
31 *Henry V*, I, Prologue, 4; *Pericles*, IV, Gower, 6; *Henry V*, III, Prologue, 1–3.
32 Ben Jonson, [*Works*], VIII, 583 (*Discoveries*).
33 Cf. A. Harbage, *Shakespeare's Audience*, p. 130: "Nowhere has Shakespeare suggested *in propria persona* that he has any quarrel with the groundlings."
34 *1 Henry IV*, II, 4, 385; *Antony and Cleopatra*, V, 2, 215; *3 Henry VI*, II, 3, 28.
35 Sonnet 110.
36 *Troilus and Cressida*, I, 3, 153–4.
37 Anne Righter, *Idea of the Play*, p. 171.
38 *Henry V*, I, Prologue, 8; *Troilus and Cressida*, Prologue, 26; *The Winter's Tale*, IV, Chorus, 20; *2 Henry IV*, Epilogue, 26; *Henry V*, Epilogue, 1–2.
39 Quoted by F. E. Halliday, *Shakespeare Companion*, p. 502.
40 *2 Henry IV*, Epilogue, 20–1; *A Midsummer Night's Dream*, V, 1, 416; *Henry V*, IV, Prologue, 50–1; *2 Henry IV*, Epilogue, 8.
41 T. Dekker, *The Guls Horn-Booke*, p. 47.
42 H. Medwall, *Fulgens and Lucres*, Part II, 30–1 (*The Plays*, p. 68). See also D. Klein, *Elizabethan Dramatists*, pp. 198ff.
43 Cf. *1 Henry IV*, II, 4, 309, 347. Concerning "Hal and the 'Play Extempore' in *1 Henry IV*," see also P. A. Gottschalk, *TSLL* 15 (1973–4), 605–14.
44 Ben Jonson, [*Works*], VIII, 643 (*Discoveries*); III, 10.
45 *Pericles*, IV, 4, 22; II, 1, 16; III, 1, 14. An interesting testimony to the non-verbal appeal of Elizabethan drama generally from an English traveller on the continent, Fynes Moryson, is discussed by A. C. Dessen, *Elizabethan Drama*, p. 12: "The English theatrical troupe which Moryson saw in Frankfort had 'neither a complete number of actors, nor any good apparel, nor any ornament of the stage, yet the Germans, not understanding a word they said, both men and women, flocked wonderfully to see their gesture and action, rather than hear them, speaking English which they understood not.'" According to Dessen, a strong visual and action-oriented appeal is built into Elizabethan dramatic language by the fact that the plays tend to show, not an action (e.g., the shipwreck in *The Tempest*) itself, "but the results or effects of that action" (*YES* 10 (1980), 9).
46 R. W. Battenhouse, in *Essays for Leicester Bradner*, ed. E. M. Blistein, p. 18.
47 Ben Jonson, [*Works*], VIII, 587 (*Discoveries*).
48 *Julius Caesar*, II, 1, 227.
49 B. Mowat quotes Thomas Wright's *The Passions of the Mind* and John Bulwer's *Chirologia* to document that behind Shakespeare's use of gesture to communicate inner emotion "lies an idea frequently

expressed by Renaissance rhetoricians: namely, that gesture is an external sign of inner passion, a direct, visible manifestation of an inner state, a signal that the body gives visually which augments or sometimes supplants a verbal signal" (*RP*, 1970, p. 43).

50 *Henry VIII*, III, 2, 111–19.

51 See, e.g., *Troilus and Cressida*, III, 3, 254; *Romeo and Juliet*, I, 1, 48; *2 Henry VI*, III, 1, 15; *Julius Caesar*, II, 1, 243; *King John*, I, 1, 192; *The Taming of the Shrew*, Induction 1, 126; *1 Henry IV*, II, 4, 373; *King John*, IV, 2, 76–7; *Julius Caesar*, II, 1, 240, 242.

52 See, e.g., *King John*, IV, 2, 192; *All's Well That Ends Well*, II, 3, 243; *Julius Caesar*, II, 1, 246; *Hamlet*, IV, 5, 6; *Julius Caesar*, II, 1, 244; *Hamlet*, IV, 5, 6; *Othello*, II, 1, 259; *A Midsummer Night's Dream*, III, 2, 238; *The Taming of the Shrew*, Induction 1, 117; *A Midsummer Night's Dream*, III, 2, 239; *King John*, IV, 2, 192.

53 *Twelfth Night*, II, 2, 19; *A Midsummer Night's Dream*, V, 1, 96; *2 Henry VI*, III, 2, 316; *Richard III*, III, 5, 2.

54 D. Wilson, *Hamlet*, p. 213.

55 *2 Henry VI*, III, 2, 316–18.

56 For a recent general discussion of "Instruction and Delight in Medieval and Renaissance Criticism," see P. Salman, *RQ* 32 (1979), 303–32.

57 *A Midsummer Night's Dream*, V, 1, 37, 52, 56–7, 356–7.

58 *The Taming of the Shrew*, Induction, I, 1, 9, 36–9.

59 *Pericles*, I, Gower, 4.

60 See J. W. H. Atkins, *English Literary Criticism*, pp. 222–3, 162, 341. See also M. T. Herrick, *Poetics of Aristotle in England*, pp. 19, 31–2, for a discussion of R. Peterson's catharsis concept and other possible allusions to the notion in Elizabethan writing.

61 B. Weinberg, *Literary Criticism*, I, 59.

62 Quoted *ibid.*, I, 289.

63 *A Warning for Fair Women*, lines 1083–6 (sig. H2). See also W. A. Ringler, Jr, in *Essays ... in Honor of Hardin Craig*, ed. R. Hosley, pp. 205–6; and A. C. Dessen, *Elizabethan Drama*, pp. 5–6.

64 L. Digges, [commendatory verses to Shakespeare's *Poems*, 1640], quoted in E. K. Chambers, *Shakespeare*, II, 233.

65 K. Muir, *Shakespeare the Professional*, p. 38; see also G. Bullough, ed., *Sources*, VI, 225; and H. J. Oliver, ed., *Timon of Athens*, pp. xiiiff.

66 See, for instance, E. C. Pettet, *ES* n.s. 3 (1950), 40 ff.; and, concerning traditional discussions of poetic mendacity from antiquity to the Renaissance, R. J. Clements, *Pléiade*, pp. 3ff.

67 *As You Like It*, III, 3, 16.

68 *Ibid.*, II, 7, 60.

Notes to Chapter III

1 Concerning Shakespeare's attitude towards the unities, see M. T. Herrick, *Poetics of Aristotle in England*, pp. 32–3; and, more recently, E. Schanzer, *SS* 28 (1975), 57–61. See also A. C. Dessen's explorations

of "Elizabethan Audiences and the Open Stage," *YES* 10 (1980), 1–20.
2 Cf. *Pericles*, IV, Gower, 44ff.; *The Winter's Tale*, IV, Time, the Chorus, 4ff.
3 *Henry V*, I, Prologue, 11–14; II, Prologue, 31–2; V, Prologue, 44–5.
4 *Love's Labour's Lost*, V, 2, 865, 866.
5 *Henry V*, I, Prologue, 29, 30–1; V, Prologue, 44, 3.
6 E. Schanzer, *SS* 28 (1975), 59.
7 F. Robortello: cf. J. Spingarn, *Literary Criticism*, pp. 91–2; B. Weinberg, *Literary Criticism*, I, 453.
8 Cf. R. M. Frye, *SQ* 31 (1980), 323–42 *et passim*.
9 R. Juneja, *RR* n.s. 4:1 (1980), 75.
10 Sidney, in *Essays*, ed. G. G. Smith, I, 197.
11 *Ibid.*, I, 199.
12 *Henry V*, IV, Prologue, 50.
13 Sidney, in *Essays*, ed. G. G. Smith, I, 197.
14 L. Castelvetro, *Poetica d'Aristotele*, pp. 679, 29, 109. Here, as in quoting Robortello, Maggi, Vettori, Beni, Piccolomini, and Buonamici, I have used B. Weinberg's translations wherever possible. See his *Literary Criticism*, I, 504, 392, 412, 464–5, 246, 547, 547–8, 549; II, 693, 695, 696–7.
15 Cf. *ibid.*, I, 175.
16 L. Castelvetro, *Poetica d'Aristotele*, p. 188.
17 Aristotle, *Poetics*, 1451, a 38, p. 234. Concerning "The Dramatic Unities in the Renaissance," see also J. E. Robinson's 1959 Ph.D. thesis of that title.
18 F. Robortello, *Explicationes*, p. 93.
19 V. Maggi and B. Lombardi, *Explanationes*, p. 131.
20 P. Vettori, *Commentarii*, p. 291.
21 P. Beni, *Disputatio*, p. 2.
22 G. Whetstone, in *Essays*, ed. G. G. Smith, I, 59.
23 Ben Jonson, [*Works*], III, 436; VIII, 647; IV, 350; V, 24.
24 Cf. G. P. Jones, *SS* 31 (1978), 100.
25 Ben Jonson [*Works*], III, 303; IV, 350; III, 438; III, 562.
26 Lope de Vega, *Arte Nuevo*, lines 11–12 (p. 11).
27 Cf. J. M. Rozas, *Lope de Vega*, p. 90. For Cinthio's similar concept of a "double thread of plot," see H. B. Charlton, *Senecan Tradition*, p. cxvii.
28 A. Piccolomini, *Annotationi*, pp. 152.
29 *Ibid.*, pp. 23–4, 222.
30 F. Buonamici, *Discorsi*, pp. 48–9, 113.
31 A. Piccolomini, *Annotationi*, p. 23.
32 F. Buonamici, *Discorsi*, pp. 111, 110.
33 Jackson I. Cope, in his otherwise stimulating *Theater and the Dream*, exaggerates, I think, Buonamici's appeals to the audience's imaginative collaboration by equating them with Theseus' in *A Midsummer Night's Dream*, V, 1, 214–15. See, e.g., p. 225.
34 F. Buonamici, *Discorsi*, p. 110.
35 Anne Righter, *Idea of the Play*, p. 80. More recent studies of illusion-

shattering devices in Shakespeare are discussed by M. Shapiro, *RD* n.s. 12 (1981), 146–7.

36 Thomas Palmer, "Master *John Fletcher* his dramaticall Workes now at last printed" (F. Beaumont and J. Fletcher, *Works*, I, xlviii). See also A. C. Dessen, *Elizabethan Drama*, p. 7.

37 T. Dekker, *Dramatic Works*, III, 121.

38 T. Nashe, *Works*, I, p. 212 (*Pierce Penilesse*): "newe embalmed with the teares of ten thousand spectators at least."

39 L. Digges, [commendatory verses to Shakespeare's *Poems*, 1640], E. K. Chambers, *Shakespeare*, II, 233.

40 For a similar view of Shakespeare's attitude toward his audience, see S. L. Bethell, *Shakespeare*, with its concept of a "multi-consciousness" of the audience (p. 29 *et passim*); also M. Mack's study of "Engagement and Detachment in Shakespeare's Plays," in *Essays . . . in Honor of Hardin Craig*, ed. R. Hosley, pp. 275–96, and numerous other more recent studies of similar orientation. (See above p. x, n. 23.)

41 Concerning the following, see the similar interpretations of R. W. Dent, *SQ* 15 (1964), 125ff.; and J. I. Cope, *The Theater and the Dream*, pp. 222–3.

42 For similar satire, perhaps inspired by Shakespeare, see *Narcissus*, the Twelfth Night play presented at St John's College, Oxford, in 1602, discussed and quoted in J. I. Cope, *Theater and the Dream*, pp. 222–3.

43 *Henry V*, I, Prologue, 23, 18; IV, Prologue, 50.

44 F. Buonamici, *Discorsi*, p. 110.

45 *Henry V*, IV, Prologue, 50–1.

46 A satirical version of how the spectator can lose himself in the spectacle is found in *The Taming of the Shrew*, where tinker Sly is made to "forget himself" (Induction, 1, 41).

47 J. W. H. Atkins, *English Literary Criticism*, p. 253.

48 Concerning the dating of the *Henry V* Chorus, see G. P. Jones, *SS* 31 (1978), 104: "The allusion in prologue V, apparently to the famous second Earl of Essex, requires that we accept the existence of the Chorus in some form or other by 1599, and possibly as early as 1598, despite its absence from the Quarto publication of 1600."

49 *Merry Devill*, sig. A3r–v.

50 *Henry V*, Prologue, 12, 13–14, 11, 13.

51 T. Dekker, *Dramatic Works*, I, 115.

52 F. Beaumont and J. Fletcher, *Works*, v, 362–4.

53 J. W. H. Atkins, *English Literary Criticism*, p. 253.

54 J. W. H. Atkins, *Literary Criticism in Antiquity*, II, 158.

55 *Ibid.*, II, 317.

56 Cf. E. H. Gombrich, *Art and Illusion*, p. 211.

57 Quoted by S. C. Hulse, *SS* 31 (1978), 16.

58 A detailed interpretation of this passage is found in W. S. Heckscher, *RORD* 13–14 (1970–1), 26. See also J. H. Hagstrum, *Sister Arts*, pp. 79–80.

59 See above, p. 13.
60 See above, pp. 20ff.
61 See above, p. vii.
62 *1 Henry VI*, III, 1, 5–6.
63 This is a question discussed by D. G. James, *Dream of Learning*, pp. 21–2.

Notes to Chapter IV

1 Cf. above, pp. 20ff., 76–7.
2 *A Midsummer Night's Dream*, V, I, 7ff.
3 Montaigne, *Essays*, p. 125 (I, 26).
4 *Ibid.*, p. 409 (II, 12); p. 186 (I, 40); p. 761 (III, 9).
5 This, no doubt, is one of the reasons why they have not received their proper recognition to date. Another reason is the general failure to see Bacon's and Montaigne's poetics in the context of their philosophical convictions, and particularly of their dismantling of traditional metaphysics. Francis Bacon, especially, is either hailed as a precursor of Romantic theorizing (e.g., by Basil Worsfold) or as an unoriginal "rationalist" incapable of appreciating poetry (e.g., by George Saintsbury). (See M. W. Bundy, *SP* 27 (1930), 245–6.) Similarly, L. C. Knights, *Explorations*, pp. 92–111, uses Bacon as an example to illustrate the "dissociation of sensibility," while J. Andrews, *NQ* 199 (1954), 484–6, 530–2, defends Hazlitt's view of Bacon's "unification of sensibility." Other critics denouncing Bacon as a rationalist with little understanding of the arts include M. W. Bundy, *SP* 27 (1930), 244–64, and P. H. Kocher, in *Essays . . . in Honor of Hardin Craig*, ed. R. Hosley, pp. 297–307.
6 Montaigne, *Essays*, p. 21 (I, 8).
7 This is a point stressed by both I. D. McFarlane, in *Essays Presented to Alan M. Boase*, ed. D. R. Haggis *et al.*, pp. 117–37, and S. J. Holyoake, *BHR* 31 (1969), 495–523, who both acknowledge, but underestimate, I think, Montaigne's overriding concern with exploring the "chimeras and fantastic monsters" of his mind. Thus Holyoake grants that Montaigne's "preoccupation with expressing the movements of his own mind" often causes him "to modify what he has said elsewhere"; but on balance, Holyoake is "inclined to guess that, more frequently than not, Montaigne viewed the imagination with moderate disfavour because it might possibly disrupt his endeavour to maintain a controlled internal serenity" (pp. 502, 521).
8 Montaigne, *Essays*, p. 68 (I, 21); p. 836 (III, 13); p. 21 (I, 8); p. 135 (I, 28).
9 Horace, *Ars Poetica*, lines 4ff. (*Satires, Epistles, Ars Poetica*, p. 450).
10 Montaigne, *Essays*, p. 574 (II, 37); p. 736 (III, 9); p. 611 (III, 2).
11 *Ibid.*, p. 61 (I, 20); p. 504 (II, 18); p. 273 (II, 6), p. 499 (II, 17); p. 504 (II, 18); p. 668 (III, 5); p. 843 (III, 13).
12 *Ibid.*, p. 720 (III, 8); p. 667 (III, 3).

13 J. Keats, *Letters*, I, 193.
14 Montaigne, *Essays*, p. 169 (I, 37). Montaigne's concept of and capacity for empathy is also discussed by I. D. McFarlane, in *Essays Presented to Alan M. Boase*, ed. D. R. Haggis *et al.*, p. 131, and by B. Hathaway, *Age of Criticism*, p. 427.
15 G. Puttenham, in *Essays*, ed. G. G. Smith, II, 20.
16 Montaigne, *Essays*, p. 251 (II, 3).
17 *Ibid.*, pp. 484–5 (II, 17); p. 761 (III, 9).
18 *Ibid.*, p. 409 (II, 12); p. 186 (I, 40); p. 761 (III, 9); p. 611 (III, 2); p. 171 (I, 37); p. 761 (III, 9); p. 135 (I, 28); p. 761 (III, 9). With customary incisiveness, H. Friedrich, *Montaigne*, pp. 352–3, notices Montaigne's idiosyncratic understanding of the *furor poeticus*. Montaigne, he writes, "prend bien soin de marquer que tout cela, à travers Platon et Plutarque, s'applique aux *Essais* eux-mêmes. Il les rapproche tous deux, et avec eux se rapproche, de l'enthousiasme poétique. Non pas à cause des visions inspirées, mais de l' 'alleure à sauts et à gambades,' de cette manière de se laisser porter et entraîner par l'inspiration du moment et le tempérament. Si on poursuit la lecture de ce passage, on y voit aussi paraître l'ambiguïté du *furor poeticus*: il est, par son côté négatif, un symptôme pathologique du vertige intellectuel découlant d'une disposition naturelle de l'homme, et il est, par son côté positif, la satisfaction de cette même disposition, source de bonheur." Regarding the traditional dissociation of the *divinus furor* from common *insania*, see above, pp. xxii–xxiii, 138ff.
19 Montaigne, *Essays*, p. 171 (I, 37).
20 *Ibid.*, p. 425 (II, 12); p. 404 (II, 12).
21 *Love's Labour's Lost*, IV, 3, 328–9. See above, pp. 120ff.
22 Spenser, "An Hymne of Heavenly Beautie," lines 1–3 (*Works*, VII (Part 1), p. 222).
23 Sidney, *Astrophel and Stella*, p. 17 (I, 10); p. 31 (XV, 10).
24 Sidney, in *Essays*, ed. G. G. Smith, I, 157, 159, 164.
25 F. Bacon, *Works*, IV, 7, 40.
26 *Ibid.*, IV, 53.
27 The possible influence Montaigne may have exerted on Bacon is discussed by P. Villey, *Montaigne et François Bacon*, p. 104. For the following, cf. *ibid.*, pp. 79ff.
28 F. Bacon, *Works*, III, 395.
29 Montaigne, *Essays*, p. 496 (II, 17); p. 425 (II, 12).
30 F. Bacon, *Works*, III, 396.
31 Montaigne, *Essays*, pp. 818–19 (III, 13).
32 F. Bacon, *Works*, IV, 61.
33 *Ibid.*, IV, 62.
34 Montaigne, *Essays*, p. 401 (II, 12).
35 F. Bacon, *Works*, III, 355.
36 Montaigne, *Essays*, p. 404 (II, 12).
37 F. Bacon, *Works*, IV, 336; III, 329; cf. V, 503–4.
38 Montaigne, *Essays*, p. 761 (III, 9).

39 F. Bacon, *Works*, v, 503. Especially critics who, like M. W. Bundy, *SP* 27 (1930), 244–64, view Bacon's poetics as intrinsically "rationalist" and unoriginal, read this and similar statements as characterizations "of poetry as a process of idealization" (*ibid.*, p. 244). By contrast, B. Hathaway, *Age of Criticism*, pp. 314–15, points out, I think correctly, that Bacon, in a tradition reaching from Tomitano to Addison, is really talking about poetry as capable of satisfying our penchant for wishful thinking rather than for idealization. See also J. L. Harrison, *HLQ* 20 (1965–7), 117: " 'Feigning' is Bacon's word, and since it is by feigning 'a more perfect order' that poetry raises the mind, the opening of the seventeenth-century onslaught on the idealistic *mimesis* of the poet may be said to begin here."

40 A. S. P. Woodhouse, *Princeton Encyclopedia*, p. 372.

41 F. Bacon, *Works*, III, 343.

42 Montaigne, *Essays*, p. 761 (III, 9).

43 Quoted by F. Bacon, *Works*, III, 382.

44 *Ibid.*

45 Montaigne, *Essays*, p. 135 (I, 28).

46 F. Bacon, *Works*, III, 343. "Pictoribus atque poetis" here is quoted from Horace, *De Arte Poetica*, line 10 (*Satires, Epistles, Ars Poetica*, p. 450). Imagination's powers to create forms non-existent in the real world by severing and rejoining common phenomena was, of course, described by other Renaissance writers, but never, so far as I know, in vindication of the kind of surrealistic conglomerates condemned by Horace. See W. Rossky, *SR* 5–6 (1958–9), 58–9. Instead, the imagination, in performing this particular function, is almost invariably "described as creating the disreputably incredible and false" (*ibid.*, p. 59).

47 See *OED* s.v. For the following, see also E. J. Sweeting, *Early Tudor Criticism*, pp. 1ff.

48 T. Lodge, in *Essays*, ed. G. G. Smith, I, 66.

49 R. Stanyhurst, *ibid.*, I, 136.

50 Sir John Harington, *ibid.*, II, 201–3.

51 Cf. J. W. H. Atkins, *English Literary Criticism*, pp. 28–9, 282–3.

52 Rabelais, *Oeuvres complètes*, p. 5.

53 Montaigne, *Essays*, 442 (II, 12).

54 Rabelais, *Oeuvres complètes*, p. 5.

55 Montaigne, *Essays*, p. 298 (II, 10).

56 Cf. Sidney, in *Essays*, ed. G. G. Smith, I, 191.

57 G. Puttenham, *ibid.*, II, 7.

58 *Ibid.*, I, xxv.

59 F. Bacon, *Works*, III, 345.

60 *Ibid.*

61 *Ibid.*, VI, 752–3.

62 *Ibid.*, IV, 344, 316, 317.

63 *Ibid.*, V, 504; IV, 316; III, 382; IV, 406.

64 For a detailed account of Bacon's changing attitudes toward myth

over the years, see P. Rossi, *Francis Bacon*, pp. 88ff.

65 F. Bacon, *Works*, III, 382; IV, 406.

66 *Ibid.*, III, 345; VI, 698, 698–9. Cf. K. R. Wallace, *Francis Bacon*, p. 84: "The imagination was not always directed, restrained, and bound by reason. It could serve a higher power than reason. Bacon saw it as the instrument of faith and divine grace and as the faculty through which God communicated directly with men."

67 See P. Rossi, *Francis Bacon*, p. 93.

68 E. Spenser, *Works*, I, 167.

69 F. Bacon, *Works*, IV, 316.

Notes to Chapter V

1 For this and the following, cf. J. L. Calderwood, *Shakespeare's Henriad*, pp. 183–220.

2 John of Salisbury, *Metalogicon*, p. 39.

3 Paracelsus, *Selected Writings*, p. 196.

4 T. Wilson, *Arte of Rhetorique*, p. 114.

5 J. C. Scaliger, *Poetices Libri Septem*, I, i, 3: "at poeta & naturam alterā ... ac demū sese isthoc ipso perinde ac Deum alterū efficit."

6 J. Hoskyns, *Directions*, p. 2.

7 Some of the terminology used in this chapter should be familiar from previous articles on *Troilus and Cressida*. See, for instance, I. A. Richards, *HR* 1 (1948–9), 362–76; and, more recently, J. O. Smith, *PQ* 46 (1967), 167–85.

8 For a discussion of *in utramque partem* or Sophistic rhetoric in classical and Renaissance literature, see C. O. McDonald, *Rhetoric of Tragedy*, *passim*; and, more recently, J. B. Altman, *Tudor Play of Mind*, pp. 3–4 *et passim*. See also J. H. Miller, *GR* 31 (1977), 44–60, about how Troilus' monologue here shows two separate language systems in conflict. One, a "monological" system, tries to preserve rational unity; another, a "dialogical" system, has a tendency to subvert such unity by creating self-division. See especially p. 51: "The 'madness' of Troilus's 'discourse' is the madness of his being forced by ocular testimony to break the 'rule' of unity, the principle of non-contradiction."

9 Cf. R. A. Yoder, *SS* 25 (1972), 24: "the speech begun in celestial and Platonic order ends with the 'greasy relics' of appetite."

10 Cf. R. A. Lanham, *Motives of Eloquence*, p. 125: "The poem is about the relation between the two poetics. A poem about defining essence – the marriage of true minds – it yet leans on its words in such a way, varying their sense with repetition, that essence dwells first in words: Love, love; alters, alteration; remover, remove. Is such a subject serious? It is and it isn't. The poem seems at once the most profound and the most playful in the sequence. Two different poems share the same words."

11 The topos derives from Horace's *Odes*, III, 30. Cf. J. W. Lever, *Elizabethan Love Sonnet*, pp. 268–9.

12 This, of course, has been noticed by several critics. See, e.g., C. Asp, *SQ* 22 (1971), 350–1. As L. Danson suggests, the play's very prologue foreshadows a concern with linguistic problems (*Shakespeare's Drama of Language*, pp. 168–70).

13 T. McAlindon, *PMLA* 84 (1969), 32.

14 *Ibid.*, pp. 35ff.

15 S. Booth, *Shakespeare's Sonnets*, pp. 86, 84, 104. For a different view of the matter, see J. D. Bernard, *PMLA* 94 (1979), 77–90. Ignoring the work of S. Booth and J. B. Leishman, Bernard argues that Shakespeare, in the Sonnets, "upholds the basic Renaissance belief in the transcendent power of the word." Here are some further findings of Bernard's along the same lines: "Having acknowledged as the source of his freedom the Logos, the Name of names by which the Godhead reveals itself to men, the poet goes on to record the petitioner's power to 'hallow' that name, that is, to certify and thus participate in its holiness. For the biblical verse echoed in Shakespeare's phrase is itself fully sacramental: it is efficacious, it fulfills itself. It is true, of course, that in the figural mode of the poem there remains a clear distinction between the actual Godhead and the beloved dressed in these borrowed words. Shakespeare is not being blasphemous here, but neither is he being muddle-headed. By identifying his own celebrations of his beloved with the devotions of the Christian worshipper, Shakespeare mimes the latter's appropriation of the *fiat*, the verbal mode of God" (p. 88).

16 Montaigne, *Essays*, p. 611 (III, 2).

17 *Ibid.*, 21 (I, 8).

18 M. M. Mahood, *Shakespeare's Wordplay*, pp. 174–5.

19 J. L. Calderwood, *Shakespeare's Henriad*, p. 5 *et passim*.

20 *2 Henry IV*, II, 4, 137–9. Cf. S. P. Zitner, in *"King Lear,"* ed. R. L. Colie *et al.*, p. 5.: "there are specifically contemporary reasons for Shakespeare's concern with the inadequacy of language. One is the impact of social change, of 'Antiquity forgot, custom not known, / The ratifiers, and props of every word' (*Hamlet* 4.5.104–5). An exchange in *Twelfth Night*, written at about the same time as *Hamlet* and full of significant parallels to it, illuminates this passage. 'Indeed,' says the Clown of *Twelfth Night*, 'words are very rascals since bonds disgraced them' (3.1.19ff.). The Clown's irony centres on the commercial and moral meanings of the word 'bond.' 'Thy reason, man?' the disguised Viola asks him. And the Clown continues, 'Troth, sir, I can yield you none without words, and words are grown so false I am loath to prove reason with them.' Shakespeare is sensitive to semantic change (see *2 Henry IV* 2.4.129ff. for example) arising from the growth of commercial enterprise and the cash nexus. He is fascinated by words like 'occupy' and 'commodity.' He doodles with the lingo of getting and spending in sonnet 30. The language of Goneril and Regan is full

of the counter and the counting house. Their terminology of 'possession and calculation' taints as it pre-empts Cordelia's language of
service and mutuality, of 'bond' and 'cause.' Language thus far
disgraced, says the Clown of *Twelfth Night*, is unfit even to think in."

21 *1 Henry IV*, V, 1, 130–40. Cf. *All's Well That Ends Well*, II, 3, 140–51; also
M. M. Mahood's comments on both passages in *Shakespeare's
Wordplay*, pp. 178–9; and G. L. Brook, *Language of Shakespeare*, p. 203.

22 Cf. *Sources*, ed. G. Bullough, III, 127–8.

23 *Twelfth Night*, III, 1, 34, 22, 56, 11–12; *As You Like It*, V, 1, 43–9.

24 *The Two Gentlemen of Verona*, II, 5, 22–8.

25 R. Berry, *Shakespearean Metaphor*, pp. 37ff.

26 A. Barton, *SS* 24 (1971), 27.

27 T. Hawkes, *Shakespeare's Talking Animals*, p. 179.

28 *Ibid.*, p. 187. For a different view on the matter, see G. R. Hibbard,
who points out that "if the other tragedies do evince a certain distrust
of language . . . on the part of their creator, this one does precisely the
opposite: in it there is unbounded confidence in the potentialities of
language, which seems capable of encompassing anything and
everything" (*Shakespeare's Styles*, ed. P. Edwards *et al.*, p. 98).

29 Margreta de Grazia, *SQ* 29 (1978), 379, 388.

30 Margreta de Grazia, *SpS* 1 (1980), 126, 130, 126, 127.

31 Quoted by J. Webster, *ELR* 11 (1981), 27. As will be obvious from my
argument, I disagree with Webster's claim that we should do away
with Stanley Fish's basic epistemological distinction between traditional (including Ramistic) rhetoric on the one hand and Francis
Bacon's "aphoristic method" on the other, and replace it by a strictly
stylistic terminology instead.

32 A. L. Deneef, in "Epideictic Rhetoric and the Renaissance Lyric,"
JMRS 3 (1973), 203–31, draws an important distinction along these
lines. In general, Deneef's findings seem to confirm E. R. Curtius'
suggestion that the "majority of lyric themes, which the modern poet
'creates' out of his 'experience,' were included in the list of epideictic
topoi by late antique theory" (*European Literature*, p. 158). But even
during the Renaissance there are important exceptions. "The latter,"
Deneef writes, "as seen perhaps in some of Shakespeare's sonnets or
in Donne's *Songs and Sonnets*, need not be complete in this sense.
They could, in fact, remain open-ended to the extent that they leave
further investigation of the subject, or even conclusions about the
significance of the subject, to the reader himself. The epideictic lyric,
however, purports to be the final word on the subject by virtue of its
dogmatic, celebratory tone and its representational, emblematic
form" (p. 222).

33 Quoted by J. Webster, *ELR* 11 (1981), 29.

34 F. Bacon, *Works*, III, 404; cf. IV, 449.

35 *Ibid.*, III, 405, 404; VII, 84.

36 J. B. Altman, *Tudor Play of Mind*, pp. 42–3 *et passim*.

37 In an essay read after I had completed the present chapter, G. J.

Greene, *SEL* 21 (1981), 273, points out the parallel between Shakespeare's attitude to language in *Troilus and Cressida* and Bacon's, as well as Montaigne's: "This sense of the arbitrary and conventional nature of language ... is expressed most clearly, in Shakespeare's day, by Montaigne and Bacon." G. J. Greene, however, only deals with these connections in passing (cf. *ibid.*, 277, 285).

38 F. Bacon, *Works*, III, 396.
39 Montaigne, *Essays*, p. 372 (II, 12).
40 F. Bacon, *Works*, IV, 61; III, 399.
41 Cicero, *De Oratore*, I, 8,
42 Ben Jonson, [*Works*], VIII, 620–1.
43 See T. Hawkes, *Shakespeare's Talking Animals*, pp. 15ff., for a convenient survey of recent studies of non-verbal communication.
44 Montaigne, *Essays*, p. 332 (II, 12).
45 *Ibid.*, p. 219 (I, 50); p. 751 (III, 9); p. 497 (II, 17); p. 392 (II, 12).
46 F. Bacon, *Works*, IV, 61.
47 Montaigne, *Essays*, pp. 405ff. (II, 12).
48 Quoted by H. Friedrich, *Montaigne*, p. 169; see also Hélène-Hedy Ehrlich, *Montaigne*, pp. 70ff.
49 Montaigne, *Essais*, p. 697 (II, 16).
50 Montaigne, *Essays*, p. 468 (II, 16). Cf. R. L. Regosin, *Montaigne's "Essais"*, p. 74: "Sebond's picture of a universe filled with symbols that lead back to their referent–author gives way to the world as obscure signs removed from their source, cut off from what they signify; they cannot point to any reality beyond themselves, they stand fundamentally as their own end."
51 Montaigne, *Essays*, p. 665 (III, 5). This "consubstantiality" or "ideal coincidence of thought and expression" in Montaigne has recently been analyzed by R. L. Regosin, *Montaigne's "Essais"*, p. 198 *et passim*.

Notes to Chapter VI

1 See J. C. Nelson, *Renaissance Theory of Love*, pp. 116ff.
2 *Ion*, 534 b 3–4 (*Collected Dialogues of Plato*, p. 220).
3 B. Castiglione, *Courtier*, p. 357.
4 L. A. Montrose, *Shakespeare's "Love's Labour's Lost"*, p. 119, describes "Berowne's paean to Love" as "a perverted analogue of Bembo's oration," but does not investigate this claim in detail. As is well known, Castiglione's *Il Cortegiano*, translated in 1561 into English by Sir Thomas Hoby, had much influence on English Renaissance literature (e.g., on Surrey, Wyatt, Sidney, and Spenser) and may also have helped inspire the Beatrice–Benedick relationship in Shakespeare's *Much Ado About Nothing*. See G. Bullough, ed., *Sources*, II, 78–80.
5 B. Castiglione, *Courtier*, p. 347.
6 Berowne's speech, of course, has often been analyzed in the context of Renaissance Neoplatonism. Most of these analyses, however,

overemphasize direct indebtedness at the expense of what a more recent critic calls Berowne's "satrical rendition of the Platonic ascent" (N. L. Goldstien, *SSt* 25 (1974) 341). See, e.g., J. Vyvyan, *Shakespeare and Platonic Beauty*, p. 65; J. Westlund, *SQ* 18 (1967), 39; and, more recently, S. K. Heninger, Jr, *SSt* 7 (1974), 38: "As though in the Academy indeed, he [i.e., Berowne] adopts the Platonic definition of love, with the steps leading to universal love so carefully laid out by Renaissance commentary." In all this, it also bears remembering that there is, as J. A. Notopoulos points out, "no evidence that Shakespeare had read Plato or Ficino; his poetry and plays reflect only a Platonism that he absorbed as part of the literary atmosphere of his time or that was reflected in his English and Italian sources" (*Platonism*, p. 108).

7 B. Castiglione, *Courtier*, p. 347.

8 N. L. Goldstien, *SSt* 25 (1974), 340, speaks of the play's "mockery of the Neoplatonic hierarchy of the senses" in this context.

9 This notion was, of course, a common one among Neoplatonists. See, e.g., M. Ficino, *Letters*, I, 44.

10 B. Castiglione, *Courtier*, p. 353.

11 J. L. Calderwood, *SEL* 5 (1965), 327, notes that Berowne's speech describes love "as a vivifying inner event, an intensification of sensory powers."

12 B. Castiglione, *Courtier*, p. 354.

13 Cf. W. C. Carroll, *Great Feast*, p. 151: "The conventional idea of love as an inspirational force is augmented by the notion that it preternaturally heightens sensibility at the same time."

14 G. Bruno, *Heroic Frenzies*, ed. P. E. Memmo, Jr, p. 40.

15 F. A. Yates, *A Study of "Love's Labour's Lost"*, p. 127.

16 For this and the following, see N. L. Goldstien, *SSt* 25 (1974), 339–40.

17 As Sears Jayne suggests in "Ficino and the Platonism of the English Renaissance," *CL* 4 (1952), 235, Florentine Neoplatonism for the most part reached England through France and was normally associated with Petrarchism.

18 As J. Grundy reminds us, criticism of Petrarchan and Neoplatonic conventions had, of course, become a tradition among continental writers long before Sir Philip Sidney (*SS* 15 (1962), 41ff.).

19 Sidney, *Astrophel and Stella*, p. 31 (15, 10).

20 Sidney, in *Essays*, ed. G. G. Smith, I, 202, 167.

21 *Ibid.*, I, 156.

22 See also D. H. Craig's recent assessment of critical theories regarding Sidney's poetics, *ELR* 10 (1980), 184: "The notion of the poet as the creator of a rival world to Nature's is not as audacious as it seems, Sidney says, since the achievement of the artificer lies in 'that *Idea* or fore-conceit of the work' and not in its execution, and the credit for this capacity to formulate ideas belongs to God." Surveying what he calls the "Mannerist," "Neo-Platonic," and "Calvinist" interpretations of *An Apologie for Poetrie*, Craig insists, I think rightly, that

"Rational and Aristotelian elements are ... the foundation of Sidney's theory" (*ibid.*, p. 200). I remain unconvinced by M. N. Raitiere's attempt to resolve the contradictions in Sidney's *Apology* by arguing that the author, foreshadowing "the romantic poetics of synthesis," pursued a deliberate rhetoric of unresolved contrast (*SEL* 21 (1981), especially pp. 38, 56–7.)

23 Joan Grundy, *SS* 15 (1962), 47, arrives at similar conclusions in comparing the implied poetics of Sidney's *Astrophel and Stella* and Shakespeare's Sonnets: "This [i.e., Sonnet 84, lines 5–12] is Shakespeare at his most Sidneyan: the central image, that of copying Nature's writing, is the same, and the conclusion, that this will make the writer famous for his style, is actually more typical of Sidney than it is of Shakespeare. (See, for example, *Astrophel and Stella*, sonnets XV and XC.) Even here, however, there is an essential difference in attitude. The implication in Sidney's sonnet that the poet has become a new and more successful kind of plagiarist – Nature's ape, not Pindar's – is missing in Shakespeare's. Instead, the point Shakespeare is making is that it is impossible for him to enhance his subject; he will do enough if he can but reproduce it. In other words, the centre of interest in Sidney's sonnet, for Sidney, is his own achievement; in Shakespeare's, it is his subject, and the key words are 'if he can tell / That you are you.'"

24 Sidney, in *Essays*, ed. G. G. Smith, I, 186; cf. I, 157, 159, 167.

25 Montaigne, *Essays*, pp. 840, 849, (III, 13).

26 Cf. R. Ellrodt, *SS* 28 (1975), 38.

27 Montaigne, *Essays*, p. 666 (III, 5).

28 *Ibid.*, p. 447 (II, 12); p. 445 (II, 12).

29 B. Castiglione, *Courtier*, p. 354.

30 As N. L. Goldstien points out, this negation and reversal of Neoplatonic conventions is all-pervasive in *Love's Labour's Lost*. None of the poems written by the aristocratic versifiers, for instance, "treats beauty as an intellectual abstraction, nor do they even successfully treat it as a mark of divinity – all of which ... effectively removes these poems from the realm of Neoplatonism" (*SSt* 25 (1974), 343).

31 See A. O. Lovejoy, *MLN* 42 (1927), 444–50; H. S. Wilson, *JHI* 2 (1941), 430–48; E. W. Tayler, *Nature and Art*, *passim*, and especially pp. 11ff.

32 H. S. Wilson, *JHI* 2 (1941), 441.

33 *Love's Labour's Lost*, ed. R. David, p. 114.

34 Thomas Lodge, e.g., paraphrased Horace's *De Arte Poetica*, 391–9, in his 1579 "Defence of Poetry, Music, and Stage Plays," written in response to Stephen Gosson's *Schoole of Abuse*; William Webbe gave a 41-point summing up of the Latin writer's poetics in his 1586 *Discourse of English Poetrie* and made "the best wryters agree that it was *Orpheus*, who by the sweete gyft of his heauenly Poetry withdrew men from raungyng vncertainly and wandring brutishly about, and made them gather together and keepe company, make houses, and keep fellowshippe together, who therefore is reported (as *Horace*

sayth) to asswage the fiercenesse of Tygers and mooue the harde
Flynts" (*Essays*, ed. G. G. Smith, I, 74, 234, 290–8).

35 Steevens quotes a striking parallel to this notion from *How a Man may
Chuse a Good Wife from a Bad* (1602) (Hazlitt's *Dodsley*, IX, 77): "Hath he
not torn those gold wires from your head, Wherewith Apollo would
have strung his harp, And kept them to play music to the gods?"
This, according to R. David, ed., *Love's Labour's Lost*, p. 114, "seems to
be a somewhat incoherent echo of the passage in the text."

36 Concerning the history of the Orpheus myth and its relation to
Renaissance literary theory, see J. B. Friedman, *Orpheus*; E. Sewell,
Orphic Voice, especially pp. 57ff.; and A. L. Deneef, *JMRS* 3 (1973),
224ff.

37 *The Merchant of Venice*, V, 1, 78–9; *The Two Gentlemen of Verona*, III, 2,
78–81.

38 J. B. Leishman, *Shakespeare's Sonnets*, p. 151. The general parallels
between Shakespeare's Sonnets and his other works have been
traced by C. Schaar, *Elizabethan Sonnet Themes*, pp. 136–82; and, more
recently, by K. Muir, *Shakespeare's Sonnets*, pp. 123ff.

39 Cf. Plato, *Republic*, x, 605 a ff. (*Collected Dialogues of Plato*, pp. 830ff.).

40 According to V. F. Petronella, *The Phoenix and the Turtle* presents us
with yet another variant of the "inverted Platonism" J. B. Leishman
noted in the Sonnets. "Incantation, magic-song, furor are all terms
that apply to the style and subject matter of *The Phoenix and the Turtle*.
But if ecstasy is supposed to be the state in which a literal separation
of soul from body takes place, then why talk of union of Phoenix
(soul) and Turtle-Dove (body), as if this were the end toward which
the poem's central characters are supposed ultimately to be headed?
Ideally the ecstatic state would find soul released from body. But in
The Phoenix and the Turtle the ecstasy is never brought off, and this is
the reason why Shakespeare speaks of 'division none' and the
'mutual flame' of death. The problem here is that body and soul are
consumed together, mutually. Never does the soul become separated
in order to enjoy observing the body from a distance as it would do if
true spiritual ecstasy took place. If any separation were to occur
(either explicitly or implicitly) in Shakespeare's poem, it would
become the kind of separation of body and soul that is in fact death.
But rather than dramatizing the soul's standing off from the body, the
poem confronts us with the death of both body and soul. Immortality, then, is out of the picture, no less than ecstatic fulfillment . . .
Instead of working toward the level of divine understanding . . . *The
Phoenix and the Turtle* takes us in the direction of a rational, rather than
a nonrational or 'enthusiastic,' vision. Shakespeare is using ecstatic
style and content for strictly terrestrial ends" (*SSt* 8 (1975), 321–2,
323).

41 Sonnet 85.

42 W. C. Carroll, *Great Feast*, p. 179.

43 It is interesting to note that Shakespeare himself, though he never

stopped playing on words, seems to have developed a new attitude to language following Berowne's bidding adieu to "taffeta phrases, silken terms precise," etc. His later puns, as G. D. Willcock, *Shakespeare as a Critic of Language*, p. 25, observes, reflect a "general apprehension of life" rather than of mere language. See also H. A. Ellis, *Shakespeare's Lusty Punning*, pp. 13–14.

44 A suggestion made by P. Cruttwell, *Shakespearean Moment*, p. 40, and other critics.

45 Compare Mercutio's "now art thou what thou art by art as well as by nature" in talking to the affected Romeo (II, 4, 87).

46 The speaker's poetics of silence, in this way, is far more than a temporary gesture valid only, as Gerald Hammond suggests, "at a time when silence is the only respectable form of expression" (*Shakespeare's Young Man Sonnets*, p. 108). Silenced by the self-reflective rhetoric of his rival, Shakespeare was only made more aware of a basic attitude, now made explicit, toward poetic language and what it is capable of expressing. See also "Beyond Words: Shakespeare's Tongue-Tied Muse" by T. R. Waldo, who, however, pursues a different perspective on Shakespeare's tongue-tied muse than that presented here. "This paper," Ms Waldo writes, will "explore in several dramatic situations the faltering language which accompanies love and advancing death" (*Shakespeare's "More than Words Can Witness,"* ed., S. Homan, p. 161).

47 As I. Ewbank reminds us, we cannot assume, of course, "that plainness of speech, or style, is the touchstone of sincerity. Plainness may itself become a convention, or an attitudinizing." But even I. Ewbank concedes that Shakespeare's "affirmation of 'true plain words' is part of a more essentialist poetic – stated *and* enacted in his sonnets – than Sidney's" (*ES* n.s. 34 (1981), 24, 25).

48 Cf. W. C. Carroll, *Great Feast*, p. 198: "The women themselves are ... fit educators for the academics ... [They] do not represent Nature alone any more than they do Art; rather, they suggest in themselves the most cunning and attractive blend of artifice and nature in the play, with the exception of the final songs."

49 Of course, there are more ways than those outlined here in which the two songs have been described as an integral part of *Love's Labour's Lost*, or even as "the ideal toward which the play's dialectic has all along been moving" (W. C. Carroll, *Great Feast*, p. 10). See, e.g., C. M. McLay, *SQ* 18 (1967), 119–27; J. Westlund, *SQ* 18 (1967), 37–46; R. Berry, *SS* 22 (1969), 69–77; S. K. Heninger, Jr, *SSt* 7 (1974), 25–53; R. G. Hunter, *SSt* 7 (1974), 55–64; M. Evans, *SQ* 26 (1975), 113–27. In terms of their implied poetics, as analyzed here, there is no evidence that the Winter song, as some critics (e.g., R. Berry and J. Westlund) have argued, points to the world beyond the Spring song and the world of the play itself. The two songs clearly transcend *Love's Labour's Lost*, but in doing so stand in a complementary rather than teleologically dialectic relationship to the play.

50 Cf. W. C. Carroll, *Great Feast*, p. 223.
51 *Love's Labour's Lost*, V, 2, 409.
52 *The Winter's Tale*, IV, 4, 91–2.
53 *A Midsummer Night's Dream*, V, 1, 9.

Notes to Chapter VII

1 Sidney, in *Essays*, ed. G. G. Smith, I, 136.
2 G. Puttenham, *ibid.*, II, 20.
3 See, e.g., W. Rossky, *SR* 5–6 (1958–9), 49–73, *passim*. As B. Hathaway, *Age of Criticism*, p. 334, points out, this general Renaissance distrust of the imagination was no doubt reinforced by English puritanism.
4 G. Fracastoro, *Navgerivs*, p. 128. For the fact that Fracastoro was basically "an Aristotelian infiltrated with Platonism," see B. Hathaway, *Age of Criticism*, pp. 316ff., and M. W. Bundy, *PQ* 20 (1941), 236–49, especially pp. 242–3.
5 Montaigne, *Essays*, p. 21 (I, 8); p. 135 (I, 28).
6 K. Muir, *Shakespeare the Professional*, p. 27. See also H. F. Brooks, ed., *A Midsummer Night's Dream*, p. cxl.
7 Cf. H. F. Brooks, ed., *A Midsummer Night's Dream*, p. 103.
8 Quoted by H. H. Furness, ed., *A Midsummer Night's Dream*, p. 202.
9 H. F. Brooks, ed., *A Midsummer Night's Dream*, p. 104.
10 K. Muir, *Shakespeare the Professional*, p. 26. See also E. C. Pettet, *ES* n.s. 3 (1950), 32–3; S. K. Heninger, Jr, *Touches of Sweet Harmony*, p. 294: "Inspired by Plato's *divinus furor*, the poet surveys the plenitude of God's creation, from heaven to earth and back again. Excited by this experience, his imagination *'bodies forth* / The forms of things unknown' – makes particular, and therefore palpable, the Platonic ideas, which otherwise would remain for us ineffable and unknowable."
11 H. F. Brooks, ed., *A Midsummer Night's Dream*, pp. cxl, 104.
12 T. Lodge, in *Essays*, ed. G. G. Smith, I, 72.
13 G. Chapman, in *Essays*, ed. G. G. Smith, II, 297.
14 *Return from Parnassus* (I, 6), pp. 22ff. *et passim*. See also Drayton's lines on Marlowe in his "Epistle to Reynolds," as quoted in H. Cuningham, ed., *A Midsummer Night's Dream*, p. 132: "And that fine madness still he did retain / Which rightly should possess the poet's brain."
15 Cf. *Phaedrus* 244b (*Collected Dialogues of Plato*, p. 491).
16 Quoted in G. Bruno, *Heroic Frenzies*, ed. P. E. Memmo, Jr, p. 19. See also J. C. Nelson, *Renaissance Theory of Love*, p. 170; M. Ficino, *Letters*, I, 42ff., 98; and, concerning the concepts of poetic frenzy in Italian literary criticism of the Renaissance, B. Weinberg, *Literary Criticism*, Index under "Furor."
17 See G. Bruno, *Heroic Frenzies*, ed. P. E. Memmo, Jr, p. 19; also J. C. Nelson, *Renaissance Theory of Love*, p. 178: "Bruno's *eroico furore* is from the beginning distinguished by its intellectuality."

18 Quoted by J. W. H. Atkins, *English Literary Criticism*, p. 108.

19 G. Chapman, *Plays*, II, 444 (*Masque of the Middle Temple and Lincoln's Inn*, Preface). For further evidence concerning the general Renaissance dissociation of the *furor poeticus* from common lunacy, see B. Hathaway, *Age of Criticism*, pp. 399ff.; M. Kemp, *V* 8 (1977), 384ff.; and the defense of poetic "feigning" and frenzy in the Epistle to Sir William Cecil, in M. Palingenius, *Zodiake of Life*, n.p.

20 G. Chapman, in *Essays*, ed. G. G. Smith, II, 297.

21 Quoted by J. W. H. Atkins, *English Literary Criticism*, p. 108.

22 According to V. F. Petronella, a similar negation of the traditional *furor poeticus* occurs in Shakespeare's *The Phoenix and the Turtle*. In the critic's view, "the Neoplatonic discussions of 'divine madness' (or what Shakespeare calls 'fine frenzy' in *A Midsummer Night's Dream* [V, 1, 12]), with the religious mystical vestiges that the term carries, are deeply involved in the thematic and stylistic constitution of *The Phoenix and the Turtle*." But such frenzy, even though reinforced by the traditional love ecstasy, never reaches its Platonic goal. "All the *furores* involve emotional intensity and are in this way related to one another, but central to *The Phoenix and the Turtle* is the all-important love-madness, which, as Ficino tells us, turns the head of the charioteer in man's soul 'toward the head of all things.' The poem's tripartite structure, a feature recognized by many of the commentators already referred to, acts as a vehicle for the theme of love-madness. Commentary on the poem's structure, however, has not touched upon the similarity between the stylistic mode of *The Phoenix and the Turtle* and that of the Orphic pastoral. A consideration of the similarity is illuminating. Richard Cody ... analyses the basic rhythm of Neoplatonic pastoral in terms of three phases: *Emanatio* (procession), *Raptio* (rapture or ecstasy), and *Remeatio* (return or recession). Poliziano, like Pico della Mirandola and Ficino, envisions the Orpheus myth as an allegory of the death and the new life of the Rational Soul, 'lost and found again in the flames of intellectual love' ... The first twenty lines constitute the *Emanatio* of Shakespeare's poem ... We then move into the anthem and its attempt to analyze the mystery of love-madness and the love-death of Phoenix and Turtle-Dove; this is the poem's *Raptio*, and rapturous it is. Union is spiritual and physical for Phoenix and Turtle-Dove; their mutual consummation, given one of the meanings of dying in Shakespeare's time, is highly erotic as well as hopefully regenerative. But although the erotic ecstasy takes place, the spiritual ecstasy never reaches its special kind of climax" (*SSt* 8 (1975), 319, 323–4). The book referred to by V. F. Petronella is R. Cody's *Landscape of the Mind*.

23 Sidney, in *Essays*, ed. G. G. Smith, I, 157. See above, pp. 20ff.

24 See also G. R. Hibbard, *SS* 31 (1978), 81: "Her [i.e., Hippolyta's] deliberate substitution of 'fancy' for Theseus's 'imagination' almost suggests that Shakespeare was on the point of making Coleridge's distinction between the two."

25 The phrase is that of T. Bright, *Treatise of Melancholie*, p. 102. See also W. Rossky, *SR* 5–6 (1958–9), p. 59.

26 Ronsard, quoted by M. W. Bundy, *JEGP* 29 (1930), 542.

27 G. Puttenham, in *Essays*, ed. G. G. Smith, II, 19.

28 *Ibid.*, II, 20.

29 Cf. D. P. Young, *The Art of "A Midsummer Night's Dream,"* pp. 133–4.

30 G. Puttenham, in *Essays*, ed. G. G. Smith, II, 20. Cf. M. W. Bundy, *PQ* 20 (1941), 239, 245.

31 *Macbeth*, V, 3, 40.

32 *2 Henry IV*, I, 3, 31; cf. *1 Henry IV*, I, 3, 199.

33 W. Pater, *Works*, V, 194.

34 W. B. Yeats, *Essays and Introductions*, p. 105.

35 W. Clemen, *Shakespeare's Imagery*, p. 55. Richard's and Bolingbroke's penchant toward play-acting is also studied by L. F. Dean, *PMLA* 67 (1952), 211–18, *passim*.

36 Gianfrancesco Pico della Mirandola, *On the Imagination*, p. 47.

37 G. Puttenham, in *Essays*, ed. G. G. Smith, II, 19–20. Gianfrancesco Pico della Mirandola, nephew of the famous Pico della Mirandola, uses a similar image in his *On the Imagination* (ed. H. Caplan, p. 63): "But those distorted and corrupted lenses I have treated in a previous chapter must generally be laid aside, and correct and clear ones selected. In other words, the habiliments of the excessive and bad affections are to be stripped off, those of the good and few assumed; for from the former proceeds false imagination, which weakens and distorts a judgment otherwise sound."

38 *The Rape of Lucrece*, 1105–6.

39 T. S. Eliot, *Selected Essays*, p. 145.

40 G. Puttenham, in *Essays*, ed. G. G. Smith, II, 20.

41 H. Dubrow, *SQ* 32 (1981), 62.

Notes to Chapter VIII

1 Quoted by M. H. Abrams, *The Mirror*, p. 275.

2 *Ibid.*, p. 382.

3 *Ibid.*, p. 275.

4 See above, p. 90.

5 For this and the following, see above, pp. 90ff.

6 See E. R. Dodds, *Greeks and the Irrational*, p. 180.

7 Quoted by G. S. Kirk and J. E. Raven, *The Presocratic Philosophers*, p. 168.

8 A definitive account of witchcraft and magic in Renaissance England is found in Keith Thomas' *Religion and the Decline of Magic*, *passim*.

9 R. Scot, *Discouerie of Witchcraft*, sig. Abr–v (pp. 52–3).

10 R. Hunter and I. Macalpine, *Three Hundred Years of Psychiatry*, p. 32.

11 L. Lavater, *Of Ghostes*, p. 9.

12 Quoted by Cyrus Hoy, ed., *Hamlet*, p. 109.

13 Quoted in Charles E. Goshen, *Documentary History of Psychiatry*, pp. 73, 74. See also R. Scot, *Discouerie of Witchcraft*, p. 66.

14 For this and the following, see R. Hunter and I. Macalpine, *Three Hundred Years of Psychiatry*, p. 47.

15 James I, *Daemonologie*, n.p.

16 This is a viewpoint also argued by R. H. West in *The Invisible World*, *passim*, and *Shakespeare*, *passim*.

17 *1 Henry VI*, I, 5, 5, 21; III, 2, 38, 52; II, 1, 15, 18; V, 4, 39–40, 42.

18 G. Bullough, ed., *Sources*, III, 77.

19 Cf. *ibid.*, pp. 93 and 124.

20 Cf. M. C. Latham, *The Elizabethan Fairies*, *passim*.

21 *Antony and Cleopatra*, III, 11, 38.

22 For the following, see J. Dover Wilson's introduction to L. Lavater, *Of Ghostes*, pp. vii–xxviii; as well as R. H. West, "King Hamlet's Ambiguous Ghost," *Shakespeare*, pp. 56–68, especially p. 65: "Shakespeare gives the Ghost 'vitality,' in part simply by reminding the audience that apparitions were a subject of current and serious experience and speculation and that anybody might find himself confonted with one."

23 *The Merry Wives of Windsor*, III, 3, 191.

24 Cf. E. Prosser, *Hamlet and Revenge*, p. 137, who argues that the ghost, much like an infernal emissary, does everything "to taint Hamlet's mind with lacerating grief, sexual nausea, hatred, and fury."

25 Cf. R. H. West, *Shakespeare*, pp. 72ff.

26 F. Kermode, ed., *The Tempest*, p. xli.

27 James I, *Daemonologie*, p. 9.

28 R. H. West, *Shakespeare*, p. 84.

29 Cf. R. H. West, *Shakespeare*, p. 89.

30 Cf. F. Kermode, ed., *The Tempest*, p. 143.

31 G. Bullough, ed., *Sources*, VIII, 245.

32 See above, p. 151, n. 1.

33 Cf. R. H. West, *Invisible World*, p. 164.

34 Cf. R. Scot, *Discouerie of Witchcraft*, n.p.: "But Robin goodfellowe ceaseth now to be much feared" ("The Epistle").

35 See above, p. 155.

36 James I, *Daemonologie*, p. 22. See also J. E. M. Latham, *SS* 28 (1975), 122–3.

37 Quoted by F. Kermode, ed., *The Tempest*, p. xli.

38 Cf. E. Schanzer, ed., *Pericles*, pp. xxiii, 97.

39 Quoted by F. Kermode, ed., *The Tempest*, p. xli.

40 See above, p. 159.

41 Cf. F. Kermode, ed., *The Tempest*, p. 104.

42 *Cymbeline*, V, 4, 92ff.

Notes to Chapter IX

1 J. H. P. Pafford, ed., *The Winter's Tale*, p. 168, gives no reasons for claiming that "it is surely wrong to assume that Shakespeare makes Time speak as the author." For a more balanced view on the matter,

see F. Turner, *Shakespeare and the Nature of Time*, pp. 146ff. See also L. G. Salingar, *RD* 9 (1966), pp. 3–4.

2 See E. Schanzer, *SS* 28 (1975), pp. 57–61, and above, p. 52.
3 F. Kermode, ed., *The Winter's Tale*, p. 93.
4 Cf. I. Ewbank, *REL* 5 (1964), 92.
5 F. Turner, *Shakespeare and the Nature of Time*, p. 183.
6 Cf. J. Lawlor, *PQ* 41 (1962), 105: "It is not, indeed, the Triumph of Time, but the human wish to triumph over time, here for once fulfilled. Time is allowed an authentic scope, evident alike in the 'wrinkled' face of Hermione (against the human wish to arrest time in a remembered perfection) and in the grief which Time will not assuage." For a different view on this matter, see I. Ewbank, *REL* 5 (1964), 93–100.
7 Montaigne, *Essays*, p. 456 (ii, 12).
8 *Pericles*, II, 3, 45–7.
9 Quoted by Ravi Ravindra, *DR* 51 (1971–2), 9.
10 Quoted by K. Rahner, *Theologie der Zukunft*, p. 69.
11 Montaigne, *Essays*, p. 77 (i, 22); p. 64 (i, 20); p. 457 (ii, 12).
12 *Ibid.*, p. 457 (ii, 12).
13 I. Ewbank, *REL* 5 (1964), 94.
14 Cf. S. L. Bethell, *The Winter's Tale*, pp. 47ff.
15 Cf. R. Proudfoot, *SS* 29 (1976), 71.
16 B. A. Mowat, *Dramaturgy*, p. 20.
17 John Jones' phrase quoted in W. Kerr, *Tragedy and Comedy*, p. 44.
18 Quoted in *Hegel on Tragedy*, ed. A. and H. Paolucci, p. 367.
19 E. Faas, *Tragedy and After*, pp. 28ff.
20 *Sources*, ed. G. Bullough, viii, 199.
21 J. A. Bryant, Jr, *Hippolyta's View*, p. 222. See also R. M. Frye, *Shakespeare and Christian Doctrine*, p. 37, *et passim*.
22 G. W. Knight, *Shakespeare and Religion*, p. 235.
23 According to G. F. Waller's investigations of "The Philosophy of Time in Shakespeare and Elizabethan Literature," Time in *The Winter's Tale* appears as "both destroyer and creator." Time and Chance, in this way, "become the play's equivalent of beneficent Providence" (*Strong Necessity of Time*, pp. 156, 161). F. Pyle draws attention to the sudden change of style coincident with the appearance of Time: "The arresting, eye-catching mode of presentation, unique in the play, interrupting the action and abruptly involving a complete change of mood and style, corresponds in its instantaneous effect upon the audience to the effect of the time shift itself" (*"The Winter's Tale"*, p. 72).
24 N. Coghill, *SS* 11 (1958), 35.
25 E. Faas, *Tragedy and After*, pp. 132ff. For a similar discussion of rebirth and transformation in *Pericles* and *The Winter's Tale*, see C. L. Barber, *SS* 22 (1969), 59–67.
26 *The Winter's Tale*, IV, 4, 88.
27 Cf. E. Faas, *Tragedy and After*, pp. 135, 137.

28 Ovid, *Metamorphoses*, p. 373. For a similar discussion of the treatment of time in Ovid's *Metamorphoses* and *The Winter's Tale*, see W. Blissett, *ELR* 1 (1971), 57.
29 Quoted by E. A. J. Honigmann, *PQ* 34 (1955), 35.
30 F. Bacon, *Works*, VI, 759.
31 E. Schanzer, *REL* 5 (1964), 74ff.; R. Proudfoot, *SS* 29 (1976), 67–78.
32 G. Bullough, ed., *Sources*, VIII, 152.
33 Cf. M. Mueller, *CD* 5 (1971), 226–39, especially pp. 235–6.
34 J. H. P. Pafford, ed., *The Winter's Tale*, p. liii.
35 As I. Ewbank, *REL* 5 (1964), 93, points out, "it is important that Perdita, who is herself almost an image of time seen as natural growth, should first appear in a world where time equals the life of nature and the cycle of the seasons."
36 F. Kermode, ed., *The Winter's Tale*, p. 33.
37 Cf. J. H. P. Pafford, ed., *The Winter's Tale*, p. 169.
38 Montaigne, *Essays*, p. 152 (I, 31).
39 G. Puttenham, in *Essays*, ed. G. G. Smith, II, 188.
40 A. O. Lovejoy and G. Boas, *Primitivism*, p. 207.
41 E. W. Tayler, *Nature and Art*, pp. 135–6.
42 Harold S. Wilson, *JHI* 2 (1941), 441–2, 447. See also R. Tuve, *Elizabethan and Metaphysical Imagery*, pp. 37–8.
43 Homer, *Iliad*, xx, 65–6.
44 *Corpus Hermeticum*, p. 29.
45 Aristotle, *Physics* 199 a 16–17; *Politics* 1337 a 41 (*Basic Works*, pp. 250, 1305).
46 Quoted by E. W. Tayler, *Nature and Art*, p. 29.
47 S. Daniel, in *Essays*, ed. G. G. Smith, II, 359.
48 Montaigne, *Essays*, p. 666 (III, 5).
49 F. Bacon, *Works*, IV, 295.
50 For the following, see J. H. Hagstrum, *The Sister Arts*, pp. 87ff.
51 Cf. E. Panofsky, *Idea*, pp. 47ff.
52 Quoted by L. Barkan, *ELH* 48 (1981), 656.
53 L. Barkan, *ELH* 48 (1981), 641.
54 J. H. Hagstrum, *Sister Arts*, p. 87.
55 *Ibid.*, p. 88.
56 E. F. Wright, *EL* 6 (1979), 147, discussing the deliberate "artificiality of the dramatic medium" in *The Winter's Tale*, also draws attention to Shakespeare's repeated use of the play metaphor (e.g., IV, 4, 655–6, 133–4, 592–4; III, 2, 33–7; V, 2, 79–80).
57 E. F. Wright, though somewhat *à rebours*, arrives at similar conclusions in her interesting essay " 'We Are Mock'd With Art': Shakespeare's Wintry Tale," *EL* 6 (1979), 156: "Old tales lack credit; their verity is in strong suspicion. Perdita, we will remember, persists in her belief that art is to be mistrusted. Autolycus's ballads, though guaranteed to be true, are obviously extravagant fictions, those who believe them, albeit charming, are ignorant rustics. In short, art generally falsifies reality. One may object that since it is a work of art –

the play itself – which communicates this truth, Shakespeare has in effect vindicated art. Perhaps, but if so, this is an art which differs strikingly from the conventional 'closed' art forms . . . [Shakespeare] has left his creation, like the philosophical debates it contains, open-ended and undecided. He has not made dogmatic pronouncements about the world of nature, nor in fact has he presented us with a clear-cut rejection of art." For an earlier discussion of the "natural art" of *The Winter's Tale*, see M. L. Livingstone, *MLQ* 30 (1969), 340–55.

58 F. Bacon, *Works*, IV, 294–5.

59 See J. A. Mazzeo, *Renaissance and Revolution*, p. 192, and D. P. Young, *Art of "A Midsummer Night's Dream,"* pp. 143–4. Such dissolution of the art–nature dichotomy, of course, becomes a common trend during the Romantic period. See, e.g., H. V. S. Ogden, *JEGP* 38 (1939), 597–616, *passim*.

60 Montaigne, *Essays*, pp. 400–1 (II, 12).

61 *Ibid.*, p. 666 (III, 5).

62 Contrary to traditional Christian interpretations of *The Winter's Tale* as a play about sin, penance, and redemption several studies have revealed the darker, or perhaps we should say fatalistic, aspects of its ending. See, e.g., E. F. Wright, *EL* 6 (1979), 149ff.; C. Leech, *SS* 11 (1958), 25 *et passim*.

63 F. D. Hoeniger, *UTQ* 20 (1950), 25.

64 E. F. Wright, *EL* 6 (1979), 154.

Notes to Conclusion

1 As G. C. Taylor suggests, reading Montaigne may well have influenced Shakespeare along these lines: "It is rather remarkable that during and after 1603 some five or six times nature and art are definitely compared and contrasted in the plays, and always to the disadvantage of art. 'Nature's above art in that respect,' cries Lear; above art also in the other references to the matter. This is one of Montaigne's favorite theses: 'There is no reason art should gain the point of honor of our great mother Nature'" (*Shakespeare's Debt to Montaigne*, p. 38).

2 Montaigne, *Essays*, p. 77 (II, 22).

3 *Love's Labour's Lost*, III, 1, 58.

4 *Henry V*, I, Prologue, 1–2.

5 A. Righter, *Idea of the Play*, p. 171. See also A. B. Kernan, *Playwright as Magician*, pp. 150ff.

6 *Troilus and Cressida*, V, 2, 140.

7 *Love's Labour's Lost*, IV, 3, 318.

Bibliography

[This bibliography only lists works cited or mentioned in the text and/or in the annotations of this study.]

Abel, Lionel. *Metatheatre: A New View of Dramatic Form*. New York: Hill & Wang, 1963.

Abrams, M. H. *The Mirror and the Lamp: Romantic Theory and the Critical Tradition*. New York: Norton, 1958 (first 1953).

Abrams, Richard. "The Tempest and the Concept of the Machiavellian Playwright." *English Literary Renaissance* 8 (1978), 43–66.

Altman, Joel B. *The Tudor Play of Mind: Rhetorical Inquiry and the Development of Elizabethan Drama*. Berkeley: University of California Press, 1978.

Anderson, Ruth L. *Elizabethan Psychology and Shakespeare's Plays*. New York: Russell & Russell, 1966 (first 1927).

Andrews, Jeanne. "Bacon and the Dissociation of Sensibility." *Notes and Queries* 199 (1954), 484–6, 530–2.

Ansari, A. A. "The Mockery of Art in *The Winter's Tale*," *Aligarh Journal of English Studies* 4 (1979), 124–41.

Aristotle. *The Basic Works*. Edited and with an introduction by Richard McKeon. New York: Random House, 1941.

Rhetoric and Poetics (*Rhetoric* translated by W. Rhys Roberts; *Poetics* translated by Ingram Bywater). New York: Random House, 1954.

Armstrong, Edward A. *Shakespeare's Imagination: A Study of the Psychology of Association and Inspiration*. London: L. Drummond, 1946.

Asp, Carolyn. "Th' Expense of Spirit in a Waste of Shame." *Shakespeare Quarterly* 22 (1971), 345–57.

Atkins, J. W. H. *English Literary Criticism: The Renascence*. London: Methuen, 1947.

Literary Criticism in Antiquity: A Sketch of its Development. 2 vols. London: Methuen, 1952.

Bacon, Francis. *The Works*. 14 vols. Edited by James Spedding, Robert Leslie Ellis, and Douglas Denon Heath. New York: Garrett Press, 1968 (first 1857–74).

Baldwin, T. W. *Shakespere's Five-Act Structure: Shakespere's Early Plays on the Background of Renaissance Theories of Five-Act Structure From 1470*. Urbana: University of Illinois Press, 1963 (first 1947).

Barber, C. L. "'Thou That Beget'st Him That Did Thee Beget': Trans-formation in 'Pericles' and 'The Winter's Tale'." *Shakespeare Survey* 22 (1969), 59–67.

Barkan, Leonard. "'Living Sculptures:' Ovid, Michelangelo, and *The Winter's Tale*." *English Literary History* 48 (1981), 639–67.

Bartlett, John. *A Complete Concordance . . . of Shakespeare . . .* London: Mac-millan, 1972 (first 1894).

Barton, Anne. "Leontes and the Spider: Language and Speaker in Shakespeare's Last Plays," pp. 131–50 in *Shakespeare's Styles: Essays in Honour of Kenneth Muir*. Edited by Philip Edwards, Inga-Stina Ewbank and G. K. Hunter. Cambridge: Cambridge University Press, 1980.

"Shakespeare and the Limits of Language." *Shakespeare Survey* 24 (1971), 19–30.

Battenhouse, Roy W. "The Significance of Hamlet's Advice to the Players," pp. 3–26 in *The Drama of the Renaissance: Essays for Leicester Bradner*. Edited by Elmer M. Blistein. Providence, RI: Brown Uni-versity Press, 1970.

Beaumont, Francis, and Fletcher, John. *The Works of Beaumont and Fletcher*. 10 vols. Edited by Arnold Glover. New York: Octagon Books, 1969.

Beni, Paolo. *Disputatio*. Patavii: Apud Franciscum Bolzetam, 1600.

Berek, Peter, "'As We Are Mock'd With Art': From Scorn to Transfigur-ation." *Studies in English Literature. 1500–1900* 18 (1978), 289–305.

Berg, Sara van den. "'The Paths I Meant unto Thy Praise': Jonson's Poem for Shakespeare." *Shakespeare Studies* 11 (1978), 207–18.

Bernard, John D. "'To Constancie Confin'de': The Poetics of Shake-speare's Sonnets." *PMLA* 94 (1979), 77–90.

Berry, Ralph. *The Shakespearean Metaphor: Studies in Language and Form*. London: Macmillan, 1978.

"The Words of Mercury." *Shakespeare Survey* 22 (1969), 69–77.

Bevington, David. *Action is Eloquence: Shakespeare's Language of Gesture*. Cambridge, Mass.: Harvard University Press, 1984.

Bethell, Samuel L. *Shakespeare and the Popular Dramatic Tradition*. London: Staples Press, 1948 (first 1944).

The Winter's Tale: A Study. London: Staples Press, 1947.

Blissett, William. "'This Wide Gap of Time': *The Winter's Tale*." *English Literary Renaissance* 1 (1971), 52–70.

Booth, Stephen. *An Essay on Shakespeare's Sonnets*. New Haven, Conn.: Yale University Press, 1969.

"Speculations on Doubling in Shakespeare's Plays," pp. 103–31 in *Shakespeare: The Theatrical Dimension*. Edited by Philip C. McGuire and David A. Samuelson. New York: AMS Press, 1979.

Booth, W. C. *The Rhetoric of Fiction*. Chicago, Ill.: University of Chicago Press, 1961.

Bridge, Sir Frederick. *Shakespearean Music in the Plays and Early Operas*. New York: Haskell House, 1965 (first 1923).

Bright, Timothy. *A Treatise of Melancholie*. New York: Da Capo Press, 1969 (first 1586).

Brook, G. L. *The Language of Shakespeare*. London: André Deutsch, 1976.

Bruno, Giordano. *The Heroic Frenzies*. A Translation with Introduction and Notes by Paul E. Memmo, Jr. Chapel Hill: University of North Carolina Press, 1964.

Bryant, J. A., Jr. *Hippolyta's View: Some Christian Aspects of Shakespeare's Plays*. Lexington: University of Kentucky Press, 1961.

Bullough, Geoffrey, ed., *Narrative and Dramatic Sources of Shakespeare*. 8 vols. London: Routledge & Kegan Paul, 1957–75.

Bundy, Murray W. "Bacon's True Opinion of Poetry." *Studies in Philology* 27 (1930), 244–64.

"Fracastoro and the Imagination." *Philological Quarterly* 23 (1941), 236–49.

"'Invention' and 'Imagination' in the Renaissance." *Journal of English and Germanic Philology* 29 (1930), 535–45.

Buonamici, Francesco. *Discorsi poetici nella Accademia fiorentina in difesa d'Aristotile*. Florence: Giorgio Marescotti, 1597.

Burton, Robert. *The Anatomy of Melancholy*. Edited with an Introduction by Holbrook Jackson. New York: Random House, 1977.

Calderwood, James L. "*Love's Labour's Lost*: A Wantoning with Words." *Studies in English Literature* 5 (1965), 317–32.

Metadrama in Shakespeare's Henriad: Richard II to Henry V. Berkeley: University of California Press, 1979.

"*Richard II to Henry V*: Poem to Stage," pp. 43–61 in *Shakespeare's "More Than Words Can Witness:" Essays on Visual and Nonverbal Enactment in the Plays*. Edited by Sidney Homan. Lewisburg, Pa: Bucknell University Press, 1980.

Shakespearean Metadrama: The Argument of the Play in "Titus Andronicus," "Love's Labour's Lost," "Romeo and Juliet," "A Midsummer Night's Dream" and "Richard II". Minneapolis: University of Minnesota Press, 1971.

Carpenter, Nan C. "Shakespeare and Music: Unexplored Areas." *Renaissance Drama* n.s. 7 (1976), 243–55.

Carroll, William C. *The Great Feast of Language in "Love's Labour's Lost"*. Princeton, NJ: Princeton University Press, 1976.

"'A Received Belief': Imagination in *The Merry Wives of Windsor*." *Studies in Philology* 74 (1977), 186–215.

Castelvetro, Lodovico. *Poetica d'Aristotele vulgarizzata, et sposta*. Vienna: Gaspar Stainhofer, 1576 (first 1570).

Castiglione, B. *The Book of the Courtier*. A New Translation by Charles S. Singleton. Garden City, NY: Doubleday, 1959.

Castor, Grahame. *Pléiade Poetics: A Study in Sixteenth-Century Thought and Terminology*. Cambridge: Cambridge University Press, 1964.

Chambers, E. K. *William Shakespeare: A Study of Facts and Problems*. 2 vols. Oxford: Clarendon Press, 1930.

Chapman, George. *The Poems of George Chapman*. Edited by Phyllis Brooks Bartlett. New York: Russell & Russell, 1962.

Charlton, H. B. *The Senecan Tradition in Renaissance Tragedy*. Manchester: Manchester University Press, 1946 (first 1921).

Cicero, Marcus Tullius. *De Oratore*. Translated by E. W. Sutton. Completed, with an introduction by H. Rackham. The Loeb Classical Library. Cambridge, Mass.: Harvard University Press, 1942.

Clemen, Wolfgang. *The Development of Shakespeare's Imagery*. London: Methuen, 1977 (first 1951).

Clements, Robert J. *Critical Theory and Practice of the Pléiade*. New York: Octagon Books, 1970.

Cody, Richard. *The Landscape of the Mind: Pastoralism and Platonic Theory in Tasso's Aminta and Shakespeare's Early Comedies*. Oxford: Clarendon Press, 1969.

Coghill, Nevill. "Six Points of Stage-Craft in *The Winter's Tale*." *Shakespeare Survey* 11 (1958), 31–41.

Cope, Jackson I. *The Theater and the Dream: From Metaphor to Form in Renaissance Drama*. Baltimore and London: Johns Hopkins University Press, 1973.

Corpus Hermeticum: The Divine Pymander and Other Writings of Hermes Trismegistus. Translated by John D. Chambers. New York: Samuel Weiser, 1975.

Cowling, George H. *Music on the Shakespearean Stage*. Cambridge: Cambridge University Press, 1913.

Craig, D. H. "A Hybrid Growth: Sidney's Theory of Poetry in *An Apology for Poetry*." *English Literary Renaissance* 10 (1980), 183–201.

Cruttwell, Patrick. *The Shakespearean Moment and its Place in The Poetry of the 17th Century*. New York: Random House 1960 (first 1954).

Curtius, E. R. *European Literature and the Latin Middle Ages*. Translated by Willard R. Trask. Bollingen Series xxxvi. Princeton, NJ: Princeton University Press, 1973 (first 1953).

Cutts, John P. "Music and the Supernatural in *The Tempest*: A Study in Interpretation." *Music and Letters* 39 (1958), 347–58.

Danson, Lawrence. *Tragic Alphabet: Shakespeare's Drama of Language*. New Haven, Conn.: Yale University Press, 1974.

Dawson, Anthony B. *Indirections: Shakespeare and the Art of Illusion*. Toronto: University of Toronto Press, 1978.

Dean, Leonard F. "*Richard II*: The State and the Image of the Theater." *PMLA* 67 (1952), 211–18.

Dekker, Thomas. *The Dramatic Works of Thomas Dekker*. 4 vols. Edited by Fredson Bowers. Cambridge: Cambridge University Press, 1953.

The Guls Horn-Booke and The Belman of London. London: Dent, 1904 (first 1608, 1609).

Deneef, A. Leigh. "Epideictic Rhetoric and the Renaissance Lyric." *The Journal of Medieval and Renaissance Studies* 3 (1973), 203–31.

Dent, R. W. "Imagination in *A Midsummer Night's Dream.*" *Shakespeare Quarterly* 15 (1964), 115–29.

Dessen, Alan C. "Elizabethan Audiences and the Open Stage: Recovering Lost Conventions." *The Yearbook of English Studies* 10 (1980), 1–20.

Elizabethan Drama and the Viewer's Eye. Chapel Hill: University of North Carolina Press, 1977.

"The Logic of Elizabethan Stage Violence: Some Alarms and Excursions for Modern Critics, Editors, and Directors." *Renaissance Drama* 9 (1978), 39–69.

Dodds, E. R. *The Greeks and the Irrational.* Berkeley: University of California Press, 1973 (first 1951).

Doebler, John. *Shakespeare's Speaking Pictures: Studies in Iconic Imagery.* Albuquerque: University of New Mexico Press, 1974.

Donawerth, Jane L. "A 'Power in the Tongue of Man': Shakespeare's Concepts of Language." *DAI* 36 (1976), 6112A (Wisconsin–Madison).

Doran, Madeleine. *Endeavors of Art: A Study of Form in Elizabethan Drama.* Madison: University of Wisconsin Press, 1954.

Dubrow, Heather. "Shakespeare's Undramatic Monologues; Toward a Reading of the *Sonnets.*" *Shakespeare Quarterly* 32 (1981), 55–68.

Dunn, Catherine M. "The Function of Music in Shakespeare's Romances." *Shakespeare Quarterly* 20 (1969), 391–405.

Edwards, Philip. "The Declaration of Love," pp. 39–50 in *Shakespeare's Styles: Essays in Honour of Kenneth Muir.* Edited by Philip Edwards, Inga-Stina Ewbank, and G. K. Hunter. Cambridge: Cambridge University Press, 1980.

Shakespeare and the Confines of Art. London: Methuen, 1968.

Egan, Robert. *Drama Within Drama: Shakespeare's Sense of His Art in "King Lear," "The Winter's Tale," and "The Tempest."* New York and London: Columbia University Press, 1975.

Ehrlich, Hélène-Hedy. *Montaigne: La critique et le langage.* Paris: Klincksieck, 1973.

Eliot, T. S. *Selected Essays: 1917–1932.* London: Faber & Faber, 1961 (first 1932).

Elizabethan Critical Essays. Edited with an Introduction by G. G. Smith. 2 vols. London: Oxford University Press, 1967 (first 1904).

Ellis, Herbert A. *Shakespeare's Lusty Punning in "Love's Labour's Lost." With Contemporary Analogues.* The Hague: Mouton, 1973.

Ellrodt, Robert. "Self-Consciousness in Montaigne and Shakespeare." *Shakespeare Survey* 28 (1975), 37–50.

Elson, Louis C. *Shakespeare in Music.* New York: AMS Press, 1971 (first 1901).

Evans, Malcolm. "Mercury Versus Apollo: A Reading of *Love's Labour's Lost.*" *Shakespeare Quarterly* 26 (1975), 113–27.

Ewbank, Inga-Stina. "'More Pregnantly Than Words': Some Uses and

Limitations of Visual Symbolism." *Shakespeare Survey* 24 (1971), 13–18.

"Sincerity and the Sonnet." *Essays and Studies* n.s. 34 (1981), 19–44.

"The Triumph of Time in 'The Winter's Tale'." *Review of English Literature* 5 (1964), 93–100.

Faas, Ekbert. *Tragedy and After: Euripides, Shakespeare, Goethe.* Montreal: McGill–Queen's University Press, 1984.

Fairchild, Arthur H. R. *Shakespeare and the Art of Design.* University of Missouri Studies. Columbia, Mo: University of Missouri Press, 1937.

Farrell, Kirby. *Shakespeare's Creation: The Language of Magic and Play.* Amherst: University of Massachusetts Press, 1975.

Felperin, Howard. *Shakespearean Representation: Mimesis and Modernity in Elizabethan Tragedy.* Princeton, NJ: Princeton University Press, 1977.

Fenton, Doris. *The Extra-Dramatic Moment in Elizabethan Plays Before 1616.* Philadelphia: University of Pennsylvania Press, 1930.

Fetrow, Fred, M. "Disclaimers Reclaimed: A Consideration of Jonson's Praise of Shakespeare." *Essays in Literature* 2 (1975), 24–31.

Ficino, Marsilio. *The Letters.* Translated from the Latin by the Members of the Language Department of the School of Economic Science, London. Volume I. Preface by Paul Oskar Kristeller. London: Shepheard–Walwyn, 1975.

Flecknoe, Richard. *A Short Discourse of The English Stage.* New York: Johnson Reprint Corporation, 1972 (first 1664). (Printed with Wright, James. *Historia Historionica: An Historical Account of the English Stage,* 1699.)

Fletcher, John: *see* Beaumont, Francis.

Fly, Richard. *Shakespeare's Mediated World.* Amherst: University of Massachusetts Press, 1976.

Fracastoro, Girolamo. *Navgerivs sive de poetica dialogvs.* Translated by Ruth Kelso. University of Illinois Studies in Language and Literature, ix. Urbana: University of Illinois Press, 1924.

Friedman, John B. *Orpheus in the Middle Ages.* Cambridge, Mass., and London: Harvard University Press, 1970.

Friedrich, Hugo. *Montaigne.* Traduit de l'allemand par Robert Rovini. Paris: Gallimard, 1968.

Frye, Roland M. *Shakespeare and Christian Doctrine.* Princeton, NJ: Princeton University Press, 1963.

"Ways of Seeing in Shakespearean Drama and Elizabethan Painting." *Shakespeare Quarterly* 31 (1980), 323–42.

Garber, Marjorie. "'Vassal Actors': The Role of the Audience in Shakespearean Tragedy." *Renaissance Drama* n.s. 9 (1978), 71–89.

Gascoigne, George. *The Complete Works.* 2 vols. Edited by John W. Cunliffe. Grosse Pointe, Mich.: Scholarly Press, 1969 (first 1910).

x242   *Bibliography*

Gerstner-Hirzel, Arthur. *The Economy of Action and Word in Shakespeare's Plays*. Bern: Francke Verlag, 1957.

Goldstien, Neal L. "*Love's Labour's Lost* and the Renaissance Vision of Love." *Shakespeare Studies* 25 (1974), 335–50.

Gombrich, E. H. *Art and Illusion: A Study in the Psychology of Pictorial Representation*. Bollingen Series xxxv. 5. New York: Pantheon Books, 1960.

Goshen, Charles E. *Documentary History of Psychiatry: A Source Book on Historical Principles*. London: Vision Press, 1967.

Gottschalk, Paul A. "Hall and the 'Play Extempore' in *1 Henry IV*." *Texas Studies in Literature and Language* 15 (1973–4), 605–14.

Grazia, Margreta de. "Babbling Will in Shakespeares Sonnets 127 to 154." *Spenser Studies: A Renaissance Poetry Annual* 1 (1980), 121–34.

"Shakespeare's View of Language: An Historical Perspective." *Shakespeare Quarterly* 29 (1978), 374–88.

Greene, Gayle J. "'Contract of Error': The Thematic Function of Language in Shakespeare's *Julius Caesar*." *DAI* 37 (1977), 4367A (Columbia).

"Language and Value in Shakespeare's *Troilus and Cressida*." *Studies in English Literature* 21 (1981), 271–85.

Grudin, Robert. *Mighty Opposites: Shakespeare and Renaissance Contrariety*. Berkeley: University of California Press, 1979.

Grundy, Joan. "Shakespeare's Sonnets and the Elizabethan Sonneteers." *Shakespeare Survey* 15 (1962), 41–9.

Hagstrum, Jean H. *The Sister Arts: The Tradition of Literary Pictorialism and English Poetry From Dryden to Gray*. Chicago and London: University of Chicago Press, 1965 (first 1958).

Halliday, F. E. *A Shakespeare Companion: 1564–1964*. Harmondsworth: Penguin Books, 1964.

Hammersmith, James P. "Language and Theme in Shakespeare's Plays." *DAI* 37 (1977), 6497A (Wisconsin–Milwaukee).

Hammond, Gerald. *The Reader and Shakespeare's Young Man Sonnets*. London: Macmillan, 1981.

Hapgood, Robert. "'Speak Hands for Me': Gesture as Language in *Julius Caesar*." *Drama Survey* 5 (1966–7), 162–70.

Harbage, Alfred. *Shakespeare's Audience*. New York and London: Columbia University Press, 1941.

Harrison, John L. "Bacon's View of Rhetoric, Poetry, and the Imagination." *Huntington Library Quarterly* 20 (1956–7), 107–25.

Hartnoll, Phyllis, ed. *Shakespeare in Music: Essays* . . . London: Macmillan, 1966.

Hathaway, Baxter. *The Age of Criticism: The Late Renaissance in Italy*. Westport, Conn.: Greenwood Press, 1962.

Hawkes, Terence. *Shakespeare's Talking Animals. Language and Drama in Society*. London: Edward Arnold, 1973.

Heckscher, William S. "Shakespeare in His Relationship to the Visual

Arts: A Study in Paradox." *Research Opportunities in Renaissance Drama* 13–14 (1970–1), 5–71.

Hegel, G. W. F. *On Tragedy*. Edited by Anne and Henry Paolucci. New York: Harper & Row, 1975 (first 1962).

Heninger, S. K., Jr. "The Pattern of *Love's Labour's Lost.*" *Shakespeare Studies* 7 (1974), 25–53.

Touches of Sweet Harmony: Pythagorean Cosmology and Renaissance Poetics. San Marino, Calif.: The Huntington Library, 1974.

Herrick, Marvin T. *The Poetics of Aristotle in England.* New York: Phaeton Press, 1976 (first 1930).

Hibbard, G. R. "Adumbrations of 'The Tempest' in 'A Midsummer Night's Dream'." *Shakespeare Survey* 31 (1978), 77–83.

"*Feliciter audax: Antony and Cleopatra, I, i, 1–24,*" pp. 95–109 in *Shakespeare's Styles. Essays in Honour of Kenneth Muir.* Edited by Philip Edwards, Inga-Stina Ewbank and G. K. Hunter. Cambridge: Cambridge University Press, 1980.

Hilliard, Stephen S. "Stephen Gosson and the Elizabethan Distrust of the Effects of Drama." *English Literary Renaissance* 9 (1979), 225–39.

Hoeniger, F. David. "The Meaning of *The Winter's Tale.*" *University of Toronto Quarterly* 20 (1950), 11–26.

Holland, Norman N. *The Shakespearean Imagination.* New York: Macmillan, 1964.

Holyoake, S. John. "Further Reflections on Montaigne and the Concept of the Imagination." *Bibliothèque d'Humanisme et Renaissance* 31 (1969), 495–523.

Homan, Sidney R. "Iago's Aesthetics: *Othello* and Shakespeare's Portrait of an Artist." *Shakespeare Studies* 5 (1969), 141–8.

When the Theater Turns to Itself: The Aesthetic Metaphor in Shakespeare. Lewisburg, Pa: Bucknell University Press, 1981.

Homer. *The Iliad.* 2 vols. With an English Translation by A. T. Murray. The Loeb Classical Library. Cambridge, Mass.: Harvard University Press, 1963 (first 1925).

Honigmann, E. A. J. "Secondary Sources of *The Winter's Tale.*" *Philological Quarterly* 34 (1955), 27–8.

Shakespeare: Seven Tragedies. The Dramatist's Manipulation of Response. London: Macmillan, 1976.

Horace. *Satires, Epistles, Ars Poetica.* With an English Translation by H. Rushton Fairclough. The Loeb Classical Library. Cambridge, Mass.: Harvard University Press, 1966 (first 1926).

Hoskyns, John. *Directions for Speech and Style.* Edited by Hoyl H. Hudson. Princeton, NJ: Princeton University Press, 1935.

Howard, Jean E. "Figures and Grounds: Shakespeare's Control of Audience Perception and Response." *Studies in English Literature. 1500–1900* 20 (1980), 185–99.

"Shakespearean Counterpoint: Stage Technique and the Interaction Between Play and Audience." *Shakespeare Quarterly* 30 (1979), 343–57.

Huarte, John. *The Examination of Mens Wits*. Translated out of the Spanish tongue by M. Camillo Camili. Englished out of his Italian, by R. C. Esquire. London: Richard Watkins, 1594.

Hulse, S. C. "'A Piece of Skilful Painting' in Shakespeare's 'Lucrece'." *Shakespeare Survey* 31 (1978), 13–22.

Hunter, Richard, and Macalpine, Ida. *Three Hundred Years of Psychiatry*. London: Oxford University Press, 1970 (first 1963).

Hunter, Robert G. "The Function of the Songs at the End of *Love's Labour's Lost*." *Shakespeare Studies* 7 (1974), 55–64.

Hyman, Stanley E. "Portraits of the Artists: Iago and Prospero." *Shenandoah* 21:2 (Winter 1970), 18–42.

Ingram, R. W. "Musical Pauses and the Vision Scenes in Shakespeare's Last Plays," pp. 234–47 in *Pacific Coast Studies in Shakespeare*. Edited by Waldo F. McNeir and Thelma N. Greenfield. Eugene: University of Oregon Press, 1966.

Jagendorf, Zvi. "'Fingers on your lips, I pray': On silence in *Hamlet*." *English* (London) 27 (1978), 121–8.

James I. *Daemonologie*. New York: Da Capo Press, 1969 (first 1597).

James, D. G. *The Dream of Learning: An Essay on "The Advancement of Learning," "Hamlet" and "King Lear"*. Oxford: Clarendon Press, 1951.

Jayne, Sears. "Ficino and the Platonism of the English Renaissance." *Comparative Literature* 4 (1952), 214–38.

John of Salisbury. *The Metalogicon*. Translated with an Introduction and Notes by Daniel D. McGarry. Berkeley: University of California Press, 1962.

Johnson, Paula. *Form and Transformation in Music and Poetry of the English Renaissance*. New Haven, Conn.: Yale University Press, 1972.

Johnson, Robert C. "Silence and Speech in *Coriolanus*." *Aligarh Journal of English Studies* 5 (1980), 190–210.

Jones, Emrys. *Scenic Form in Shakespeare*. Oxford: Clarendon Press, 1971.

Jones, G. P. "'Henry V': The Chorus and the Audience." *Shakespeare Survey* 31 (1978), 93–104.

Jonson, Ben. [*Works*]. 11 vols. Edited by C. H. Herford and Percy and Evelyn M. Simpson. Oxford: Clarendon Press, 1954 (first 1925).

Jorgens, Elise B. "On Matters of Manner and Music in Jacobean and Caroline Song." *English Literary Renaissance* 10 (1980), 239–64.

Joseph, Sister Miriam. *Shakespeare's Use of the Arts of Language*. New York: Columbia University Press, 1947.

Juneja, Renu. "The Unclassical Design of Jonson's Comedy." *Renaissance and Reformation* n.s. 4 (1980), 74–86.

Keats, John. *The Letters 1814–1821*. Edited by Hyder E. Rollins. Cambridge, Mass.: Harvard University Press, 1958.

Kemp, Martin. "From 'Mimesis' to 'Fantasia': The Quattrocento Vocabulary of Creation, Inspiration and Genius in the Visual Arts." *Viator* 8 (1977), 347–98.

Kennedy, William J. *Rhetorical Norms in Renaissance Literature.* New Haven and London: Yale University Press, 1978.

Kernan, Alvin B. *The Playwright as Magician: Shakespeare's Image of the Poet in the English Public Theater.* New Haven and London: Yale University Press, 1979.

'Shakespeare's Essays on Dramatic Poesy: The Nature and Function of Theater within the Sonnets and the Plays," pp. 175–96 in *The Author in His Work: Essays on a Problem in Criticism.* Edited by Louis L. Martz and Aubrey Williams. Introduction by Patricia Meyer Spacks. New Haven and London: Yale University Press, 1978.

Kerr, Walter. *Tragedy and Comedy.* New York: Simon & Schuster, 1968 (first 1967).

Kirk, G. S., and Raven, J. E. *The Presocratic Philosophers: A Critical History with a Selection of Texts.* Cambridge: Cambridge University Press, 1977 (first 1957).

Klein, David. *The Elizabethan Dramatists as Critics.* New York: Greenwood Press, 1968 (first 1963).

Knight, G. Wilson. *Shakespeare and Religion: Essays of Forty Years.* New York: Simon & Schuster, 1968 (first 1967).

Knights, L. C. *Explorations: Essays in Criticism Mainly on the Literature of the Seventeenth Century.* London: Chatto & Windus, 1963 (first 1946).

Kocher, Paul H. "Francis Bacon on the Drama," pp. 297–307 in *Essays on Shakespeare and Elizabethan Drama in Honor of Hardin Craig.* Edited by Richard Hosley. Columbia: University of Missouri Press, 1962.

Laan, Thomas F. van. *Role-playing in Shakespeare.* Toronto: University of Toronto Press, 1978.

Lanham, Richard A. *The Motives of Eloquence: Literary Rhetoric in the Renaissance.* New Haven and London: Yale University Press, 1976.

Latham, Jacqueline E. M. "*The Tempest* and King James's *Daemonologie.*" *Shakespeare Survey* 28 (1975), 117–23.

Latham, M. C. *The Elizabethan Fairies.* New York: Columbia University Press, 1930.

Lavater, Lewes. *Of Ghostes and Spirites Walking by Nyght.* Edited with Introduction and Appendix by J. Dover Wilson and May Yardley. London: Oxford University Press, 1929.

Lawlor, John. "*Pandosto* and the Nature of Dramatic Romance." *Philological Quarterly* 41 (1962), 96–113.

Leech, Clifford. "The Structure of the Last Plays." *Shakespeare Survey* 11 (1958), 19–30.

Leggatt, Alexander. *Ben Jonson: His Vision and His Art.* London and New York: Methuen, 1981.

Leishman, J. B. *Themes and Variations in Shakespeare's Sonnets.* London: Hutchinson, 1963 (first 1961).

Lever, J. W. *The Elizabethan Love Sonnet.* London: Methuen, 1974 (first 1956).

Lewis, C. S. *The Discarded Image: An Introduction to Medieval and Renaissance Literature.* Cambridge: Cambridge University Press, 1967 (first 1964).

Livingston, Mary L. "The Natural Art of *The Winter's Tale.*" *Modern Language Quarterly* 30 (1969), 340–55.

Long, John H. *Shakespeare's Use of Music: A Study of the Music and Its Performance in the Original Production of Seven Comedies.* Gainesville: University of Florida Press, 1961 (first 1955).

Shakespeare's Use of Music: The Final Comedies. Gainesville: University of Florida Press, 1961.

Shakespeare's Use of Music: The Histories and Tragedies. Gainesville: University of Florida Press, 1971.

Lope de Vega. *Arte Nuevo de Hacer Comedias. La Discreta Enamorada.* Madrid: Espasa–Calpe, S. A., 1967.

Lovejoy, Arthur O. " 'Nature' As Aesthetic Norm." *Modern Language Notes* 42 (1927), 444–50.

and Boas, George. *Primitivism and Related Ideas in Antiquity.* New York: Octagon Books, 1973.

Lyly, John. *The Complete Works.* 3 vols. Edited by R. Warwick Bond. Oxford: Clarendon Press, 1967 (first 1902).

Lyons, Clifford. "Stage Imagery in Shakespeare's Plays," pp. 261–74 in *Essays on Shakespeare and Elizabethan Drama in Honor of Hardin Craig.* Edited by Richard Hosley. Columbia: University of Missouri Press, 1962.

McAlindon. T. "Language, Style, and Meaning in *Troilus and Cressida.*" *PMLA* 84 (1969), 29–43.

Shakespeare and Decorum. New York: Barnes & Noble, 1973.

McDonald, Charles O. *The Rhetoric of Tragedy: Form in Stuart Drama.* Amherst: University of Massachusetts Press, 1966.

McElveen, Idris B. "Shakespeare and Renaissance Concepts of the Imagination." *DAI* 35 (1974), 409A–410A (South Carolina).

McFarlane, I. D. "Montaigne and the Concept of the Imagination," pp. 117–37 in *The French Renaissance and its Heritage: Essays Presented to Alan M. Boase.* Edited by D. R. Haggis, S. Jones, F. W. Leakey, E. G. Taylor and G. M. Sutherland. London: Methuen, 1968.

Mack, Maynard. "Engagement and Detachment in Shakespeare's Plays," pp. 275–96 in *Essays on Shakespeare and the Elizabethan Drama in Honor of Hardin Craig.* Edited by Richard Hosley. Columbia: University of Missouri Press, 1962.

McLay, Catherine M. "The Dialogues of Spring and Winter: A Key to the Unity of *Love's Labour's Lost*." *Shakespeare Quarterly* 18 (1967), 119–27.

Maggi, Vincenzo, and Lombardi, Bartolomeo. *In Aristotelis Librvm De Poetica Commvnes Explanationes*. Venice: In officina Erasmiana Vincentij Valgrisij, 1550.

Mahood, M. M. *Shakespeare's Wordplay*. London: Methuen, 1957.

Marston, John. *The Works*, 3 vols. Edited by Arthur Henry Bullen. New York: Georg Olms Verlag, 1970 (first 1887).

Massinger, Philip. *The Plays and Poems*. 5 vols. Edited by Philip Edwards and Colin Gibson. Oxford: Clarendon Press, 1976.

Matchett, William H. "Some Dramatic Techniques in *King Lear*," pp. 185–208 in *Shakespeare: The Theatrical Dimension*. Edited by Philip C. McGuire and David A. Samuelson. New York: AMS Press, 1979.

"Some Dramatic Techniques in *The Winter's Tale*." *Shakespeare Survey* 22 (1969), 93–107.

Mazzeo, Joseph Anthony. *Renaissance and Revolution: The Remaking of European Thought*. New York: Pantheon Books, 1965.

Medwall, Henry. *The Plays*. Edited by Alan H. Nelson. Cambridge: D. S. Brewer, 1980.

Mehl, Dieter. "Emblems in English Renaissance Drama." *Renaissance Drama* n.s. 2 (1969), 39–57.

"Visual and Rhetorical Imagery in Shakespeare's Plays." *Essays and Studies* n.s. 25 (1972), 83–100.

Merchant, W. Moelwyn. *Shakespeare and the Artist*. London: Oxford University Press, 1959.

The Merry Devill of Edmonton. Issued for subscribers by the editor of the Tudor Facsimile Texts, 1911. New York: AMS Press, 1970 (first 1608).

Miller, J. Hillis. "Arachne's Broken Woof." *Georgia Review* 31 (1977), 44–60.

Moncur-Sime, A. H. *Shakespeare: His Music and Song*. London: Kegan Paul, 1920.

Montaigne, Michel de. *The Completed Essays*. Translated by Donald M. Frame. Stanford, Calif.: Stanford University Press, 1965 (first 1958). *Essais*. Texte établi et annoté par Albert Thibaudet. Paris: Gallimard, 1950.

Montrose, Louis Adrian. *"Curious-Knotted Garden": The Form, Themes, and Contexts of Shakespeare's "Love's Labour's Lost"*. Salzburg: Institut für Englische Sprache und Literatur, 1977.

Mowat, Barbara A. "The Beckoning Ghost: Stage-Gesture in Shakespeare." *Renaissance Papers*, 1970, 41–54.

The Dramaturgy of Shakespeare's Romances. Athens: University of Georgia Press, 1976.

Mueller, Martin. "Hermione's Wrinkles, or, Ovid Transformed: An Essay on *The Winter's Tale*." *Comparative Drama* 5 (1971), 226–39.

Muir, Kenneth. *Shakespeare's Sonnets*. London: George Allen & Unwin, 1979.

Shakespeare the Professional and Related Studies. London: Heinemann, 1973.

Musgrove, S. *Shakespeare and Jonson.* Auckland: Auckland University College, 1957.

Nashe, Thomas. *The Works.* 5 vols. Edited by Ronald B. McKerrow. (Revised by F. P. Wilson). Oxford: Basil Blackwell, 1958 (first 1904–10).

Nassar, Eugene P. *The Rape of Cinderella: Essays in Literary Continuity.* Bloomington: Indiana University Press, 1970.

Naylor, Edward W. *Shakespeare and Music: With Illustrations from the Music of the 16th and 17th Centuries.* New York: AMS Press, 1965 (first 1896).

Nelson, John Charles. *Renaissance Theory of Love: The Context of Giordano Bruno's "Eroici furori."* New York: Columbia University Press, 1958.

Ness, Frederic W. *The Use of Rhyme in Shakespeare's Plays.* Hamden, Conn.: Archon Books, 1969 (first 1941).

Noble, Richmond. *Shakespeare's Use of Song: With the Text of the Principal Songs.* Oxford: Clarendon Press, 1967 (first 1923).

Nosworthy, J. M. "Music and Its Function in the Romances of Shakespeare." *Shakespeare Survey* 11 (1958), 60–9.

Notopoulos, James A. *The Platonism of Shelley: A Study of Platonism and the Poetic Mind.* New York: Octagon Books, 1969.

Ogden, Henry V. S. "The Rejection of the Antithesis of Nature and Art in Germany, 1780–1805." *Journal of English and Germanic Philology* 38 (1939), 597–616.

Ovid. *Metamorphoses.* Translated by Rolfe Humphries. Bloomington: Indiana University Press, 1955.

Pafford, J. H. P. "Music, and the Songs in *The Winter's Tale.*" *Shakespeare Quarterly* 10 (1959), 161–75.

Palingenius, Marcellus. *The Zodiake of Life.* Translated by Barnabe Googe. With an Introduction by Rosemund Tuve. New York: Scholars' Facsimiles & Reprints, 1947.

Panofsky, Erwin. *Idea: A Concept in Art Theory.* Translated by Joseph J. S. Peake. Columbia: University of South Carolina Press, 1968.

Paracelsus. *Selected Writings.* Edited, with an Introduction, by Jolande Jacobi. Translated by Norbert Guterman. London: Routledge & Kegan Paul, 1951.

Pater, Walter. *The Works.* 8 vols. London: Macmillan, 1901.

Petronella, Vincent F. "Shakespeare's *The Phoenix and the Turtle* and the Defunctive Music of Ecstasy." *Shakespeare Studies* 8 (1975), 311–31.

Pettet, E. C. "Shakespeare's Conception of Poetry." *Essays and Studies* n.s. 3 (1950), 29–46.

Piccolomini, Alessandro. *Annotationi . . . nel libro della Poetica d'Aristotele.* In Vinegia: Presso Giouanni Guarisco, & Compagni, 1575.

Pico della Mirandola, Gianfrancesco. *On the Imagination.* The Latin Text

With an Introduction, an English Translation, and Notes by Harry Caplan. Westport. Conn.: Greenwood Press, 1971 (first 1930).

Plato. *The Collected Dialogues, Including the Letters.* Edited by Edith Hamilton and Huntington Cairns. Bollingen Series lxxi. Princeton, NJ: Princeton University Press, 1973 (first 1961).

Porter, Joseph A. *The Drama of Speech Acts: Shakespeare's Lancastrian Tetralogy.* Berkeley: University of California Press, 1979.

Prosser, E. *Hamlet and Revenge.* Second Edition. Stanford, Calif.: Stanford University Press, 1971.

Proudfoot, Richard. "Verbal Reminiscence and the Two-Part Structure of 'The Winter's Tale'." *Shakespeare Survey* 29 (1976), 67–78.

Pyle, Fitzroy. *"The Winter's Tale": A Commentary on the Structure.* New York: Barnes & Noble, 1969.

Rabelais, François. *Oeuvres complètes.* Texte établi et annoté par Jacques Boulenger. Edition revue et complété par Lucien Scheler. Paris: Gallimard, 1955.

Rahner, K. *Die Theologie der Zukunft.* Munich: Deutscher Taschenbuch Verlag, 1971.

Raitiere, Martin N. "The Unity of Sidney's *Apology for Poetry." Studies in English Literature. 1500–1900* 21 (1981), 37–57.

Ravindra, Ravi. "Time in Christian and Indian Traditions." *Dalhousie Review* 51 (1971–2), 5–17.

Reese, Gustave. *Music in the Renaissance.* New York: W. W. Norton, 1959 (first 1954).

Regosin, Richard L. *The Matter of My Book: Montaigne's "Essais" as the Book of the Self.* Berkeley: University of California Press, 1977.

The Return from Parnassus: Or, The Scourge of Simony. Edited with Introduction, Notes and Glossary by Oliphant Smeaton. London: J. M. Dent, 1905.

Richards, I. A. "*Troilus and Cressida* and Plato." *Hudson Review* 1 (1948–9), 362–76.

Riggs, David. "'Plot' and 'Episode' in Early Neoclassical Criticism." *Renaissance Drama* 6 (1973), 149–75.

Righter, Anne. *Shakespeare and the Idea of the Play.* London: Chatto & Windus, 1962.

Ringler, William A., Jr. "Hamlet's Defense of the Players," pp. 201–11 in *Essays on Shakespeare and Elizabethan Drama in Honor of Hardin Craig.* Edited by Richard Hosley. Columbia: University of Missouri Press, 1962.

Robinson, Forrest G. *The Shape of Things Known: Sidney's "Apology" in Its Philosophical Tradition.* Cambridge, Mass.: Harvard University Press, 1972.

Robinson, James E. "The Dramatic Unities in the Renaissance: A Study of the Principles, with Application to the Development of English Drama." *DAI* 20 (1959) 292 (Illinois).

Robortello, Francesco. *In Librum Aristotelis de Arte Poetica Explicationes:*

Paraphrasis in Librum Horatii, Qui Vulgo de Arte Poetica ad Pisones Inscribitur. Munich: Wilhelm Fink Verlag, 1968 (first 1548).

Rossi, Paolo. *Francis Bacon: From Magic to Science*. Translated from the Italian by Sacha Rabinovitch. London: Routledge & Kegan Paul, 1968 (original Italian edition 1957).

Rossky, William. "Imagination in the English Renaissance: Psychology and Poetic." *Studies in the Renaissance* 5–6 (1958–9), 49–73.

Rozas. Juan M. *Significado y Doctrina del Arte Nuevo de Lope de Vega*. Madrid: Sociedad General Española de Libreria, S. A., 1976.

Sacharoff, Mark. "Critical Comment in Response to T. McAlindon's "Language, Style, and Meaning in 'Troilus and Cressida'." *PMLA* 87 (1972), 90–3.

Salingar, L. G. "Time and Art in Shakespeare's Romances." *Renaissance Drama* 9 (1966), 3–35.

Salman, Phillips. "Instruction and Delight in Medieval and Renaissance Criticism." *Renaissance Quarterly* 32 (1979), 303–32.

Scaliger, Julius Caesar. *Poetices Libri Septem*. Faksimile-Neudruck der Ausgabe von Lyon 1561 mit einer Einleitung von August Buck. Stuttgart–Bad Cannstatt: Friedrich Frommann Verlag, 1964.

Schaar, Claes. *Elizabethan Sonnet Themes and the Dating of Shakespeare's "Sonnets"*. Lund Studies in English, xxxii. Lund: C. W. K. Gleerup, 1962.

Schanzer, Ernest. "Shakespeare and the Doctrine of the Unity of Time." *Shakespeare Survey* 28 (1975), 57–61.

"The Structural Pattern of *The Winter's Tale*." *Review of English Literature* 5 (1964), 72–82.

Scot, Reginald. *The Discouerie of Witchcraft*. New York: Da Capo Press, 1971 (first 1584).

Seltzer, Daniel. "The Actors and Staging," pp. 35–54 in *A New Companion to Shakespeare Studies*. Edited by Kenneth Muir and S. Schoenbaum. Cambridge: Cambridge University Press, 1971.

Seng, Peter J. *The Vocal Songs in the Plays of Shakespeare: A Critical History*. Cambridge, Mass.: Harvard University Press, 1967.

Sewell, Elizabeth. *The Orphic Voice: Poetry and Natural History*. London: Routledge & Kegan Paul, 1960.

Shakespeare, William. *Hamlet*. Edited by Cyrus Hoy. New York: Norton, 1963.

Love's Labour's Lost. Edited by Richard David, based on the edition of H. C. Hart. New Arden Edition. London: Methuen, 1960.

A Midsummer Night's Dream. Edited by Harold F. Brooks. New Arden Edition. London: Methuen, 1979.

A Midsummer Night's Dream. Edited by Henry Cuningham. The Arden Edition. London: Methuen, 1905.

A Midsummer Night's Dream. Edited by Horace Howard Furness. New York: Dover Publications, 1963.

Pericles, Prince of Tyre. Edited by Ernest Schanzer. The Signet Classic Shakespeare. New York: New American Library, 1977.

The Tempest. Edited by Frank Kermode. New Arden Edition. London: Methuen, 1979 (first 1954).

Timon of Athens. Edited by H. J. Oliver. New Arden Edition. London: Methuen, 1959.

The Winter's Tale. Edited by J. H. P. Pafford. New Arden Edition. London: Methuen, 1963.

The Winter's Tale. Edited by Frank Kermode. The Signet Classic Shakespeare. New York: New American Library, 1963.

and John Fletcher. *King Henry VIII.* Edited by R. A. Foakes. New Arden Edition. London: Methuen, 1957.

The Two Noble Kinsmen. Edited by Clifford Leech. The Signet Classic Shakespeare. New York: New American Library, 1977.

Shapiro, Michael. "Role-Playing, Reflexivity, and Metadrama in Recent Shakespearean Criticism." *Renaissance Drama* n.s. 12 (1981), 145–61.

Shirley, James. *The Dramatic Works and Poems.* 6 vols. Edited by William Gifford. Additional notes by Alexander Dyce. New York: Russell & Russell, 1966 (first 1833).

Sicherman, Carol M. "*Coriolanus*: The Failure of Words." *ELH* 39 (1972), 189–207.

Sidney, Sir Philip. *Astrophel and Stella.* Edited by Kingsley Hart. London: The Folio Society, 1959.

Sipe, Dorothy L. *Shakespeare's Metrics.* New Haven, Conn.: Yale University Press, 1968.

Sloan, Thomas O., and Raymond B. Waddington, eds. *The Rhetoric of Renaissance Poetry: From Wyatt to Milton.* Berkeley: University of California Press, 1974.

Smith, G. Gregory: *see Elizabethan Critical Essays.*

Smith, J. Oates. "Essence and Existence in Shakespeare's *Troilus and Cressida.*" *Philological Quarterly* 46 (1967), 167–85.

Smith, Warren D. "Stage Business in Shakespeare's Dialogue." *Shakespeare Quarterly* 4 (1953), 311–16.

Spenser, Edmund. *The Works of Edmund Spenser: A Variorum Edition.* 9 vols. Edited by Edwin Greenlaw, Charles Grosvenor Osgood, Frederick Morgan Padelford, and Ray Heffner. Baltimore, Md: Johns Hopkins Press, 1966.

Spingarn, Joel E. *A History of Literary Criticism in the Renaissance.* New York: Columbia University Press, 1908 (first 1899).

Spurgeon, Caroline F. E. *Shakespeare's Imagery: And What It Tells Us.* Cambridge: Cambridge University Press, 1935.

Sternfeld, Frederick W., ed. *Music from the Middle Ages to the Renaissance.* London: Weidenfeld & Nicolson, 1973.

Music in Shakespearean Tragedy. London: Routledge and Kegan Paul, 1963.

"Shakespeare and Music," pp. 157–67 in *A New Companion to Shakespeare Studies.* Edited by Kenneth Muir and S. Schoenbaum. Cambridge: Cambridge University Press, 1971.

Stroup, Thomas B. *Microcosmos: The Shape of the Elizabethan Play*. Lexington: University of Kentucky Press, 1965.
Suckling, Sir John. *The Works of Sir John Suckling in Prose and Verse*. Edited by A. Hamilton Thompson. New York: Russell & Russell, 1964 (first 1910).
Sweeting, Elizabeth J. *Early Tudor Criticism: Linguistic & Literary*. New York: Russell & Russell, 1964 (first 1940).

Tayler, Edward W. *Nature and Art in Renaissance Literature*. New York: Columbia University Press, 1966 (first 1961).
Taylor, George C. *Shakespeare's Debt to Montaigne*. Cambridge, Mass.: Harvard University Press, 1925.
Thomas, Keith. *Religion and the Decline of Magic*. Harmondsworth: Penguin Books, 1970.
Tigerstedt, E. N. "The Poet as Creator: Origins of a Metaphor." *Comparative Literature Studies* 5 (1968), 455–88.
Tomkis, T. *Albumazar: A Comedy. As it is Now Revived at the Theatre-Royal in Drury-Lane with Alterations. A New Edition*. London: T. Becket, 1773.
Lingua. Edited by John S. Farmer. New York: AMS Press, 1970.
Tourneur, Cyril. *The Works*. Edited by Allardyce Nicoll. New York: Russell & Russell, 1963 (first 1929).
Trousdale, Marion. "A Possible Renaissance View of Form." *English Literary History* 40 (1973), 179–204.
Turner, Frederick. *Shakespeare and the Nature of Time: Moral and Philosophical Themes in Some Plays and Poems of William Shakespeare*. Oxford: Clarendon Press, 1971.
Tuve, Rosemund. *Elizabethan and Metaphysical Imagery: Renaissance Poetic and Twentieth-Century Critics*. Chicago, Ill.: University of Chicago Press, 1963 (first 1947).

Vettori, Pietro. *Commentarii, In Primum Librum Aristotelis de Arte Poetarum*. Munich: Wilhelm Fink Verlag, 1967 (first 1560).
Vickers, Brian. "Shakespeare's Use of Rhetoric," pp. 83–98 in *A New Companion to Shakespeare Studies*. Edited by Kenneth Muir and S. Schoenbaum. Cambridge: Cambridge University Press, 1971.
Villey, Pierre. *Montaigne et François Bacon*. Geneva: Slatkine Reprints, 1973 (first 1913).
Vyvyan, John. *Shakespeare and Platonic Beauty*. London: Chatto & Windus, 1961.

Waddington, Raymond B. "Shakespeare's Sonnet 15 and the Art of Memory," pp. 96–122 in *The Rhetoric of Renaissance Poetry: From Wyatt to Milton*. Edited by Thomas O. Sloan and Raymond B. Waddington. Berkeley: University of California Press, 1974.
Waldo, Tommy Ruth. "Beyond Words: Shakespeare's Tongue-Tied Muse," pp. 160–77 in *Shakespeare's "More Than Words Can Witness"*:

Essays on Visual and Nonverbal Enactment in the Plays. Edited by
Sidney Homan. Lewisburg, Pa: Bucknell University Press, 1980.
Wallace, Karl R. *Francis Bacon on the Nature of Man.* The Faculties of Man's
Soul: Understanding, Reason, Imagination, Memory, Will, and Appetite.
Urbana: University of Illinois Press, 1967.
Waller, G. F. "Romance and Shakespeare's Philosophy of Time in *The
Winter's Tale.*" *Southern Review: An Australian Journal of Literary
Studies* 4 (1970), 130–8.
*The Strong Necessity of Time: The Philosophy of Time in Shakespeare and
Elizabethan Literature.* The Hague–Paris: Mouton, 1976.
A Warning for Fair Women. 1599. Issued for subscribers by the editor of the
Tudor Facsimile Texts, 1912. New York: AMS Press, 1970 (first
1599).
Webster, John. *The Complete Works.* 4 vols. Edited by F. L. Lucas.
London: Chatto & Windus, 1927.
Webster, John. "'The Methode of a Poete': An Inquiry into Tudor
Conceptions of Poetic Sequence." *English Literary Renaissance* 11
(1981), 22–43.
Weimann, Robert. *Shakespeare and the Popular Tradition in the Theater:
Studies in the Social Dimension of Dramatic Form and Function.* Trans-
lated by Robert Schwartz. Baltimore, Md: Johns Hopkins University
Press, 1978.
Weinberg, Bernard. *A History of Literary Criticism in the Italian Renaissance.*
2 vols. Chicago, Ill.: University of Chicago Press, 1963 (first 1961).
West, Robert H. *The Invisible World: A Study of Pneumatology in Elizabethan
Drama.* New York: Octagon Press, 1969 (first 1939).
Shakespeare & the Outer Mystery. Lexington: University of Kentucky
Press, 1968.
Westlund, Joseph. "Fancy and Achievement in *Love's Labour's Lost.*"
Shakespeare Quarterly 18 (1967), 37–46.
Whitaker, Virgil K. *Shakespeare's Use of Learning: An Inquiry Into the Growth
of his Mind and Art.* San Marino, Calif.: Huntington Library Publi-
cations, 1953.
Willcock, Gladys D. *Shakespeare as a Critic of Language.* London: Oxford
University Press, 1934.
Wilson, J. Dover. *What Happens in Hamlet.* Cambridge: Cambridge Uni-
versity Press, 1960 (first 1935).
Wilson, Harold S. "'Nature and Art' in '*Winter's Tale,*' IV, iv, 86ff."
Shakespeare Association Bulletin 18 (1943), 114–20.
"Some Meanings of 'Nature' in Renaissance Literary Theory." *Journal
of the History of Ideas* 2 (1941), 430–48.
Wilson, Thomas. *The Arte of Rhetorique.* Revised Edition (1560). Edited by
G. H. Mair. Oxford: Clarendon Press, 1909.
Wolfley, Lawrence C. "Sidney's Visual–Didactic Poetic: Some Complex-
ities and Limitations." *Journal of Medieval and Renaissance Studies* 6
(1976), 217–41.
Woodhouse, A. S. P. "Imagination," pp. 370–7 in *Princeton Encyclopedia*

of Poetry and Poetics. Edited by Alex Preminger. Princeton, NJ: Princeton University Press, 1974 (first 1965).

Wright, Ellen F. " 'We Are Mock'd With Art': Shakespeare's Wintry Tale." *Essays in Literature* 6 (1979), 147–59.

Yates, Frances A. *A Study of 'Love's Labour's Lost'*. Cambridge: Cambridge University Press, 1936.

Yeats, William Butler. *Essays and Introductions*. New York: Macmillan, 1961.

Yoder, R. A. " 'Sons and Daughters of the Game': An Essay on Shakespeare's 'Troilus and Cressida'." *Shakespeare Survey* 25 (1972), 11–25.

Young, David P. *Something of Great Constancy: The Art of "A Midsummer Night's Dream"*. New Haven and London: Yale University Press, 1966.

Zitner, Sheldon P. *"King Lear* and Its Language," pp. 3–22 in *Some Facets of "King Lear:" Essays in Prismatic Criticism*. Edited by Rosalie L. Colie and F. T. Flahiff. Toronto: University of Toronto Press, 1974.

Index